STREET SMART

THE PRIMER FOR
SUCCESS IN THE NEW WORLD

JOHN POSITANO AND ROCK POSITANO

SAVIO
REPVBLIC

A SAVIO REPUBLIC BOOK
An Imprint of Post Hill Press
ISBN: 978-1-63758-364-7
ISBN (eBook): 978-1-63758-365-4

Street Smart:
The Primer for Success in the New World
© 2022 by John Positano and Rock Positano
All Rights Reserved

posthillpress.com
New York • Nashville
Published in the United States of America

1 2 3 4 5 6 7 8 9 10

TABLE OF CONTENTS

When I wrote *Carlito's Way*, I wanted to instill the same values in the book as espoused by the Positano brothers here: that sense of the "Stand-Up Guy" conveyed in all these works can be best described as a keen awareness of what is possible and even natural in the Street Smart environment.

The "Stand-Up Guy" didn't rat out his friends, or even his enemies. He was silent but deadly, and no bravado here. It just happens that the Street Smart guide to success has deep roots in *Carlito's Way*.

My "Carlito Brigante" was a man born of the streets, who used his wits—now sharpened and also saddened by his serving time in prison—to re-emerge on the same mean streets he was raised in. Carlito lived the Stand-Up Guy! He stood by his friends and could not evade his roots of poverty, gangs, and drugs. But Carlito's world was my world, though I successfully evaded it and prospered.

I'm not proud of this, but it reminds me of an incident as a teenager in Harlem. You had to be Street Smart in Harlem, you just had to be. Or you were dead.

I was about fifteen to sixteen years old fishing in the lake on 106th Street. A Harlem gang, the Copians, came on bicycles.

One of the punks came over and said to me, "Let me hold a quarter, motherfucker."

I said, "Your father, motherfucker."

He smacked me in the face. His "back up" came over on the bikes. I said, "Any one of you motherfuckers come around my way, I'll pop y'all."

This guy then pulled out a zip gun (a homemade and dangerous pistol made of wood and scrap metal) and I had to turn tail. They called me "Fast Eddie" 'cause I ran track back then, but when I was scared, I was even faster!

They chased me up to 110th Street, but I got away.

The next day, my closest buddy Orlando and I went on the roof, and we saw the Copians going up and down the block looking for me. Someone ratted on me and told them where I lived. I connected with my main man, one of the baddest guys in Harlem, Johnny Guinn. The Copians biked over later that day when he and I were hanging out. Johnny grabbed one of their "stingy brim" hats, threw it on the street, and we saw it get run over by a car. Soon, they all started laughing, as if it was a big joke all around.

"We was just kiddin'!"

Guinn wasn't falling for it. "That's my boy (me). You ain't touching nobody."

No one messed with me after that.

I learned that in the street, you needed "back up"; friends who are always there for you. It goes both ways. I have stayed friends with some of these cats over fifty years. Sadly, most have passed, but you never forget who had your back when you needed them. I've been blessed.

Such is the way of the street.

One day, I was sentencing a very dangerous defendant. This guy had a very long rap sheet and was a hard ass among hard asses. So, he asked to approach the bench. I was a little nervous!

"Your Honor, may I approach the bench?" he asks.

I was curious!

"You may approach the bench."

He saunters on up and asks his question. I craned my neck downward. The court was perfectly quiet.

"Your Honor, I just want to know when I will be up for parole?"

I had to lean off the front of the bench, just for effect. Nice and personal!

Bad Ass craned up his neck, accordingly.

"Sucker, *your parole officer hasn't been born yet.*"

He got the point, and the quote became a legendary response for both jurists and defendants.

I learned from bitter personal experiences that one hand washes the other in life. On the street, maybe that's not so true. A favor will kill you faster than a bullet, so watch whom you grant them to. That's Street Smart written in stone. Pass it on. No use getting into empty trouble or a lost cause.

Street Smart is intuition mixed with common sense, but not necessarily intelligence. There are plenty of smart people, educated types, who you'll surely meet. But, you'll meet very few Street Smart guys.

The biggest asset I brought to the bench was my exposure to the streets. It served me well on the bench for thirty years and over 60,000 cases. What I learned on the streets, you can't get out of a book, law school, or college. I learned about the criminal mind, human nature, all of it.

Ain't no wise guy gonna run a game on me, and after reading *Street Smart*, no wise guy is gonna run a game on you, neither.

The Honorable New York State Supreme Court
Judge Edwin Torres, Author of *Carlito's Way*

WELCOME TO THE ASPHALT JUNGLE

This book is not the usual Horatio Alger "happy horseshit" notion of the self-help, self-image, self-reliant school of getting ahead. In some ways, this book is a little tart and blunt, so it is not eternally "happy," and definitely not "horseshit." Its contents are based on countless hours of successes, failures, conversations, and confrontations. They're not derived from reading a "how to" book.

It won't tell you that everything will be alright if you just work even harder, network like a fiend, lean on business contacts, tie on the old-school tie, smile harder, and think optimistically. You can buy the other "self-improvement" books for that reason. Other advisors, gurus, books, "influencers," DVDs, and internet sites were obsolete before the various and sundry waves of COVID hit you in your home and business, and now, these other advisors have become dangerous. Whether or not the world tomorrow gets a "magic bullet" killing COVID, this is the present reality.

Instead, what our "Street Scholars" are telling you, directly and without a filter, is that using your Street Smart to spot, seize, exploit, and create a lucky break is mandatory not just for success, but for survival. To our knowledge, no other "personal advice" book has ever connected success to survival; but in today's world, it seems more relevant and crucial than ever.

Before we introduce ourselves and these Scholars, let's get to definitions....

We define "success" as such: being exemplary in your field, accomplishing goals amidst any obstacles and trepidation, and taking advantage of these achievements to improve humanity and the world they inhabit. Wealth and access to people in high places are only a few pieces of the jigsaw puzzle. There are other definitions, but this is not a book on philosophy. For that, feel free to read Plato or Socrates, who both practiced their own version of Street Smart back in their day.

These Street Scholars, who will tell you how they directly achieved success, come from every walk of life that you can imagine: several races, ethnicities, and income levels.

So, what exactly are our Street Scholars directly recounting to you in these pages?

They're telling you, after a brief introduction from us about our own street education, that they not only believe in the concept of being Street Smart, but that they also use it every day of their successful lives. They further tell you exact examples of how being Street Smart has been useful to them, without mincing words. For the purpose of emphasis, the rules of present-day political correctness and cancel/woke culture are suspended here. So, for those who might be offended, we apologize in advance. These "chapters" are their Street Smart Memoirs. They use, for the most part, their own words—raw but powerful. Amazingly, their stories overlap in many ways but also are distinctly different.

These Street Smart Memoirs are powerful and perhaps even relatable, because you may very well have been aware of being Street Smart in your life.

You have always said that you spotted a brilliant idea like Stephen A. Schwarzman, Bill Gates, Warren Buffett, or those young tech billionaires, and you didn't take advantage of such an opportunity. Especially in the era of COVID, or post-COVID, you may have heard other people tell themselves, regarding a person, industry, or firm that did not survive the years of COVID, "Unlucky bastards, better them than me!"

The traditional "personal advice" books and speakers don't seem to work post-COVID. The old ways of attaining success were: attend "personal advisor" workshops; view movies and videos in conference centers dispensing personal advice; "glad-hand" possible influential people during luncheons and fundraisers; "read" facial gestures and body language for clues; smile and think positive thoughts; work the "magical" overtime and over-weekend hours for guaranteed success; struggle with that school tie; grin inanely like the village idiot; and network, network, network!

During COVID, it was almost impossible to go to "personal advisors," except on the internet; it was also legally and physically risky to network personally; attend big meetings of any type; observe facial and body language through triple-masked faces; gauge the strength and sincerity of handshakes through gloves or telephones; read body language through a MOPP suit, or hold brainstorm sessions in person. "Optimistic" thinking, which was wishful thinking on an international basis, was worse than merely ineffective...it may have killed millions.

Now the obsolete becomes dangerous in a real way. You can be true to the old ways, but as Benjamin Franklin said in *Poor Richard's Almanack*, "Who has deceived thee as oft as thyself?"

With that out of the way, let's continue reading the treatise that you really did help to write. The topic at hand: how famous, accomplished, and successful people in various fields spotted, seized, exploited, and created their lucky breaks.

So, what got people through difficult and troubling times? Being Street Smart, able to spot an opportunity and navigate accordingly in wholly unlucky times. Stephen A. Schwarzman, philanthropist and co-founder of Blackstone, perhaps says it best in his own book, *What It Takes: Lessons in the Pursuit of Excellence*: "For me, the greatest rewards in life have come from creating something new, unexpected, and impactful. I am constantly in pursuit of excellence. When people ask me how I succeed, my basic answer is always the same: I see a unique opportunity, and I go for it with everything I have. And I never give up."[1]

When first conceived, being Street Smart was applicable merely to business success. But as you'll soon read, being Street Smart applies to success in all other walks of life. You'll discover that it's not the number of degrees and diplomas you have hanging on your wall, but the number of times you've been knocked on your ass and found the will to get up again, strategize, and put yourself back in the game.

The concept of a primer actually comes from the early American history of Ben Franklin, hailed as an intellectual and practical war leader. He also suffered from the dreadful gout, which some say may have affected his writings (and perhaps even United States history).

A primer is a short book that contains everyday wisdom on how to adapt to the world. In Franklin's time, both New York and Philadelphia were frontline battlegrounds, and the actual frontier—meaning wild animals and hostile enemies—was a stone's throw away. Franklin and a small staff toiled away at creating a

---

[1]   Stephen A. Schwarzman, *What It Takes: Lessons in the Pursuit of Excellence* (New York: Avid Reader Press, 2019), 8.

primer, which were originally just corny religious sayings, into a practical, lifesaving guide to survival. These writings were immediate bestsellers, rolling off printing presses in the little towns and villages.

That's why we call this book a primer. COVID, certain violent world events, and high crime make survival critical. Boiling down the blubber from the usual self-help or self-improvement book just yields useless fatty oils today. Success means survival, and many have not survived in this era. The difference between survival and failure is the use of Street Smart. The three dozen or so Street Scholars you meet here are directly, and without a soft buffer, passing on the primer. Like Ben Franklin, they do not mince words. Because while the advice of merely one successful person is worthy of respect, the synchronized advice of several dozen successful people is much more compelling, impactful, and far-reaching.

STREET SMART MEMOIR OF JOHNNY AND ROCKY

Johnny and Rocky

THE BEGINNINGS OF BEING STREET SMART

THE BENEFITS OF AN IVY-LEAGUE EDUCATION ON THE ROUGH-ASS STREETS OF OLDE BROOKLYN: STREET SMART ELEMENTARY SCHOOL

We grew up as working-class kids during the '70s and early '80s in Brooklyn, an outer borough of New York City. It was the neighborhood known as Bensonhurst, roughly divided between Jewish communities, Italian Americans, a few Irish Americans, and a handful of WASPs. Everyone was poor or working class. Stores were entirely "mom and pops" with a sprinkling of small groceries. It was lucky to own a single car, let alone the fleets of cars families expect now. Our father worked as a window trimmer (a field now buried by malls) at stores such as Saks Fifth Avenue, B. Altman and Company, and Macy's, famous for his design of the Christmas windows, among many others. Dad was also an accomplished musician who played piano with the "Big Bands" in the '40s. He was a high school dropout, yet he was the only father in our neighborhood who read the *New York Times*. He taught us the value of understanding a more sophisticated vocabulary than the one that we were exposed to in the neighborhood.

Our mother, a Depression-era baby, was a stay-at-home mom, but she worked at a fledgling computer-data-entry company called Interstate Computer in another rough neighborhood to make ends meet. We were both prehistoric latchkey kids, when most moms stayed home and made chocolate pudding. We were out in the schoolyard, playing hoops and avoiding all the bad influences imaginable during the turbulent late '60s and '70s. These influences included: drugs, drinking, petty larceny, discrimination, unsafe sex, among others. You name it. We saw it and passed. No place for this crap in our lives. These vices were for the spoiled brats in the neighborhood.

There's no doubt in our minds that being cheek to cheek with other ethnicities and races, being exposed to other cultures, and being accustomed to the "New York minute" made us sharper when compared to people from slower-paced neighborhoods. New York is the Petri dish of ideas in politics, music, the arts, medicine, and even crime. That follows from the premise here that New York "outer borough life" brings an innate need for being Street Smart. It's the hidden and unwritten curriculum that nobody talks about but is unquestionably present in the mosaic of the "university without walls." Surviving into adulthood equates graduating from this particular "school." Not everyone makes it, but those who do are well-equipped for what lies ahead.

Brooklyn, being a vibrant part of New York City, at least in our day, now looms as a major reason for developing one's Street Smart. It is no accident that many of the Street Scholars lived as neighbors.

Which brings us forward to the dilemma: an entire generation of Americans has been raised without development and appreciation of their own Street Smarts. And they desperately need it. Luckily, an older generation has developed what is needed: direct advice from their collective experiences and mentoring that helped propel them to success amidst setbacks, obstacles, and barriers that seemed unbreakable and insurmountable. This advice is not available in school, not codified in any books, and not given to the newer generations anywhere else. Much of the younger generation has been deprived of exposure to this invaluable skill. It's not their fault. We can blame ourselves as doting parents and teachers, protecting our kids from all the adverse and bad things out there in the real world that we had to endure and overcome. For example, you wouldn't leave a puppy alone in the middle of the woods, would you?

People always lived by their wits, using their own Street Smarts to live better and now to live safer. Back in "Olde Brooklyn," meaning Brooklyn in the '60s/'70s, when no one cared to acknowledge our existence, we each followed our own Street Smarts religiously.

Literally.

Take the example of a poor Jewish "shul," meaning a very small, ill-attended synagogue that was located in our old neighborhood of Bensonhurst. The shul had seen better days, frequented by a rapidly dwindling and aging population of older Jewish people, including many survivors of the Holocaust from Southern Europe. It occupied a ground-floor "open door" premises with the rabbi living on the second floor. Our third base on the punchball court was located directly outside the entrance, and many a Spalding or Pennsy Pinky ball would end up inside the synagogue.

This was not one of the marble super temples of the Upper East and West Side, attended by suited-up celebrities and industry "masters of the universe." No, there were never more than a few dozen poorly dressed old people crammed into a worshiping area all of eighty feet deep and twenty feet wide. Bensonhurst—indeed, most of Brooklyn—was a genuine melting pot of Jewish, Italian, and Irish cultures, where people accepted and even enjoyed differences where politically correct heightened sensibilities were plainly not observed, relevant, or important.

Us streetwise kids saw that the shul needed protection from neighborhood hooligans. It was common for the shul to receive firework and smoke-bomb barrages in the summer, snowball attacks in the winter, and catcalls throughout the long rolling year. This was completely unacceptable and intolerable behavior for the both of us. The neighboring streets were busy Sixty-Fifth Street and Twenty-Fourth Avenue, only twenty feet away through open doors. The congregants competed with eternal truck traffic and honking horns from the streetcars and motorcycle gangs, and the street always won. So, it was easy to disrupt the nighttime services.

One winter day, the rabbi in charge of the shul was walking up Sixty-Fifth Street to shop at the kosher fish market near Bay Parkway and attracted the dubious attention of one local rascal. The rabbi had on a very tall and very wooly fur hat that made him a conspicuous target, even above mountains of newly plowed snow from a recent New York blizzard.

The neighborhood ruffian, a kid about ten, sized up wind direction and distance, blocked street traffic, and hurled a snowball about a hundred feet to its destination. We saw the snowball make contact with its intended target, and the oversized hat ended up in a mound of snow. We gotta admit, we admired the accuracy of the *throw* but not the *dirtbag* who threw it...the kid was a punchball expert who threw a snowball from the east side of Sixty-Fifth Street to the west side, taking enough lead to hit a moving target about a hundred feet away. Naturally, even in Brooklyn, clergy were exempt from attack (yes, how naïve this is today), so we cuffed the kid, picked up the rabbi's hat, got a "thank you" from the holy man, and went home.

Now this was all minor hooliganism, but it goes to prove that force is also an effective language when all else fails. You can turn the proverbial other cheek and end up with two shattered cheekbones and a short "vacation" in the local hospital.

The delinquent in this case was attending a parochial school, so he should have known better. He never showed up again, though. We waited at the unspoken behest of the rabbi, who was certainly of the "turn the other cheek" theology. You can look to Darwinism with the extinction of the dodo bird, whose only response to aggression by humans was being even friendlier, thereby becoming extinct. "Reasonable" is sometimes a cover-up for being dangerous. Certainly, in the streets, the dodo-bird reflex is dangerous enough.

This expanded to protection from snowballs and fireworks tossed into the shul itself. Now, we were "good bullies" as kids, meaning we extended protection from attacks to people that needed it: senior citizens, younger kids, and those with special needs. The start of every school year had the first street fight between the two biggest boys in the grade: Fran Apicella and Paul Fontana, the two best athletes in the class of '72 at St. Athanasius.

We happened to pick up the moniker "good but rough" kids, and we made good money from it, too. Hey, who does something for nothing in a working-class neighborhood? But, it was better than stealing.

So, we were now *Shabbos goyim*, meaning young non-Jewish kids, who on the Sabbath would perform very ordinary household chores on Fridays and Saturdays so the Jewish people could observe appropriately. For a price of course, always for a price! The Jewish families could not attend to very ordinary chores because the Old Testament said it was illegal to do so on the Sabbath.

We were the only Catholic school kids who loved Chanukah more than Christmas. To us, Chanukah meant Chanukah gelt, which tasted far better than the Italian cookies and other delicacies of the season. We knew every major and minor Jewish holiday of the Old Testament as well as the Christian holidays we celebrated. It was good for both business and neighborhood harmony. It was extremely important to know the ways of your neighbors as well as your enemies.

Protection is important. As Catholic school kids, we embraced that the foundation of our religion was based on a Jewish man, Jesus Christ. We always asked our parents, "Why do we go to Catholic school if we were being taught to follow the life and examples of a Jewish man?"

There was never a response, just a nod of the head. and a shrug of the shoulders

Our mother swore that we were running numbers or betting in the streets, as the Sanka coffee jar on our kitchen windowsill was always filled with dollar bills and coins. Our Jewish neighbors taught us the value of entrepreneurship: identifying a need and filling it.

We'd get a quarter for things like turning off light switches, opening mail, lighting a gas burner, or throwing out garbage. Good work if you could get it, and we got it, for the unspoken reward for being decent, caring, and protective, even though we were rough-edged kids. There was no room for religious discrimination on our block. And it was bad for business!

So we spotted and created the lucky break, seized and exploited it, and gained the rewards of being Street Smart, courtesy of our revered Jewish neighbors.

Now no one ever spoke of this, but the link was clear enough for us kids. We were being Street Smart. Brooklyn (and New York) kids grew up being more resilient and resourceful because we lived by our wits. More people meant more interplay. That meant more interaction, schemes, dishonesty, and more reason to employ what we had learned from our experiences. To this day, we regard this as urban evolutionary, Darwinian "Survival of the Fittest" at its best, and it is.

Faster-paced and more cosmopolitan surroundings equate to Street Smarts being exercised on a daily basis. And we lived it in a real-time fashion.

Practically every one of our Street Scholars stresses that using their own version of being Street Smart helped them overcome their social and economic disadvantages, becoming successful enough for us to want to include them in this book.

THE SCIENCE BEHIND STREET SMART

Street Smart is always born and honed in urban or crowded environments, where intense and constant interaction with diverse populations is the norm. It is never forgotten in childhood. It is never hard to define being Street Smart as it is always present. This specific skillset almost always separates the successful from the ordinary.

Extrasensory perception (ESP) is a staple of American folklore. ESP is roughly defined as perception of facts and thoughts not actually derived from the usual senses of sight, smell, hearing, taste, and touch.

Street Smart is itself derived, we believe, from ESP. In other words, people believed that a capacity for Street Smarts existed, and they knew of it. And, of course, they said so. The polls are older but certainly informative and overwhelmingly favorable to the belief that being Street Smart is relevant. As we have stated, the capacity to read a situation or a person beyond mere physical features is a critical component of being Street Smart.

A 2005 Gallup Poll related that 73 percent of Americans believed in some kind of paranormal phenomena, with 41 percent of those polled saying they believe in ESP or used it themselves in their lives. A 2002 Gallup showed a 57 percent belief, as reported in *CBS News*. More polls as in the Baylor Survey (2007) indicated a 63 percent belief in Street Smart as expressed in ESP. The decade before, belief always hovered favorably in the 60–67th and even 70th percentiles.

The *New York Times*, in an issue dated January 10, 1984, traced military applications of ESP from an order from President Jimmy Carter in 1977 to the Central Intelligence Agency to close a perceived "ESP gap" between the United States and the then-Soviet Union. The CIA supposedly responded with several projects accordingly to close the "gap."

Similarly, *CBS News* televised in 2018 the news that the Defense Intelligence Agency (DIA) initiated "Project Star Gate" with a dozen or so ESP-talented individuals in intelligence gathering.

From several media accounts, "Star Gate" existed. In fact, the CIA declassified over twelve million pages of "Project Star Gate" (now defunct under its former name but continued under top secret designation elsewhere), including a program tracking Islamic terrorists. Twelve million pages is a lot of information based on a frivolous topic, by anyone's measure.

One of the authors participated in an early-1970s version of "Star Gate," as reported in the *New York Times* from November 25, 1973. The concept explored and proved statistically is called remote viewing: reading a person's mind from another, sealed, isolated room in the building.

In this article, "Federal Grant Supports ESP Dream Research at Maimonides," *Times* reporter Gordon T. Thompson recounted the basic outline of the experiments that had been conducted in 1974–75.

With a major grant from the National Institute of Mental Health, the Maimonides Medical Center of Parapsychology and Psychophysics conducted both experiments. Maimonides is a major hospital in, of course, Brooklyn. The NIMH is another major player, not given to frivolous causes. It was, and is, notoriously tightfisted in giving away money. Its spokesman told the *Times*:

> The evidence of ESP, not only from our work but from a dozen other experiments, establishes beyond any reasonable scientific doubt that it occurs. It is important that research on ESP now shifts from attempts to demonstrate that something unusual is happening—which has been the argument over the last 90 years—to what kind of situations and individuals are necessary for it to be obtained.
>
> Many scientists have argued that parapsychology—the term commonly applied to ESP research—is not a true science and point to its long years as the exclusive province of carnival mind readers and charlatans. But the American

Association for the Advancement of Science, the country's largest scientific association, has recognized it as a discipline and admitted it as an affiliate, in effect recognizing ESP research as a legitimate scientific enterprise.

This was the program one of the authors participated in as part of a joint Long Island University (Brooklyn Center, of course!) cooperation between Maimonides Medical Center and LIU's Honor Programs, with "unofficial assistance" from the United States Army.

Effectively, one "sender" tries to mentally project a glimpse of a registered image to another person (a receiver) in a neighboring room, with a crew tape recording both persons as they recount what is going through their mind. They are sensory deprived otherwise (wearing eye coverings and earmuffs) and kept in relative darkness for concentration. People are "statistically psychic" when their "hit scores," meaning when they exactly match the image projected to what they were sent, in such accuracy that it can't be explained away by mere chance. (Seeing the *Mona Lisa* or Malibu at the same exact time without clues is psychic.) And the same ability termed Street Smart, registered similarly, is the capability to see an opportunity or avoid a trap.

Last, but hardly least, the US Marine Corps (USMC) participated in an Office of Naval Research (ONI) program exploring the "Spidey sense" (ESP of Marvel superhero "Spiderman") of Marines and sailors that lasted four years and cost several million dollars. "Spidey sense" or not, this was Street Smarts for Marines.

In popular culture, ESP was fictionalized in the 2009 film *The Men Who Stare at Goats*, starring Jeff Bridges and George Clooney. The movie accurately, if in a tongue-in-cheek way, depicts a remote reading program undertaken by the United

States military in the aftermath of 9/11. The military used Street Smarts to track down terror cells. This involved actual combat in Street Smart tactics during the invasion and pacification of Iraq. The official word is that such programs have wound down to basically caretaker administration. The unofficial word is that the programs still exist, though not advertised in military literature.

Similarly, both the Russian government and the Chinese government have unpublicized Street Smart programs. The *New York Times* picked up the lead way back in the '70s in an article titled, "Émigré Tells of Research in Soviet in Parapsychology for Military Use," by veteran reporter Flora Lewis. In that *Times* article, the old Soviet KGB (national Russian secret police) drafted sixty experts in many scientific fields. Physics was the primary emphasis. It was eventually termed "Special Department Number Eight."

Further research is found in "Unconventional Research in the USSR and Russia," by Serge Kernbach, archived at ARXIV. org, with over three hundred scholarly citations (Dec. 5, 2013). Curiously, a specific Soviet Army unit based at Novosibirsk (Russia) and tagged unit "715 A2" was employed for Street Smart purposes. Soviet, then Russian, research focused on Street Smart mental emissions.

In short, the CIA, DIA, USMC, ONI, our Street Scholars (including Bo Dietl, Detective, NYPD), various other national governments, and most Americans believe or at least publicly believed in a version of being Street Smart. But, being Street Smart isn't taught or scripted, and it can certainly be fleeting.

STREET SMART CLASSICS: GUYS WHO WEREN'T LUCKY ENOUGH TO BE BORN IN BROOKLYN, OR WHO ARE DEAD RIGHT NOW

There's Street Smart wisdom from ancient China and Middle Ages Europe, well quoted over the centuries, but which has been adapted in various self-help and business strategies. Sun Tzu, Chinese military general and part-time philosopher, is considered a timeless doyen. Niccolò Machiavelli, more quoted for his political savvy, was a philosopher whose thoughts served great influence over the sixteenth, seventeenth, eighteenth, and nineteenth centuries. Both men's ideas adapt well to Street Smart, the school of thought of the twenty-first century.

SUN TZU, STREET SMART, AND SEIZING LUCKY BREAKS

Work smart, not just hard. Only work smart at what you can win.

Self-Knowledge Is Critical to Seizing Luck

If you know both the enemy and yourself, victory will come easy. If you know yourself but not the enemy, you will win as often as you lose. If you know neither the enemy nor yourself, you will always lose. Make no mistakes; conquer an enemy already defeated by your planning. The moment you seize will defeat the wiliest enemy.

Seize Luck Before Another Does

Leave nothing to chance. Seize luck first. He who seizes luck first wins.

STREET SMART IN THE RENAISSANCE

Machiavelli on Luck

While quoted essentially for politics, with his book used by every political party in the world, Machiavelli can be seen as a precursor of Street Smart for his contemporaries. Luck was a "traditional" woman to Niccolò: fickle, malleable, and absolutely unpredictable. We think this is nonsense, but he conceptualized that luck was largely a matter of being attuned to "the times." Cautious strategies work in some instances and lead to ruin in others. Bold strategies come into play at other times. "The Mac" also noted that bold men sometimes get their heads handed to them, literally, in a basket. He uses archaic but effective examples from Europe:

Machiavelli's Chapter 25: What Role Fortune Plays in Human Affairs and How to Control Her

People believe that luck rules all endeavors and can't be influenced by human willpower. But Machiavelli believed that only half of our fate is luck. Luck is like a wild and raging river which sweeps onto the land. Those prepared for her ravages will survive; these preparations include canals and other defenses. Luck attacks those unprepared for her wiles. She turns her force mostly against weakness. Some court luck by force and skill, but this often fails. Some court luck by patience, but this too is subject to failure. One must accommodate oneself to change itself: hence the adaptable survive, because they choose either caution or force. Divining which approach is successful is paramount. Here, the Duke is a sadistic masochist: he states that luck, being like a woman, needs to be beaten into submission. He certainly wouldn't have made it with this attitude in present-day society.

STREET SMART AND WAR

Ernest Hemingway said that war was the province of chance. The generals and military strategic thought confirm the legendary writer's thoughts. But chance is hardly blind. Generals and admirals know this better than anyone, matched possibly by entertainers and some businesspeople.

Of course, the military calls this "opportunism," which is not a dirty word to them, or now, to you. Opportunism means a lot of things. To the military, it means taking advantage of a friendly strength or an enemy weakness.

Leading examples of this include three great World War II generals: General George S. Patton, General Erwin Rommel, and Soviet Marshal Georgy Zhukov. Also, one American Civil War general, William Tecumseh Sherman.

What they knew is still valuable, if not imparted to you personally.

George S. Patton: You Make Your Own Luck

The four-star general was born to a military family and was the wealthiest officer in the United States Army, though he also suffered from dyslexia. The Nazis were more frightened of him than any other opposing officer of equal rank. The reasons were many: General George S. Patton was unpredictable, in an army of very assured formulaic American and British generals; he was always planning several campaigns in advance; he did not accept laxity or unprofessionalism in his own generals or his men; and he knew his business. He also was keenly aware of the tactics, strengths, and weaknesses of his adversaries.

Street Smart characteristics all. But more to the point, Patton believed in the lucky break.

He said so at great length in his books, official orders, and comments to his superiors and his own troops. To a point, he reflected the adage you will read here of making your own luck. But that always oversimplified the process of Street Smart. The lucky break is *always* there. Spotting it, seizing it, and exploiting it are what is often missing.

Patton Street Smarted the entire war. It was reported in recent histories that his campaign in Sicily relied on information reported to him by the Sicilian Mafia.

Yes, the Mafia, the "Mano Nera."

They semi-ruled Sicily and provided Patton's troops with better intelligence on German defenders that couldn't be gotten anywhere else. The Mafia passed the information onto classified sources who, in turn, told Patton, who then used the information to bypass strongpoints. The Germans were totally baffled because he knew more about their troop dispositions than they did. In France, without a Mafia, Patton used thousand-year-old maps to plan modern campaigns flawlessly. In the Battle of the Bulge, when everyone else assumed the war against Germany was over, Patton smelled a rat and prepared his army to relieve American troops trapped in Bastogne by a revitalized Nazi army. He always demanded more of his troops and received it. He was always two campaigns in advance of the one he was currently embroiled in.

Each episode, and there are many more, revealed a capacity to use one's Street Smart in war. Patton's troops hated him in many ways, but they also loved him because he always won and spared their lives. Patton, in fact, believed in the adage, "Hit them where they ain't," meaning find the hole in the enemy line and then push your troops through.[2] Somehow, he always knew where the gap was, a talent that eluded every other American general, except General Douglas MacArthur, who served in the Pacific against the Japanese warlords. MacArthur also believed in the "hit them" adage, flinging American troops (including our father) against lightly occupied islands.

Erwin Rommel: War Is in Your Fingertips

Rommel was an honorable man in a dishonorable and cruel war. But he believed, as most great warriors, that your "fingertips" guide the war. Rommel was always upfront with his men: he spotted weak places in the enemy (British) defenses in Africa and exploited their weaknesses. He could not do this, he argued, waiting for news back at headquarters. He was credited by his troops with a "Sixth Sense." There are comical stories, even in war, about Rommel's front-line antics. Once he found himself inspecting, as generals in all wars do, an army hospital to encourage the troops. He only then realized that the hospital was an enemy hospital.

In another instance, Rommel's command car was on one side of a road while a heavily armed British armored convoy was passing him to the front. Rommel just waved and sped up. The British soldiers waved back and not a shot was fired though the convoys were all of ten feet apart.

Rommel spotted as a lucky break a seam between armies defending against him and thus saw a weak spot. This won him many battles. Acting as his own scout was dangerous, but even the British enemy admired him for it. "You've got to hand it

---

[2] Basil Liddel Hart, *Strategy* (New York: Plume, 1991).

to the bastard Rommel," they said.[3] While he served a vile and evil Hitler, his comportment with war was strictly honorable. Prisoners were humanely treated. It was unknown for Rommel to be cruel, besides killing or wounding for military necessity.

Georgy Zhukov: War and Luck Must Be Bent to Your Will

Zhukov's humble origins and his Street Smart can be divined from a sample of his personal life which he allowed historians a glimpse of: he marveled, in his own old age, how his mother used to heft hundred-pound bags of produce on her back when he lived with her as a child. For Zhukov, life was hard but could be conquered by being Street Smart, though he never called it that.

In the Soviet Army, the slogan arose "Where there is Zhukov, there is victory." He was even called *Spasitel*, or "savior," by the ordinary Russian people when he beat the Nazi armies invading Russia in 1941–45. The Street Smart reasons are many.

He insisted on perfect performances with no mistakes. He insisted on bravery in the face of impossible odds. He expected his men to stand or die. As proof of this, he issued strict orders to station military police behind his own lines to shoot anyone found retreating, even if it was really reasonable to do so. He did so to actually save Russian lives—when the Nazis found a gap, they exploited it and killed far more soldiers than before. He insisted on spotting, seizing, and exploiting lucky breaks, even when his superiors yelled at him otherwise. He used the firing squad for officers and suicidal "punishment battalions" of soldiers who showed less-than-perfect courage for the most difficult

---

[3] David Fraser, *Knight's Cross: A Life of Field Marshal Erwin Rommel* (New York: Harper Perennial, 1994), 309-311.

jobs. "It was hard not to be brave in the Soviet Army," even his commander Joseph Stalin stated. Zhukov, for example, always tried to put himself in the shoes of his enemies. At Stalingrad, a great trap was laid for the Nazis because Zhukov read the mind of the more conventionally-trained Nazis.

William Tecumseh Sherman: Pick Your Fights Carefully and Attack the Enemy as a Nation, Not Just Its Soldiers

In the American Civil War, victory was measured in men killed, which brought no end to the battle. After suffering a nervous breakdown, General Sherman, a Union officer fighting the Confederate troops, had a Street Smart moment:

Why attack the soldiers when we can attack the support systems of the rebel armies...their farms, factories, ports, livestock?

Accordingly, Sherman went on a great and damaging rampage, with an army, through the civilized South. He avoided enemy strongpoints and destroyed factories, farms, and productive assets of the South. He was screamed at by both friend and foe as a monster. But it worked. Enemy troops started deserting their commands to travel home to defend their farms.

The remaining Southern armies ran out of supplies, like food and shoes. Clothing became ragged. Bullets were now scarce. Sherman saw the South as his enemy. Not just the Southern soldiers.

STREET SMART DIARY

OLDE BROOKLYN STYLE

t's how it all began. Thankfully, we were not "fortunate" enough to have grown up in a privileged and comfortable neighborhood or household. We had a very untraditional way of learning in Brooklyn that was nowhere near the Ivy League colleges of Yale and Harvard. We could only dream about these places and read about them in our history books. We had no connections to prestigious institutions like this or role models to emulate. We couldn't go to sleepaway camp and swim in the lake or play tennis on the clay or grass courts. Instead, we went to the asphalt schoolyard to play punchball, stickball, stoopball, kickball, and arc softball. We received an education that can't be replicated anywhere else.

During the hazy and hot days of summer, we cooled ourselves under the fire hydrant that had a cap adapter drilled with many holes, made by the fire department, that created a great sprinkler and cooling system. We would lie in the street and bathe in the cold fire-hydrant waterfalls. We would wash the passing cars as a token of neighborhood etiquette, making sure their windows were up to protect them from the strong water stream of the hydrant.

The opposite was also true. If we didn't like you as a neighbor, you and your passengers would receive a free shower along with the car.

We knew nothing of country club swimming pools, but we were still happy and content. You don't miss what you never had. This was our camp, our learning outside of the classroom, on the toughest playing field of them all. The ice cream from the Good Humor truck was our version of s'mores. The unforgiving and unpredictable streets gave us street kids an advantage for what was to come later in life. This was our version of being able to live on a handful of rice.

Elementary school nuns taught us how to read and write, but not speak eloquently. Our accent, language, body movements, and word inflection were our defining traits. We had to go to elocution lessons to learn how to pronounce our words and "drop the slang." Brooklyn College professors were more than happy and accommodating to turn us into "Little Lord Fauntleroys," at least until we were angered by someone, and then the "Brooklyn brogue" reappeared. Proper pronunciation went right out the window. We transformed from speaking the Queen's English back to Kings County Brooklyn English. Our high school English teacher from Xaverian High School, Mr. Jim Martin, once told our class, "The only difference between you and the prep school boys is that they talk and dress better than you do."

We received our education in the best classroom of them all: the concrete stoop. Six cool steps where the biggest of us kids would sit at the top in the "power pecking order" while the smaller ones took their places at the bottom rung. This is the place where we learned about loyalty, love, shrewdness, forgiveness, tolerance, compassion, and so many of the vital subjects that comprised our Street Smart education. Every neighborhood had their stoop—our version of a university—where ideas were exchanged and plans were made. We all taught each other these important and life-saving skills, sharing our dreams with one another and with our families while sitting on the stoop, fixated on the summer Van Gogh sky, wondering one day where we'd all end up. Growing up, it was our classroom and university.

That was the unique thing about the streets; none of us were experts in all the important survival areas, but at least we exposed one another to our talents and shared the many tidbits of surviving the asphalt jungle. We were essentially pack animals. The local stores and shops knew us. They were our watchdogs. One bad move and your parents were told the next time they made their trip to the bakery or butcher. That was an unbelievably efficient way of policing the area. Everyone's parents went to the same shops and stores, so there was no escaping the word getting out. Everyone's parents looked out for the other kids, not just their own. It wasn't unusual to be reprimanded more than once for the same offense: your pal's mom down the block and again by your own parents, with the addition of a kick in the ass when you arrived home.

Brooklyn has evolved over the many decades. Unlike Philadelphia, Chicago, Detroit, and Boston (all of which served as valuable training grounds in their own right), Brooklyn has probably conferred the most degrees for being Street Smart of any city in the country and, probably, the world. Barbra Streisand, Neil Diamond, Donna Karan, Joe Torre, Dr. Salvatore Ferrera, and so many others are considered "graduates" of Street Smart education.

The candy store was another interesting place. It was the command central of the neighborhood. In between chocolate egg creams and tuna salad on a Kaiser roll, the kids would get the latest on the sporting world and what teams won and lost. Many times, the local bookies would act like sports newscasters regarding baseball, football, horse racing, and the like. Tennis, squash, golf, and soccer were foreign games to us, and these were way above our social strata. No betting on these sports, as most of us had no clue about how these games were played and we lacked a point of reference. These sports were for kids that came from educated homes, means, and wealth. We could only dream that one day we could go from caddying and washing cars at the country club to actually being a member.

Sonya and Milton, an elderly Romanian Jewish couple, owned our neighborhood candy store. They made the best chocolate egg creams on a hot summer day and the best chicken soup during an extreme cold front. The candy store was never very busy, so we always wondered how Sonya and Milton made a living.

It appeared that little kids were not the only customers in the candy store. So were "big kids," like our fathers and uncles. This became painfully clear one summer day. We accompanied our father to the candy store, where Dad met a couple of his buddies. We left Dad in the store after seeing some of our friends. Suddenly, the empty candy shop was taken over by police cars from our local 66th precinct, sirens blazing and people yelling as lookouts, trying to warn everybody that the cops were about to invade.

It turns out that chocolate egg creams and tuna salad sandwiches weren't the only items on the menu.

This was the day we learned how they made their actual living: the shop was a front for the local bookies to take bets on horse racing and arrange for loan sharking. We were stunned, seeing all the policemen and well-dressed detectives putting our handcuffed neighbors in the paddy wagon.

When they went to bust Dad, we hysterically explained to them that this was our father and that our mother wasn't around. Who would take care of us? The sergeant heard us out and realized that it wouldn't look good for little kids to come out of the police wagon. He looked at us, stared at my father, and told us to get lost and disappear from his sight. We beat them on this account, and Dad came a hair close to having to explain to Mom why she would have to bail him out at the police precinct. His friends were not as fortunate.

Anyway, this set a precedent. Fathers who planned on playing the ponies knew never to go and place a bet at the candy store without bringing one of their young kids. It was the best form of protection against incarceration. What it did demonstrate to Dad was that we could keep our mouths shut better than anyone. He saw that his sons possessed one of the most important traits to survive the mean streets. We never even told Mom—or anyone else, for that matter. But Mom Positano will be finding out once she reads this passage....

Now, all the "mom and pop" shops have been replaced with higher-end ritzy and preppy boutiques. A cup of coffee has been replaced with fancy caffeinated and non-caffeinated beverages, many of which are tongue twisters and difficult to pronounce. What happened to just asking for a simple cup of coffee?

OUR OLD NEIGHBORHOOD

The neighborhood was an interesting place: a real melting pot. Italian and Jewish cultures were the two biggest ethnic communities. The Italian street guys were very protective of their Jewish neighbors. We were *mishpocha*, meaning family.

Religion played a big part in growing up. All the parishes and synagogues in the city acted like independent states. People knew who you were, where you lived, and what you were made of depending on your parish or synagogue. Social casting at its best. If you came from a certain parish, it defined who you were socially and economically. It was simple. People in certain parishes lived in beautiful homes while others lived above a candy or shoe store. God forbid a kid from a poorer parish would hook up with a kid from a richer one. This was a version of the UN with the priests and rabbis acting as ambassadors and senators. The way you prayed at one parish was different from other parishes. We thought God and the saints played by different rules from house of worship to house of worship. The local priests and rabbis would have no problem accepting a dinner invitation from the wealthy congregants, but they also wouldn't hesitate to oversee the funeral services of the poorer, less elite, and working-class worshippers. But breaking bread with us was very unlikely except at the communion breakfast, where powdered eggs and burnt potatoes were the fare of the gathering. Remember, we were from the wrong side of the tracks.

The relationship between our communities was very special. Orthodox Jewish girls always had a thing for Italian street guys and vice versa. The poor darlings couldn't have too much fun with Zach or Moshe, but with Tony and Johnny, the sky was the limit for one very good reason: these girls had to be very careful about their virtuous behavior within their community. One indiscretion, and they'd be ostracized and no one from their clan would want to marry them. Translated, this meant a boring existence. However, when they hung out with us, their secret was safe. We respected these girls as fine young ladies, and as gentlemen, we never even attempted to "go the distance" or cross the line of decent and respectable behavior. They could dance and party as well as any other girl. What most impressed the guys were the beautiful clothes they wore. They were fashion plates. No sneakers, cut-off jeans with patches, daisy duke shorts, or tank-tops for these girls. They were impeccably dressed with gorgeous skirts, blouses, and elegant fashion shoes. It was an oasis to the eyes of an Italian street boy. We only saw clothing like this in our Mom's fashion magazines.

This was the Brooklyn version of the movie *Dirty Dancing*. Nobody ever snitched. We were just having some good clean fun, but never on a Friday after sundown, because we knew the traditions and the customs associated with Shabbos. There has always been a strong attraction between the opposite sexes of both groups.

Streetwise Italian men always loved the sophistication found in Jewish women. It was about lifestyle, culture, tradition, and knowing how to dress to the *nines*. Jewish women loved the rough, tough, and tumble found in Italian street boys. In Yiddish, an Italian guy is known as "Italyeinish zachor." The ladies always felt safe and secure, and there was no doubt that the Italians were always protective of their Jewish neighbors dating back to World War II Italy, especially in towns like Positano and Sorrento.

Our mother, Frances, always says that the best and most stable marriage on the Positano and Bagnuola sides of the family was between our cousin, the educator and loyal Yankee fan, Roger Aiello and his bride of over fifty years, the former Betty

Postrion. When they first started dating, Roger had to change his name to a faux Jewish name, and hence Roger Aiello became Roger Gershon during the courtship, because Betty's mom would not have approved of the match otherwise. This was before the controversial TV program *Bridget Loves Bernie* was in vogue. Betty's mom loved Roger "Gershon," and eventually she was told the truth that her daughter had fallen in love with a *thaliana* (Yiddish word for Italian man). It had a lot of do with the fact that Roger came from Bensonhurst originally, where mixed religious marriages were more commonplace than in other locals. This was plainly accepted because Jew and Italian cultures shared what can only be seen now as an old-fashioned worship of family and family ties. Organized religion sometimes took second place based on the circumstances.

There was also a lot of anti-Semitism in the neighborhood, but we didn't allow it on our block and especially in front of our Jewish lady friends. Their community was a pillar of strength. They ran all the major businesses in the neighborhood and were the most formally educated. We took an anti-Semitic kid to task after he insulted one of our lady friends for being Jewish. What made it worse was that she had just lost her brother in a fraternity hazing accident in upstate New York. The word spread very fast that this type of activity would not be tolerated. In our neighborhood, Italians protected the Jewish communities and vice versa, which is still true to this day, but in a different way and manner.

During the late '60s, there was an Italian American movement called Italian American Unity Day. All of these *paisani* would get together in Manhattan's Columbus Circle to demonstrate Italian unity and pride. Unfortunately, the day was also an excuse for some of the local hoodlums to terrorize the merchants, which was the complete antithesis of what the day was supposed to represent. One of their gang rules was that on this Unity Day, all neighborhood businesses had to close down for the afternoon out of "respect" for the Italian community. The Jewish merchants were terrified and were often threatened that if they didn't close their shops, their store windows would be broken and vandalized with graffiti.

One of our favorite Jewish merchants in the neighborhood was named Maxie, owner of Maxie's Dry Goods. He was blind as a bat and had spectacles as thick as Coca-Cola bottles. A young local hoodlum visited Maxie the day before the rally, trying to shake him down. Maxie refused to be scared because he had our group as a protection agency. He summoned us to his store to tell us about the threats. We wouldn't dare let anything happen to Maxie's store. Where else could we buy our mothers their handkerchiefs or hair combs on credit for Mother's Day? We took it upon ourselves to go to the social club in the area and speak with the local mob chieftain. We were assured that nothing would happen to Maxie's store, and nothing did. We never stiffed Maxie; even if we bought something on credit and couldn't pay for it, we'd make good by washing the windows of the store. Let's just say that when all was said and done, Maxie always had the cleanest windows in the entire neighborhood.

The Chinese laundry was a different story. It seemed that no one in the area embraced or socially interacted with the Chinese merchants very much, most likely because it appeared that they didn't seem to understand our traditions. Even though we didn't always see eye to eye, us Italians and our Jewish neighbors knew that the Asian community was incredibly hardworking and industrious.

The owner of the laundry was warned about staying open for Unity Day. This laundry was known for their hand pressing.

They would hand press sheets and shirts in the front of the store for the public to see. On this Italian American Unity Day, the Chinese laundry owner was pressing and starching his shirts. In one instant, three fellows went to the foot of his door and let fly a barrage of water balloons, not bullets, on all of the shirts and sheets he was pressing. Interestingly, the next year, the Chinese laundry observed Unity Day and remained closed.

The Chinese were best known for their laundries and, of course, the local Chinese restaurant, Taeng Fong, located on Bay Parkway across from Smolenski's kosher deli.

To an Italian family, the idea of going out to eat in a Chinese restaurant, or any restaurant for that matter, was as foreign as one could imagine. That was usually reserved for gatherings at Bamonte's on Withers St. in Brooklyn after a family funeral. As a matter of fact, if it weren't for our reformed Jewish neighbors, most Italians would have never eaten Chinese food. Sunday night was the night that our Jewish friends would flock to the Chinese restaurant. There was always a line out the door. Like the Italians, Jewish people knew where to eat.

Italians owe a lot to the Jewish faith and vice versa. We loved their adherence to and respect for traditions and family values, their cohesiveness as a group, and we were totally intrigued by their outlook on death and dying. They handled death with a great mystique. If you were dead at eight in the morning, you were in the ground by three in the afternoon. No fancy double-spring mattresses in the casket, but instead, a simple and degradable pine box. No fancy three-piece suit, Hermès tie, and shirt, but instead, a simple burial shroud. No Aunt Millie or Uncle Tony trying to pull Grandma Nettie out of her open casket the morning of the funeral, but instead, a closed casket. No embalming, eye make-up, lipstick, lip glue, or anything else like that.

One of the funeral directors who would visit the neighborhood regularly was an Italian guy named Joe. Joe was extremely unusual because, unlike most funeral directors of Italian extraction, he worked in one of the major Jewish funeral chapels in the city. His pick-ups were always the easiest, as he would refer to his Jewish bodies as the "in and outs." We had once asked him, kidding around, if there was a difference between Jewish and gentile bodies. He gave an answer stating that Jewish cadavers had the most crooked and worst-looking feet and toes. He really did believe this, but we thought that distinction belonged to Italian grandparents with their overlapping second and third toes and huge bunions stuffed into an ill-fitting shoe.

In addition, he was a crazy opera fan. After picking up his bodies, he would blast Italian opera tapes and sing along in the hearse going north and south on West End Avenue while his Jewish customers were trying to rest in peace.

Next to the priest and mobster, the funeral director was the most respected guy in our neighborhood. Keep in mind, we say "respected," not liked or even welcomed into the home. Italians had these superstitions about inviting the mortician over to the house for a cup of espresso or a quick bite. This was taboo. The undertaker was *persona non grata*. He got to see all your body parts and dirty secrets when you died. In the end, you couldn't hide anything from him. He wasn't welcome in the home because one had the distinct impression that when he was speaking with you, he was also sizing you up for the right casket size and funeral attire for a later date.

We will never forget that when our maternal grandfather, Danny Bagnuola, the gravedigger, was dying, one of our aunts innocently invited "Goomba" Jimmy Anastasio, the family undertaker, to visit from Lorimer Street in the Greenpoint area in Brooklyn. We will never forget how crazy Grandpa got when he saw Goomba Jimmy ringing his doorbell for a social visit. He already realized that his days were numbered, as he was suffering from end stage lung cancer. To the Italian people, knowing who was going to take care of you in death was just as important as who took care of you in life. Our family had this obsession that only Goomba Jimmy could see our bodies and prepare our corpses for burial.

Jimmy had a young grandson named Andrew who was the complete opposite of Joe from the Jewish chapel. Andy was inheriting his grandfather's funeral business. He frequently visited the morgue to pick up his customers. Andy dressed like a *GQ* model—tailored suits, monogrammed shirts, silk ties, and Napoleon shoes. He treated his bodies with the same sense of style and fashion. He personally embalmed the bodies, washed them, dressed them, manicured their nails, and coiffed their hair. His bodies looked better in death than they had in life.

One day, Andy went to his funeral parlor to check on a wake in progress. Because he spent so much time there, it wasn't unusual for him to have his suits and shirts delivered to the funeral home. He checked all the clothes that were delivered and noticed that his favorite suit was missing. After frantically calling the cleaners, they assured him that by the evening his suit would appear.

Well...it sorta did....

Two hours passed, and Andy still had no suit. He went around the chapel to check on the various wakes in progress.

After searching through two services, he entered a third parlor, and as he stood in the door, he noticed something familiar about the man lying in the casket. Andy approached slowly, and to his amazement, he found his favorite custom-tailored suit on the body of one of his customers. He internally went ballistic, leaving the parlor in a huff, and summoned his dresser about finding his favorite suit on one of the customers. The dresser explained that the suit had to be "cut" on the body because it was way too small for the obese deceased man and he had mistakenly thought the designer suit belonged to the stiff. Andy screamed at him, making the point that the man now wearing his favorite suit happened to weigh fifty pounds more than Andy did, which would explain why the suit had to be split down the back of the jacket and the pants. Even Andy had to admit, though, that this was one well-dressed good-looking corpse.

The local funeral parlor wasn't always about death. It did have other benefits. As teenagers, a group of us started a rock band. A huge problem was that there was no place to rehearse in Brooklyn, especially for kids like us. We didn't have a garage, and no way would our parents let us drag our instruments and amps into their houses (as if we had any space in our tiny apartment, anyway). However, one of our bandmates' fathers owned the neighborhood funeral home, which turned out to be more beneficial for us aspiring rock stars than we thought.

One day after softball practice, we went back to the funeral home for ice water from the cooler, and we saw one of the workers rolling a casket out of the elevator in preparation for a wake. Our friend said that the casket room upstairs was where bereaved families would go to pick out the best casket for their loved ones to rest as comfortable as one can in the afterlife with their double mattress spring lining that would guarantee eternal comfort.

We all had a Street Smart thought: Band rehearsal in the casket room. It was available, cheap, and we couldn't wake anyone up. They were already dead.

Why not? The room had great acoustics and a natural reverb. It was air-conditioned, had a high ceiling, and was spacious. So, we moved a Gretsch drum set, Marshall guitar amps, a Fender bass, and a Farfisa organ all up into the casket room. This was our version of the Grateful Dead.

It was a great place to rock out.

Well...almost.

During a wake (and rehearsal), some of the grieving family members complained about a steady thumping sound clearly emanating from the bass drum pedal. Our musical venture was at risk.

It did work for a while, until we got a little adventuresome. To create a better vibe amongst all the depressing caskets, we thought adding a strobe light would really lighten the mood. The owner of the funeral home didn't exactly agree with us. His face turned red and rightfully so. The lights flashing from the upstairs windows made his business look like a Brooklyn disco, one that was definitely visible to the bereaved guests. "Casket Room" concerts had now come to an end, just like the funeral for the fellow downstairs that was laid out. Of course, the dead don't complain.

The Street Smart lesson we learned? Don't push the envelope when you already have a sweet deal going. We were lucky enough to have the casket room rehearsal space, but we messed it up by adding the unnecessary light show. Instinct and experience should dictate the next move, if any.

Italians also like to use a wake as a place to meet potential spouses. Everyone is dressed to the nines and on their best behavior. Hey, you are going to see the best in most of these mourners. Many a match was made at an Italian wake, as well as many a personal vendetta resolved, because of the deceased's wishes for family members and friends to resolve their differences. Nobody, however, would ever fess up that they met their future spouse at Aunt Millie's wake.

One morning, our Uncle Joe was being buried. His widow, Aunt Rosie Ansanelli, was inconsolable, and she became very emotional and demanding at the last moment. Joe's casket was a "halfie," meaning that it was only opened from above the waist and up. Rosie made this big scene and she demanded to see that Joe was buried in his favorite trousers and shoes. She had memories of going to a funeral in her younger years where the deceased was being buried without shoes and pants on—a sin in Aunt Rosie's eyes (and an embarrassing one, too). That specific funeral had been put together in a "rush job," hastily coordinated to accommodate one of the grieving family members leaving town, and in such a rush, the dresser neglected to add shoes and pants to the deceased's ensemble. He erroneously assumed that nobody would ever know. Luckily, Joe was buried with both on.

Italians have these funny quirks about burials and wakes. They're notorious for burying their loved ones with some object that the deceased loved during their lifetime. You may see pictures, jewelry, sacred religious ornaments, and baseballs lined neatly in the casket before it is finally sealed.

These quirks also explain why Aunt Rosie went nuclear (again) when she realized Uncle Joe was going to be buried without his favorite hat. Not wanting her husband to go into the afterlife without it, Aunt Rosie sent one of her cousins to the house to retrieve the hat. However, Joe's dog and closest companion Pepe wasn't so keen on giving up his best friend's hat and wouldn't give in so easily. After nearly being bitten and attacked, Aunt Rosie's cousin raced back to the funeral parlor with no hat. Goombah Jimmy had to think fast, and without telling Joe's widow, took one of his own hats and put it on the deceased, right before his casket was sealed. Aunt Rosie spent the rest of her days convinced that her husband was buried with his absolute favorite hat.

Speaking of Aunt Rosie, who passed in her nineties, she had wits sharper than a straight-edge razor. She got to be so old because, frankly, she outlived most everyone else by intimidation. She earned the family nickname, "The General." Basically, all the men in the family were scared shitless of her and never had the balls to confront her or disagree with her.

An Italian's biggest concern (second to where they would retire), was where they were going to be buried. Aunt Rosie saw this fear as an opportunity and took full advantage. Through shrewd horse trading, she amassed many cemetery plots in the various and sundry New York area Catholic and civil cemeteries. Some were left to her as a bequest, it was rumored, through card sharking our most dimwitted neighbors and kin. As Aunt Rosie stated it, "The law is the law, but swag is swag," which puts her in the elite of New York civil service, government, and the judiciary. The "swag" here was the cemetery plots. Everyone needs one eventually. That's the law part. But you had to get them through Aunt Rosie.

Accordingly, she parsed them out miserly and played by her own rules. It absolutely terrified some husbands to be buried with their wives, thinking they'd nag them through three or more feet of New York soil. The dead are usually quiet enough, but why take chances? Being buried for eternity with some husbands was too much for some wives. If he was sloppy or crude, he would probably be the same after he died. Now this went the same for *gumbas* and *goomaras*, essentially lovers. The same for dismal siblings. For some reason, being buried with Mom and Dad was usually a safe bet.

To avoid unpleasant interment, some people begged Aunt Rosie for alternate resting requirements, usually for a trade or some cash or an insurance policy. But that could be arranged, as complaints were muffled by either satisfaction or the cold earth of the grave. The dead don't complain. This we noticed right off hand.

But there were other considerations. Like the geographic earth—besides the usual where to bury in what named cemetery. Location, location, location is what the realtors desire, and here it was really so because once planted, the choices became limited enough. St. John's, St. Raymond's, Calvary, and Green-Wood were all A-List cemeteries in New York that were part of her real estate grave portfolio. She would have even impressed Count Dracula and his Carfax Abbey with her stakes in these places.

If you were born in Brooklyn, Queens, or the Bronx, you wanted to be buried as close to home as possible when the time came. Family and friends could always visit, and loved ones would never be separated from each other, even in the afterlife. So, Staten Island and New Jersey weren't the most desirable places for us Brooklynites to be put six feet under. Those from Manhattan couldn't seem to care less.

Accordingly, Aunt Rosie kept supply and demand sharpened by intimidation, making sure that people were kept on her limited good side. This deferment to her wishes, honed by death and aging, held her in good stead until she died as well. This was how the General kept law and order in the family. Rock once told this story to Woody Allen, who found it hysterically funny and ironic.

***

Religion played a central role in our neighborhood. Going to a Catholic school made it very difficult not to be a practicing Catholic. Whether you liked it or not, you were going to practice your faith. One of the mandatory things was confession. This was what Catholic kids feared most. The school made it mandatory that once a month we would be paraded across the street to St. Athanasius, forced to wait in lines, and confess our sins, whether we had any or not. As a matter of record, we can't be accused of being disrespectful to religion, as we came from a prominent religious family where one of our uncles, Father John Positano, was a very well-known and respected clergyman.

What scared us the most was which priest would hear our confessions. Sometimes, this created havoc. There were our favorite priests that everyone would try to get on their line outside of the confessional, and then there were the one or two priests from Hell that everyone would try to avoid. In a small church, it was very easy to tell who the popular priest was. All you had to do was look at the line outside one of the confessional boxes.

Another problem we had with confession was thinking of what sins we had committed since our last confession a month before. What this meant was that most of us were making up sins to tell the priest because the majority of us at this age really weren't committing major sins. Most of our "sins" were fabricated. If you went into the confessional and told the priest that you hadn't committed a sin, you knew you were in for a grilling. We all convened and decided which "sins" we were going to tell in confession so as not to cross our wires and confess to the same sins.

On one occasion, we were on one of the very long lines waiting to confess to one of our favorite priests. We saw one of the confessional doors swing open, and out staggered one of the more unpopular priests to give your confession to. He called over one of our nuns and said that he had no one coming to his confessional. The nun promptly came over to us and pulled us out from the line. She insisted that young Rocky go over to Father Bill's confessional of doom. He was scared shitless of this priest. Father Bill would condemn his own mother to Hell, and he was known for giving these marathon penance obligations like a thousand Hail Marys, five hundred Our Fathers, or worse.

Rocky was now in a very uncomfortable dilemma. He was about to confess his fictitious sins to a very mean priest who also had a drinking problem. Rocky went into this small confessional box separately and was immediately struck with the scent of alcohol. This was going to be a long and painful confession. He was expecting to receive the Holy Ghost, not the Holy Spirits.

Rocky had decided that our made-up sin for the day was that he missed mass two Sundays ago. When Father Bill asked why, Rocky told him that we had to go to our Aunt Mary's for dinner. He began to yell at Rocky, lecturing him about what a bad Christian he was. This lasted for five minutes. By the end of the priest's angry speech, Rocky felt that he had undergone a second circumcision and was ready to convert to Judaism. Father Bill ended by asking a final, but loaded, question.

"Young man, who do you love more, God or your Aunt Mary?"

Rocky could not have picked a worse fucking time to tell the truth.

"Aunt Mary."

Father Bill was outraged, so it was time for Rocky to do a quick escape for fear of five thousand Hail Marys and five thousand Our Fathers.

The church came in handy on many occasions. Our softball field was directly across from the church. Playing ball for four or five hours on a ninety-five-degree day was no fun. Occasionally, the schoolyard water fountains would be locked, which meant no water. As a group, we would improvise. The solution was simple: walk two hundred feet to the church, open up the doors, go directly to the holy water fountains, and drink to your heart's content. The head of the church, Monsignor Elwood Purick, wasn't as amused with our ingenuity. As penance, he quickly purged us from the building.

The rectory and the convent were other interesting places. Only the best students and altar boys were allowed entry into these palatial edifices. These priests and nuns lived very well, compliments of the local butcher, baker, and candlestick maker. They had the best furniture, the best carpets, and their food was second to none. You would never see a supermarket brand ice cream container, but instead Breyers®, the equivalent to today's Häagen-Dazs. They ate the best of meats, none of the crap that our mothers would buy wrapped in plastic. Only the top of the line for our humble and pious parish priests and nuns. As we say in the street, it was all "on the arm." But why not? These Fathers and Sisters made a huge impact on our lives, and we wanted to give them their due.

We can vividly remember our uncle, Father John Positano, bringing us copious amounts of tomatoes, peppers, and eggplants, among many other fruits and vegetables from the extremely generous Progresso family (as in Progresso Soup) in East Vineland, New Jersey. So, safe to say, this was a practice that we had first-hand familiarity (and approval) with.

HOW STREET SMART BROUGHT TWO LEGENDS TOGETHER: SONNY GROSSO MEETS HIS HERO, JOE DIMAGGIO

A primer here: Sonny Grosso, like our later-day friend Det. NYPD Bo Dietl, was a legendary New York City Police Department detective. He was a man who was literally "of the streets," hence Street Smart. You know Sonny without remembering his name. He served as the inspiration for the character Buddy Russo, played by Roy Scheider, in the film *The French Connection*. Sonny also supplied the famous hidden "pull-chain toilet" gun used in *The Godfather*, where Michael Corleone murders drug kingpin Virgil Sollozzo and the corrupt police Captain Mark McCluskey, thus beginning Michael's ascent into becoming the Don himself.

All action, like the movies: Sonny broke the greatest heroin ring in history in the early '60s.

Yankees legend Joe DiMaggio, you know already: the greatest all-around ball player of all time, and irrefutably the last legitimate American icon and hero. He may be more famous to you as the failed husband of movie legend Marilyn Monroe, for whom he held a torch until his dying breath.

In addition to being considered two of the most Street Smart individuals of all time (which is why you'll see their names mentioned throughout this book), the two men also shared Rock as a confidant. All three of them shared a working-class Street Smart origin.

It just so happened that Grosso, a man who dismissed the rich, the powerful, and the famous with barely disguised contempt, was a hero worshiper of Joe DiMaggio. Once he waited for Joe to get a signed autograph when Joe was returning to New York and was balked because neither man had a pencil. That smarted Sonny, a man not used to failure, for most of his life until Rock happened to mention to Sonny that Joe was a friend of his.

Detective Sonny Grosso

Sonny's gun, used by Michael Corleone in the
famous pull-chain toilet scene in *The Godfather*

The relationship between Joe the ball player and Rock actually started many years before. Rock was setting up a medical practice in the upper reaches of Manhattan and used his Street Smart accordingly.

Fear nothing or nobody and take no prisoners. That was his mantra. Rather than follow "common sense" and set up a medical practice in his hometown of Brooklyn, or one of the other outer boroughs, Rock decided to go for it. He ended up tending to pro athletes, corporate and business executives, and other wildly successful Street Scholars with foot problems. There are indeed two New York Cities: the wealthy Manhattan and the outer boroughs. There were no hassles with tightfisted and legalistic medical insurance companies. It didn't hurt, either, that he was a graduate of Yale University and developed the specialty of non-surgical musculoskeletal foot and ankle care while at Yale School of Public Health and the Hospital for Special Surgery in New York City. Yet, he never forgot his childhood pals from the old neighborhood and to this day, takes care of them on a handshake.

Rock learned the Street Smart economics of the medical profession just out of medical school, burdened by several hundred thousand dollars of student loans. Upon his exit interview from Yale, he was asked by the financial aid officer, "Dr. Positano, we're concerned. How are you going to pay off such a large amount of debt?"

Rock had a Street Smart answer. "Don't worry about me. I come from a very tough environment and it won't be a big deal."

Ole Brooklyn Street Smart Survival was more like it. No better motivator than fear of failure.

"If you were going to bust your ass," Rock figured, "you might as well do it for the big picture and having a couple hundred thousand dollars in student loans is a great incentive and motivator."

Anyway, after this first exercise of Street Smart, he made powerful, accomplished, and wealthy friends. One was the legendary

New York Daily News sports columnist and cartoonist Bill Gallo. Gallo took a liking to Rock and mentioned, name unspoken, a fellow who had a foot injury problem. The person was sportsman and legendary New York Yankee Joe DiMaggio.

Long and short of it, Joe showed up at Rock's office and explained what turned out to be the holy grail of all sports injuries: his heel spur, which crippled Joe in his last three seasons. A botched heel spur surgery definitely didn't help the situation.

Not only did this injury take down one of the most famous baseball players of all time, it has become immortalized in history, even being referenced all throughout Ernest Hemingway's *The Old Man and the Sea*.

Safe to say, this new patient of Rock's was simply like no other. And he never would be.

It didn't start out so easy, though. Rock was at first treated with skepticism by Joe because as a Sicilian-American, Joe considered everyone suspicious when he didn't know them well. However, he soon found out that Rock had the Street Smart that was most familiar and comforting to him. Rock was Italian, educated, loyal, and he could read a room better than anyone. He was able to see trouble coming from a mile away and keep Joe safe and sequestered. But the most important was his ability to keep his mouth shut. DiMaggio was most attracted to Rock because of this Brooklyn-honed Street Smart trait. Joe even tested him a few times by sharing personal and professional things with him to see if they showed up in the press or anywhere else. Rock passed the DiMaggio test with flying colors.

Rock won over Joe, not an easy feat, by curing Joe's heel problem. And, though he wasn't a doctor, DiMaggio knew a thing or two about treating elite athletes. He wasn't afraid to guide Rock on what *not* to do.

"Doc, if you ever have a pro athlete as your patient, no matter what, *never* let them know you're a fan. If they get that sense, good luck trying to get them to listen to you. They won't fear, respect, or listen to any medical advice you have to offer them."

Rock took this sage advice well.

The two formed what can be only called a symbiotic relationship: Joe wanted to leave his sometimes boring Florida retirement life and enjoy glamorous New York City, because the city had been largely unavailable to him when playing ball up in the Bronx. Rock, in turn, got to know Joe and vice versa.

This was happy for Sonny, who wanted a "makeup" call for screwing up when he asked for Joe's autograph when he was a kid.

So, Rock helped arrange Sonny Grosso's meeting with Joe DiMaggio in New York. Of course, Rock didn't tell Sonny, the most jaded of cops, who he was about to meet. It caught Sonny entirely by surprise when he met his idol, after so many years, at a New York family-owned-and-operated Italian restaurant called Manducatis in Queens.

Rock noticed, with great and sardonic amusement, how Sonny latched onto Joe's hand in a white-knuckled death grip. So did Joe.

"Nice to meet you," said Joe gently but a little perturbed. "You can let go of my hand now...."

Sonny, the starstruck and hardboiled detective, who was the bane of some cops and the New York Mafia, remained latched onto Joe's hand until he was reminded again. Joe and Sonny remained confidants under Rock's guidance, of course, and exchanged many stories at their Manducatis dinner which can never be repeated here or anywhere else for that matter. If anything from that night was ever brought up again, certain historical events would have had to be written. If only there had been a fly on the wall.

STREET SMART PEARLS: TACTICS OF STREET SMART

All that being said, we know that Street Smart may not be easy to apply. After speaking to some youngsters who may not know where to start, or wanted some guidance, we set to compile a few "tricks of the trade."

We thought it best to introduce these pearls of wisdom, certain guidelines, and edicts that we discovered growing up in the '70s and early '80s that we think could serve as a toolkit of sorts for those kids who want to study up.

It's definitely easy to see the streets that we grew up on have certainly changed. We learned these pearls in different times, but the lessons behind them are perpetual and their disciples descend from all walks of life. The culture may have become far more diverse, but the foundation of social interactions hasn't.

The cover chosen for this book, taken in the early '80s by famed street photographer Alfred González and a favorite photo of writer/director Spike Lee, demonstrates a perfect display of the timeless hunger and ambition in the subjects' eyes and their badass body language that mirrors the same aspirations and determination in today's world. Sadly, we can't change history, but these street pearls have weathered the test of time and can certainly be applied to contemporary days. And we've all heard it before: history always repeats itself.

They may not all apply to your life right at this moment, but the basic tenets of these pearls can definitely be carried from generation to generation, and we can all learn and re-learn them.

BAIT AND SWITCH

Beware of the bait and switch. It's one of the oldest tricks in the book, but it works. When someone is trying to get information from you about your personal stuff or other people, they will often set it up by telling you one of their "secrets" to get you to fess up intel about other people. It's used as a confidence move, like, "Hey, I just told you something that nobody knows, and I trust you, now tell me something." Don't step on this land mine and blow yourself up. Nine times out of ten, what they tell you is either bullshit, half-true, or something that is irrelevant and pales in comparison to the information they're trying to get from you.

The way to tell if someone is really on the square is to give them specific misinformation and see where it shows up. If it shows up, then you know for sure that the "confidant" you shared the privileged info with is a rat and a snitch who can't be trusted.

This is a survival technique in the streets, as everyone often knows the real deal, but it also isolates them as not trustworthy people, exposing them as culprits. It's amazing how fast this can get around. Almost as fast as the speed of light.

This also happens within corporate America, where the stakes may be a little higher. Your business associates may be checking you out. Bottom line: don't fall for this trick. Better to say nothing that will be misconstrued and used against you later.

IF YOU PLAY OTHERS, THEY WILL PLAY YOU TOO

Pick your battles. For ego's sake, don't start expensive battles at bargain basement prices. Take one example:

We had a neighbor on Louisa Street in Brooklyn. We'll call him "Pete." Pete was a retired cigar roller who decided to start a handyman service. His house shared a common easement and driveway with ours. His detached garage shared a common wall with Dad and Mom's garage. That was his business headquarters.

Now, Pete picked a battle with Dad, and we still don't know why. Dad was a good soul, a man who went out of his way to do right by others. Pete kept saying that Dad bought a "pig in a poke" house. That meant a run-down house that needed a lot of work, which, because Dad was hardly handy—he rented the first twenty years of his marriage—both men took as an insult. Pop was a little down about this.

Pete rubbed this pearl o' wisdom into dad's skin at every opportunity.

It just so happened that Pete's own garage roof had a leak that opened up with every rainstorm. He decided to showcase his handyman talents, fixing that same leak. It did stop for a while. That is, until we decided to give him a man-made leak later.

Pete showed a lot of people his leak as a "before" picture. After he fixed the leak, it was an "after" moment and advertisement for his home repair service. He showed the garage to potential customers who really liked the work. Now this bothered the hell out of us kids—we were high schoolers—waiting to get back at the "King of Home Repairs."

So, we jerry-rigged a pipe which went from Pete's garage to ours, all of a few feet, and an army surplus canteen full of tap water. We poured the water into the pipe, which ended at a decline on Pete's side of the common garage. There was a two-inch gap between the garages. We waited for the next bad thunderstorm for the attack.

Lo and behold, Pete opened his garage door for a potential sucker awaiting a leak repair. Pete did it with a Hollywood flourish.

There was a leak in the garage, water on the floor, but no leak marks on the ceiling.

The customer was left with a laugh, and Pete began scratching his head.

We repeated this about a half-dozen times, and each time, Pete lost a roof leak customer. He must have worked on that goddamned leak as many times as Michelangelo worked on the Sistine Chapel ceiling. No matter how much plaster he threw on that ceiling, he still got a leak.

Finally, during a dry spell in the summer, "Michelangelo" returned with confidence to his garage. He had a customer, a man as idiotic as he was. But Pete figured that no matter what, it hadn't rained in weeks, so it would be a sure bet that no leak was possible.

Of course, Pete opened the door and there was a leak in the middle of a drought!

The client left laughing, and Pete had NO SALE on his forehead. He wrapped up "Pete's Home Improvement Empire" accordingly.

Served him right! So, learn the lesson. Make an enemy only if you have to.

WATCH WHO YOU'RE MESSING WITH

We've seen this so many times in the street. You have a confrontation with someone and lock heads with them, only to realize later on that you have more than one enemy, and they can all cause trouble for you and your inner circle. The classic example is what's "waiting around the corner" for you. You think you've won the battle, only to find out that waiting around the corner for you is someone waiting to give you a physical, vocational, or mental beating. This was totally unexpected because you didn't do your homework on your adversary.

This flows over to corporate as well. People will have you blocked and blackballed very easily. You have to assess and know your enemy. Is it worth it to go after them and inherit all their network of bad blood as well? Smart people look at the ramifications and measure the benefit-to-risk ratio.

Reminds us of a time when we were growing up. There was a neighborhood bully who was a weightlifter and always under the influence of drugs and alcohol. One day, one of the local studious kids was walking home from school with his book bag and minding his own business. This bully, trying to impress his girlfriend, decided to pick on this innocent and well-meaning kid. He assaulted him, drawing blood from a headshot and a sucker punch. There was no contest. The bully thought it was funny and figured this kid was a local nobody and would go running home to his mother, crying.

This asshole was about to learn the lesson of his life: you don't size someone up because of their looks or disposition.

It turns out this bookish kid was the nephew of one of the local "big boys." So, two days later, a group of guys went into the local candy store and tattooed this bully with a 34 oz Louisville Slugger baseball bat and taught him the lesson of his life. He and his bullying ways were never to be seen again in the neighborhood.

He committed the fatal error: he didn't know who he was messing with.

Needless to say, this innocent kid became a neighborhood hero. He didn't have to use his fists. What'd he do instead? He used his brains. Be careful of who you decide to declare war on. It's not the person that you have the beef with. Be aware of who their friends are, as you're more likely to be dealing with repercussions from their network of friends and associates. That's often a fatal error and should be part of the "pick your wars wisely" strategy. Always find out who their "Rabbi" is in house.

EVERY JOB IS A LEARNING EXPERIENCE IN THE NEW WORLD ORDER

Because you get a Street Smart experience from everyday life, it follows that even a menial, unrewarding job can teach valuable lessons. Every job is a learning experience, where making mistakes is necessary, and no job is a total and meaningless waste of time. Joseph Conrad, hailed as one of the greatest novelists in the English language, sums it up well: "It's only those who do nothing that make no mistakes, I suppose."

Similar experiences abound in almost all the Street Smart Memoirs. Indeed, the origin of almost every one of our Street Scholars is working- or lower-middle-class. Their jobs started out quite ordinary and sometimes menial.

Quite often, people in the service business such as restaurants, social clubs, sporting events, and the like have the real experience of having to deal with the meanest, rudest, and most condescending people while still having to smile and be polite. Hospitality industry is one way to put it, but a more appropriate title would probably be, "the hostility trade." Don't be afraid to shoot back, and if you're going to insult these idiots, do it in a way where they didn't realize they were insulted until later on.

Or "someone" can always spit in their food before bringing it to the table.

It provides the perfect classroom environment to learn how to deal with difficult, demanding, and sometimes unreasonable people. We call it the AH (for "asshole") factor.

So, we always insisted on working with people who had at least their own share of mistakes. No mistakes to us means either no effort or an inflated sense of performance. You can have a perfect record because you didn't do much. This is the lesson of more than a handful of our Scholars, who learned from their mistakes and thrived because they made that effort. Of course, we'd rather learn from other people's mistakes because there is less pain and expense involved.

Practically speaking, people who haven't had that effort and are later confronted by a mistake fall apart quickly and usually fatally. In boxing, they call it having a "glass jaw." One punch to the weak spot, the boxer goes down and is out for the count. They're overloaded by failure, not knowing Street Smart resilience. The military calls this "seeing the elephant." This was a powerful feature of the opening of the American Civil War: troops and officers seeing combat for the first time, pumped up by feelings of superiority against the other side, quickly fell apart. They derived this wisdom from over two thousand years earlier, when during the Punic Wars, Roman troops ran in panic from rampaging elephants of the war leader Hannibal, who sought to destroy Rome. When they got over the anxiety, however, and realized that just making vulgar noises and getting out of the way of the animals rendered them ineffective, the Romans rallied and won.

When the bombs start dropping, you want someone next to you in the foxhole who has legitimate experiences of successes and failures. They're less likely to fall apart and have already been tried, true, and tested. You'd much rather be fighting alongside someone who's lost and learned, than someone who's never stepped foot on the field to begin with.

FIND OUT WHO YOUR REAL FRIENDS ARE

Our rule of thumb: never ask a person for a favor unless you were sure they could handle it without difficulty. This was a great litmus test. If they accommodated the request, you knew they were on your side. If they didn't, that was the quickest way to Siberia and the end of the relationship.

Unfortunately, the authors experienced this firsthand when writing this very book, as some people failed the ultimate litmus test. Hopefully, they'll read this account....

In the case where an accommodation far exceeded the person's capability, this was a major defining moment. We go over the top to help our friends, and it's all about the relationships. If someone does a solid for a friend and they ask you, what do you say? You always want to make a true friend look good. That's all part of doing the right thing. We found ourselves in these predicaments so many times, that if someone was important to someone we cared about, we would never say no. Even if we hated their guts. We may ask our friend not to tell them where the favor originated from, as that could be perceived as weakness or caving on our account.

DiMaggio would always tell us to put everyone you meet in the negative column and let them work themselves out of the ditch over time through a series of good deeds. This was pretty good advice, even in today's times.

Don't ever judge a book by its cover. It sounds old and worn out, but it is truer today than it ever was. The person who is understated and underdressed is never to be underestimated. The guy with the fancy clothes and shoes is often more for show and not necessarily substance. Beware the guy who dresses down; they usually have the power and the wealth. History has shown that staying under the radar and not being flamboyant offers a level of protection that sometimes can't be matched. This is a version of "hiding in plain sight." Basically, it comes down to, "Sometimes it doesn't pay to advertise." Don't show what you have.

It reminds us of a situation that happened in the '90s. A friend of ours had a very well-known food business that was around for many years and was one of the most popular gathering places in the area. It seems though in the adjacent building there was a hangout for the local "boys" where they were conducting other types of "business" like betting, loan sharking, and extortion.

It turns out the mountains had eyes in this neighborhood. There were some law enforcement present and surveillance of these guys going in and out of the shops. These boys were always dressed to the nines: the most expensive shirts, custom-made five-thousand-dollar Brioni suits, handmade shoes from E. Vogel, and, of course, late-model big-ass luxury cars. The law enforcement guys were Street Smart, as they were soon able to piece together an inconsistency. Many of the impeccably dressed people under surveillance were on the record as being factory workers, car mechanics, and disabled.

So how could they all afford to be dressed so well on their reported earnings?

Clearly there must have been some other invisible revenue stream. This created a red flag, and the rest was history. These guys all got pinched. They learned their lesson, though. A few years later, they were wearing dungarees, sneakers, and baseball caps so as not to create the same image that screwed them over a few years earlier.

Years ago, a colleague of Rock's had a similar experience in his office at the hospital. Doctors were always instructed to wear a shirt and tie along with clean and polished shoes. One day, a patient approached this colleague and noticed his very expensive watch (that actually had been given to him as a gift) and went on to say, "Now I know why the hospital prices are so high... because of your fancy dress and fancy jewelry! Someone has to pay for this."

This was an eye opener, and the doctor got it.

He changed his attire to a surgical scrub shirt, basic pants, and simple loafers with no watches or jewelry of any kind. We are proud to say that he has never heard that comment again. Plastic surgeons, cosmetic dentists, and dermatologists can get away with this because their practices are often built on aesthetics. Few would dispute that going to a plastic surgeon that dressed like a schlub would create the exact opposite impression.

The other takeaway is you must know your audience and the circumstances for your interaction. Someone with a broken knee won't appreciate a fashionable doctor dressed to the nines because of the nature of the practice, whereas a person considering a facelift, breast reduction, nose job, new veneers, or Botox would almost certainly expect it.

We have always learned from a very early age to treat everyone with respect and kindness unless they deserve or act otherwise. Maybe it was our parochial education at St. Athanasius in Brooklyn, where to their credit, our teachers, nuns, and priests never demonstrated favoritism toward people of greater means. We treated the janitor, crossing guard, and parking lot attendant with the same reverence paid to the local doctor or clergy.

Why? Because life has shown us that you can learn valuable lessons from people of all walks of life. Getting advice only from the formally educated and financially successful can leave a big gap. Applied knowledge is what counts. Book smarts are important, but people's instincts are just as crucial, and in certain situations, even more so.

Don't ever underestimate anyone. You never know their life experience. This has triggered the downfall of many important people, while launching the success of someone who appreciates the value and friendship of every person they meet.

The ability to strike the balance is essential. Just look at Leona Helmsley. Who brought her down? Not the corporate raiders, but the lobby workers, janitors, cleaning staff, cooks, and secretaries. They were clearly more adept and educated in observing abhorrent behavior. The main caveat is always being most wary and mindful of the person who has nothing to lose. They are usually the most dangerous and treacherous, which is why the "elite-thinking" people often mistreat, dismiss, and underestimate people of lower socio-economic standing, who end up being the most effective and stealthiest assassins.

The paradigm is straight and simple: don't get involved with anyone, on any level, unless they have as much to lose as you do.

People who have positions of power should think twice before they do something that could potentially affect their social, vocational, and corporate standing.

As they say in the street, the person who threatens you outright isn't the dangerous one, but the person who maintains a stealth profile. Keep an eye out.

Look at all the assassinations over the years. The street person won't give you notice. They will just show up one day and take you out without any heads-up or warning.

The other scenario is psychological assault. Make someone think you're going to hurt them, but in most cases, nothing goes down. We used to call it "psyching out" someone. It was effective, but after a while, you learned how serious a threat it was or wasn't. Intimidation only works on the weak-minded. We weren't afraid to call your bluff.

Don't feel obliged to tell people what you're thinking. It may seem like the polite thing to do. This sets you up as a target and potential competitor for someone with the same goals.

A perfect example of this is a longtime friend of ours. He was fortunate enough to attend NYU in the late '70s, when it was not only a great university but also where to learn how to get slammed and scammed.

Our friend was pre-med, but he noticed how many students were also pre-med and he had heard stories about the "throats": the cutthroats who wouldn't help you in class, conceal notes from you, not share old exams that were floating around, and more.

NYU was unusually difficult because of this fierce street-like competition and warfare among the students. So, our friend had to decide between being the typical pre-med student or strategizing differently. He wisely chose the latter and used the foundation of not being obvious but instead presented himself in a much less threatening way to his classmates.

So, instead of belonging to pre-med and science clubs, where internal distrust and anxiety was at an all-time high, he decided to become active in school politics. His pre-med classmates looked at him in a different light. He was acting and doing things that a pre-law student would do, instead. The pre-med students actually embraced him and were helpful because his actions and activities were not those of someone in their major and thereby posed a significantly lesser threat. He found the same in the laboratory classes, which were "career-killers" such as inorganic and organic chemistry, biochemistry, physics, and biology where graduate students worked as teachers' assistants.

Our pal observed that many of these TAs weren't successful in their attempts to enter medical or dental school. So, he thought, *Why make them feel bad?* Of course, they were going to have a hard-on for all of their students, knowing that they were going to get accepted into medical school. The TAs were extra nice and helpful to him because he was "pre-law." This strategy clearly worked, and in addition, our friend eventually went on to also earn his law degree.

THE GATSBY EFFECT

A concept that we think is important, and has largely been forgotten, is the idea of loyalty. Today, it seems that everyone is for themselves, and they've decided to lose the people along the way who've been good and kind to them. Loyalty is a two-way street, and it can be a costly error when you don't match someone else's kindness.

There's nothing more unforgivable than turning your back on a person who is struggling, especially after they've been good to you and have consistently done the right thing. We all go through hardships in our lives, and we remember those who were there for us, and more importantly, those who decided to suddenly forget about us, leaving us to suffer all on our own. Those who suddenly don't seem to care about you may very well have made a costly mistake. The payback in this situation could certainly be quite devastating and compounded with interest over time. You can be sure they will have no problem broadcasting out to your network.

But those who are always in your corner, always there to defend you, will find the rewards greatly outweigh any risks. Because, as we said, loyalty is a two-way street.

We've coined this "The Gatsby Effect," paying homage to the ultimate act of loyalty: Jay Gatsby from F. Scott Fitzgerald's *The Great Gatsby* remaining faithful to his one true love, Daisy Buchanan.

In our lives, we've seen that keeping trusts and loyalties has been instrumental to our own successes, even if the person whose secrets and confidences we've been keeping isn't in our lives anymore. And that happens: no matter if someone is in your life or not, any sacred information and secrets shared should be kept away and not repeated. There is even honor among enemies.

In the "Olde Neighborhood," the Stand-Up Guy, the guy you could trust to keep a secret, did not rat out even an enemy to "outsiders" like parents, police, or community leaders. These rules held up even if these outsiders could be useful to the Stand-Up Guy. We've come to learn that the phrase "Stand-Up Guy" is dated, because following this rule transcends gender and gender identity. From now on, we're going to call them a "Stand-Up Person."

DiMaggio and Rock's friendship was outlined by the notion of being a Stand-Up Person. The two men realized they both grew up by the same code, and this only brought them closer.

One night, Joe told Rock, "Doc, I know you're a loyal friend."

Rock was apprehensive, but curious. "What brings up that observation?"

"You aren't a snitch. You don't pry into matters or ask me questions. That was your upbringing."

From Joe's street in San Francisco to Rock's neighborhood in Bensonhurst, separated by four decades, the rules of being a Stand-Up Person were carved into their philosophies.

Even if you held the secrets of someone who wasn't in your life anymore, a confidence remains a confidence.

JUST BECAUSE THEY SMILE DOESN'T MAKE 'EM FRIENDLY

Dad contributed to the Street Smart syllabus as well as Mom did. It all had something to do with backstabbers, those charming people who smile at you benevolently while mentally sizing you for a pine box on Boot Hill.

Dad was a sharpshooter in the Second World War. During the campaigns in New Guinea, he and his friends were housed at the outskirts of a full-on jungle surrounded by what they assumed were friendly Stone Age natives. These natives would appear at the edge of the jungle and smile at the soldiers. Since no one spoke anyone else's language, smiling and gesturing were the vogue. It just so happened that one native...very much unlike the others...was very pretty in a savage type of way, especially as she wore no top and was young. Dad noticed this, of course, and so did the "Romeo" of the outfit, who smiled hardest at the comely savage. And we do mean savage. And everyone smiled. They smiled harder and harder.

One night, Romeo left camp without permission. Then he went AWOL for several days. The military police went looking for him in the jungle, and that was fruitless. But Romeo did show up one fine morning—though dead.

He had his throat cut from ear to ear. That ended the romance, no doubt. The rest of the natives vanished into the jungle. Dad's wisdom: Just because they smile doesn't make 'em friendly.

That's good Street Smart wisdom, from a man who, prior to the war, thought the edge of the world was the far terminal of the New York City subways in the Bronx.

That brings up, tangentially, the concept of "backstabbing." It is a Street Smart certainty that any hostile attack on you will begin with a smile. The Polish people say that the Devil is always attractive...and smiles have something to do with it. People on the street will attempt to distract you with a smile. They will never start with a frown.

In a more historic way, we observed how DiMaggio kept a psychic distance from everyone except Rock when meeting with others. He always insisted that the pair, when eating out or at functions, kept a lookout forward while being safely kept quiet in the back. That controls the situation. The situation doesn't control you.

A corollary here: Cautiously give out information to the public. Leave the blueprints of your plans in the vault of your mind. And always leave out some of the ingredients.

Our Aunt Rosie and Aunt Phyllis Capasso would always leave out an ingredient or two so that their recipes could never be reproduced.

A famous example was Aunt Rosie's sesame cookies, which would be booby-trapped if you ever attempted to make them with her listed ingredients. We mean *booby-trapped* here. They were tougher to bite than the hardest diamond and could easily take out your front teeth.

Some harmless information could be used against you accordingly. That, we learned from DiMaggio, who routinely censored and rerouted personal information in such a way that made his private life unavailable. Hostile biographers had only creative hearsay, meaning bullshit, to throw at Joe's wall to see what could stick. Nothing did.

Learn to compartmentalize your life as he did. Tell certain people some things and others different things so that nobody has the complete picture. Napoleon would have been proud of this strategy.

Information can always be used against you. What appears harmless to you is dynamite to another. Coca-Cola and Pepsi practice with the same caution. No one person has all the ingredients for these internationally famous soft drinks. We knew a fellow who was a chemist for Pepsi, and he would always amaze us when speaking about protecting the Pepsi brand and proprietary formula. No one individual knew all the ingredients. Instead, various people each had a piece of one of the many components that made the product.

Likewise, always have an escape hatch, no matter whom you are dealing with. That means friend or foe. In the modern world, post-COVID, friends become foes overnight. Some call them "frenemies." We all learned from the *Godfather* movies to keep your friends close but your enemies closer. Look at the masked versus unmasked, vax versus antivax, and similar new hate points. Did you ever dream these hatreds would exist a few years ago? You would be lying to say yes.

Let's face it: a time may come when you are sleeping with the enemy. There are enough stories out there to remind us that nothing lasts forever, such as relationships and business partnerships, and information that you shared that you would never tell anyone suddenly becomes public knowledge and even lethal ammunition.

Recently, the highly successful (and now defunct) Cellino & Barnes personal injury law firm breakup is a perfect example. Two friends from the onset who together built a huge law practice, were bitter enemies in the end with all the cloak-and-dagger intrigue one could imagine.

In effect, keep your escape route open and clearly marked as you might need it one day. Nothing good lasts forever.

CRITICISM IS CRUCIAL

We are offering this book as an intergenerational primer for a younger, Street Smart generation. Part of the gift is a better appreciation of benign criticism. Winston Churchill said it best: "Criticism may not be agreeable, but it is necessary. It fulfills the same function as pain in the human body; it calls attention to an unhealthy state of things." Beautifully said and truer today than ever.

Having "thin skin" implies that a person is not able to handle criticism well, constructive or not. In the street, having thin skin is perceived as a major weakness.

Millennials, who are presently filling positions of trust and responsibility, may perceive benign criticism as a personal affront. While stinging at times, benign criticism fulfills the same function as pain in human events. If you don't know something is wrong and needs fixing, there is no shame in being advised otherwise. Take it or leave it. People of all ages must accept criticism accordingly. The value of critique is increased efficiency. Otherwise, you are constantly reinventing the wheel, which can often be burdensome in tranquil times. It could fatally delay a proper response. It's always better to embrace criticism as constructive communication, and in most cases, it indicates that a person may care enough about you to tell you the truth.

There is nothing more damaging than people providing "lip service" to gain favor with you very much like the message conveyed from the famous Hans Christian Andersen folktale, *The Emperor's New Clothes*. Tell me like it is, not something you think I want to hear.

DON'T EVEN THINK ABOUT IT

What's the absolute quickest way to become a neighborhood pariah? Desiring the person dating one of your best friends. This is absolutely *unforgivable* in the streets and can cause more bad blood than one can imagine, even though the saying goes that "the grass is greener on the other side, and what's not in your possession always looks better." These grudges are usually lifelong and can mutate into a host of other vendettas that concern not only the two people involved, but also their entire families.

Affairs of the heart cut the deepest, perhaps of all tragedies. There's really no repair, even decades later. Those devastating feelings can never go away. Anyone who hits on a friend's partner can never be trusted again.

The same rules apply after a break-up of a serious relationship. Don't Even. *Think*. About. It.

Off-limits. The same with an ex-spouse; there's simply no explanation for why you want to date the ex of one of your closest friends. If someone's spouse dies, then exceptions can be made, but not always.

We can think of a few prime examples in life where we had a front-row seat:

When Rock was in college, he was managing a restaurant on the weekends to help pay for tuition. There was a beautiful hostess who was happily married (or so we thought). She would come in on her day off with her husband and another couple who were their best friends. He always enjoyed watching the four of them laughing and telling jokes over a few drinks. How great was this?

He thought to himself, *Wow, is this what I have to look forward to when I grow up?*

Rock changed his schedule, coming in a day earlier to work. One day, to his surprise, he walked in and there was the wife of one couple with the husband of the other hanging at the bar. They were as surprised to see Rock as well. It didn't take long for Rock to figure out what was going down. He played it cool and didn't even give a hint when the two "happy" couples were coming in together on the weekend. The only thing that changed was that Rock's tip tripled. The elusive couple knew he would never say a thing or rat out anybody.

This play was going on for a year or so. One night, when the two "forbidden lovers" were sitting at the bar, they both turned white. Crossing the street was the gal's husband. Safe to say, they probably both crapped their pants. They pleaded for help from Rock.

The man (let's call him "Tony") said, "Rocky, you gotta hide me. How about the bathroom?"

Rock almost laughed in his face. "No way! That's the first fucking place he's going to look!"

Rock had to use his Street Smarts very, *very* quickly. He brought lover boy to the kitchen and decided that the walk-in meat freezer was the safest place to hide. He gave Rock an incredulous look while impeccably dressed in his beautiful three-piece suit and Hermès tie with the shiniest black shoes you could imagine. Rock cast about and was able to find a white gallon pickle bucket that, when flipped over, turned into a makeshift chair. He put him in the refrigerator safely and later brought him a bottle of his favorite red wine to keep him warm.

Needless to say, the husband of Juliet just happened to be in the area and wanted to give his wife a kiss hello. How noble of him! He ended up drinking at the bar for almost an hour with his wife while the other guy was freezing his fancily-dressed ass off.

When Rock went back to save Tony, he couldn't have seen a more humbling sight. The guy was frozen and the bottle of *Tignanello* was empty.

Rock remembered asking him, "Tony, is all of this really worth it?"

"No, but I made the huge mistake of falling in love with the wife of my best friend. Remember this lesson in your future. My balls are so frozen, I may never be able to use them again, so it may not matter anymore."

One of our friends, "Tommy," worked at a bar where he befriended a patron with a problem: a girlfriend who was drunk over martinis and needed an escort home.

Tommy was entrusted with that escort duty.

After his shift, he dutifully drove the girl home and pulled up outside her apartment, promising not to leave until she was safely inside. According to her, it wasn't good enough. Of course, Tommy had to ward off potential burglars and rapists and needed to physically enter the premises at her side. He complied, went inside, and promptly noticed that the entrance door was locked on both sides.

Realizing he was stuck for the time being, Tommy was offered a drink that he politely declined. That was it! She got angry, dropped the keys down her blouse, and started to dance in a sexually suggestive manner. Tommy then noticed a very large pair of men's shoes nearby and instantly got the bad feeling that they might not have been alone.

He asked again to leave, but the young lady refused, laughing drunkenly. Obviously, reason and courtesy were not working. Thinking Street Smart fast, Tommy noticed a couch and threatened to urinate on the furniture unless he was let out.

The woman refused, again. After her refusal, Tommy went straight to relieving himself right on her couch.

As Tommy was keeping his promise, the girl sobered up at lightning speed, reached down her blouse, produced the keys, and let him leave.

Soon after, she called Tommy, apologized, and promptly enquired if he happened to rat her out to her jealous boyfriend. Of course, he was absolutely silent on the matter. That was a happy Street Smart solution because the woman in question is now happily married and lives in New Jersey!

Then there was the classic story of the Sinatra/DiMaggio feud, which was a real tragedy. Two revered icons who hated each other until their last breathing moments. It wasn't always that way. They were buds that often hung out with each other, bonded by their concern for the sons of each who were cursed with both the same name and unimaginable burden to be as successful as their fathers.

That all changed rapidly as Sinatra broke the *unforgivable* rule of wanting to date DiMaggio's former wife and one true love, Marilyn Monroe. This was reprehensible in DiMaggio's world and created a vicious feud that could never be healed, even with interventions from their closest mutual friends. The wound would never close for as long as both men lived. This bad blood was a throwback to street rules that both Sinatra and DiMaggio lived by.

DiMaggio would often speak about this *virgognosa* and *disgrazia* to Rock. The fire never left his eyes no matter how many times he recounted this story. Every year, a Christmas card was sent to Rock's office from Frank addressed to Joe, and every year it wound up in the garbage can, ripped to shreds. Not even a sit-down mediated by Henry Kissinger would be able to resolve this perpetual dispute. Joe would forever be scarred and devastated by what he perceived to be Frank's betrayal.

KNOW YOUR OPPONENT AND HIS CULTURE

A very celebrated media event of 2022 was the clash of Dr. Anthony Fauci and Senator Roger Marshall (Republican of Kansas) during one of those interminable COVID briefings.

Fauci was called to the witness table in Congress, and Marshall started asking heated questions about public disclosures of Fauci's salary as COVID raged. And the questioning raged, as well.

If Senator Marshall were from Brooklyn (like us and like Dr. Fauci), what happened soon would make perfect sense.

Marshall kept at it, pestering Fauci, and his usual Street Smart composure began to fray at the edges.

Slowly but surely, Fauci's *Brooklynese* vocabulary came back, like our Brooklyn accents invariably do when we are all pissed off. It just does!

Fauci was beginning to tire, and his usual Brooklyn "cool as a cucumber" composure began to waver. Fauci didn't really fathom that he was on a "hot mic," meaning the microphone at the hearing was picking up everything at his end.

Finally, Fauci muttered under his breath, "What a moron, Jesus Christ!"

A news event heard round the world! And Dr. Fauci was not expressing the opinion that Jesus Christ was a moron! Marshall and the media took this as a heated exchange. The COVID-maddened mobs on both sides shrieked in horror! Or glee! But both are wrong.

Dr. Fauci was not insulting Senator Marshall. So, MSNBC and CNN and the *New York Times* should not be so happy.

None of them speak Brooklynese or understand what Fauci's words meant.

And probably neither did you, but we are dutifully explaining.

What Bensonhurst's Dr. Fauci was saying to Kansan Marshall was not a curse. It was a supplication to Jesus Christ to help a Brooklyn denizen deal with a dense colleague in government. Like, "You gotta be kidding me!" and, "I need to look toward the heavens for some divine intervention to understand what this guy is trying to say."

Enlisting the aid of the Almighty in dealing with difficult people is not unusual in Brooklyn or if you're Street Smart. It is best if you are both, but Fauci was in Washington, the very opposite of Street Smart Brooklyn. So, Marshall and his tribe misunderstood the basic Street Smart and deep-dyed Brooklyn in Dr. Fauci. The lesson: understand the idiom and the culture of the Street Smart or be embarrassed in front of millions of people.

When another Street Scholar, Anthony Scaramucci, was appointed to be White House Communicators Director, he suddenly received a crash course education in dealing with the Washington bureaucracy and the national media. Scaramucci had no significant familiarity with these two entities and had to learn the hard way.

He spoke about his brief experience in the White House with writer Todd Shapiro for the A-list Long Island Hamptons publication *Dan's Papers*. "Perhaps the most direct reason for my short stint in Washington was my naivete about how Washington operates – both relating to politics and media. My strength as a communicator and my first White House press briefing backfired as both journalists and bureaucrats sought to take me out of the game. If I had been more attuned to the Washington scumbaggery, I would have lasted longer, and I believe I would have had a positive impact on Trump administration policymaking."

Speaking further about understanding the culture of people you interact with reminds us of a very unique situation that Rock experienced in Harlem in the '80s, when Harlem was a very different place than it is today. The renowned New York College of Podiatric Medicine Foot and Ankle Clinic was located on East 124th Street. You wouldn't think this was the type of neighborhood that you went out for a stroll in the afternoon or at night, but amazingly that wasn't the case. The local heavies—one nicknamed "Flash"—made sure that if any of the local gangs were going to rough up the boys and girls dressed in white medical coats, there was going to be a huge price to pay.

Rock was part of a very small group that provided essential medical care to this neighborhood, and if they were forced out, there would be no medical care and the residents would be left with nothing. The message from Flash was quite evident: Leave our medical care specialists alone or you'll wind up in the trauma room at Harlem Hospital.

It worked. There wasn't a single incident involving Rock's medical team. As a matter of fact, every Tuesday night, Flash took over a dance club on 2nd Ave in the East 60s, and he invited many of us who worked in the clinic to socialize with the Harlem street guys to cultivate good will and solidarity among the community.

THERE'S ABSOLUTELY NO PRIMER AMONG THE GENERATIONS

In our day, the older generation, though old fashioned in our eyes then, did share some commonality with our younger generation. We used to sit on the stoop on those hazy, hot, and humid nights in the summer and actually entertain the senior elders in the neighborhood. We would serenade them with songs, and they would compensate us with their time and infinite wisdom.

They taught us that there is no more valuable a gift than giving your time to someone. It is perpetual currency that can last an entire lifetime. We realized that these older folks knew more about life, strife, hardship, and change than anyone in the neighborhood, including our own contemporaries. They were the real "Street Scholars," and we learned at a very early age that their advice was accurate and timeless.

DON'T KISS AND TELL

This is advice you don't hear, but it's Street Smart and comes from the intimacy of our homes. We've got two great Italian American quotes from our mom over the years, confirmed by Joe DiMaggio, who undoubtedly followed the street adages in his two failed marriages: to his first wife, Dorothy Arnold, and then Marilyn Monroe.

You have seen so many politicians, celebrities, and businessmen brought down by romances. There are indisputably many, and every week brings another. Our mom says, "There are always two heads on one pillow."

What does that mean? Okay, in any sexual relationship, the intimacy under the sheets is also matched by an intimacy of conversation. This is small talk, of course, but a lot of dynamite is in small talk. In spying, governments invariably use the information gleaned from romances using planted lovers. These lovers usually are inserted into the failing or mundane marriages of individuals with a propensity to cheat on their spouses. These inserted lovers now pump the gullible spouses for information. A lot of information is passed before and after the lightning bolts under the bed covers. And it usually ends up at some conference table peopled by spymasters.

But you've read those stories and it can't happen to you.

Mom's second quote is also practical. And it's harder to follow. But here it is:

"If two people know a secret, it is no longer a secret."

Okay, you're laughing. But you shouldn't, because it is also terribly true. If you let any really dangerous secret be known to anyone, a good person or a bad person, there is always the heavy risk that the two-sided secret becomes three-sided, or worse, shared with a community that is hostile to you.

A gabby or loquacious person, any person, is a genuine and present danger. He or she lets loose the secret with a hairdresser, business colleague, traveling salesman, mother-in-law, or enemy agent.

This leads to blackmail and personal ruin. It is definitely not Street Smart, and we dare you to find these wisdoms in any other "self-improvement" or "personal advice" book.

But you will follow them, of course. The United States government did for a project that won World War II: the Manhattan Project, which built the atomic bomb dropped on Japan. Naturally, America tried to keep atomic secrets away from the Nazis, the Japanese, and also the Russians. No fewer than one hundred thousand people were involved in this project. How do you keep a secret among a hundred thousand people?

Isolate them and their families in Manhattan Project "cities," of course. Their phone calls, mail, and everyday shopping kept internal to each city, which were all heavily guarded by the US Army. This worked very well. The enemy was baffled.

So shut up in bed. Or otherwise pay the price.

DiMaggio followed this rule perfectly. He broke up his many relationships into self-sealing compartments. The "New York crew" had only a fourth of his secrets. Rock had a fourth as well. California, another fraction. Finally, Florida had its share. Joe kept them all separate and did not mingle them. He was a control freak, and it worked. Hostile people had no chance to defeat this foolproof system. Rock probably had Joe's best-kept secrets. But even he was stunned to find out that Joe kept some things from him in other places.

Speaking of "Don't Kiss and Tell," know that *someone* is watching your illicit behavior. Unless you live at the foot of a glacier in Greenland, you have neighbors, and neighbors are nosy and have internet access. They also have cell phones with cameras.

One of the dilemmas facing our youth today is that quite often we may not know who the enemy is, as they are stealthy and not overtly visible. It's difficult and sometimes impossible to identify and hit a target that is invisible. As M says in James Bond's *Skyfall*, "...our enemies are no longer known to us. They do not exist on a map. They're not nations, they're individuals. And look around you. Who do you fear?"

As we've already talked about, when we were growing up, we had the stoop. Even we as kids parked our little butts on the bricks and noticed many societally critical issues. For example, the toughest and the most powerful husbands in the neighborhood were nagged by their wives to throw out the garbage every night. We also noticed how during daytime, certain women in the neighborhood, husbands slaving away in the city, would get visits from male callers the same hours. The guys always looked so merry and carried gifts from afar. We had those guys pegged! And a lot of those women were regular church and novena goers.

Hey, we noticed that, even as kids. Give your soul to Jesus but your ass to a mailman.

That's interesting theology. But not Street Smart. Now you even find people freaking out on airplanes, store lines, in traffic, and then being broadcast around the world to billions of COVID shut-ins. That's "Kiss and Tell" wrought in electronics!

Another funny example of Brooklyn kids not ratting each other out? Wait until you hear about our time at St. Athanasius Elementary School. It involves one of the nuns, let's call her "Sister Barbara," who was being very difficult on our class. A few of our classmates were fed up, so they decided to take matters into their own hands.

Every morning, we would each file in and hang our coats and hats on a designated hook in our own cloakroom, where we'd also keep boots if we had to come to school in rain or snow.

One day, some of the girls decided to have some fun, so they brought in four jumbo AA eggs to class, placing two eggs in each of Sister's boots.

You could hear her screaming from two avenues away when she experienced the surprise of her feet "beating the eggs."

As punishment, she held every one of us for one week in detention with our heads placed on our desks until someone fessed up. Not a word from anybody! Even with our heads down, anonymity an option, no one ratted out the offenders!

To fall on the sword, a Stand-Up Person in our class falsely confessed to this atrocity and took the punishment that the holy sisters dished out. His sacrifice made him extremely popular, but we still didn't know who the culprits were.

It wasn't until a class reunion dinner fifty years later at Rao's, a world-famous restaurant in East Harlem (known for having been booked solid for four decades without a single reservation available), that our female guests, Camille Nowak, Carolyn D'Amico, Mary Pellegrino, Janet Puntorieri, Cathy DeMattia, and Theresa Kelly fessed up and identified the two gals who committed the parochial school caper of the century. But at least they weren't rats. In following this important rule, note how we still won't reveal the offenders' identities, just in case Sister Barbara happens to be reading this account. She will enter the eternal life not knowing who put the eggs in her boots.

Of course, we have another story of how keeping our mouths shut paid unusual dividends. Mom had a refined soup tureen, which we used for many years as the centerpiece for many a working-class dinner party. It invariably drew much praise for its style and function, having been hand cast in some foreign land and of impeccable workmanship. The whole neighborhood waxed poetic in its appraisal.

We also had a demented dog, a wire-haired fox terrier called Pedee (named after the dog in the *Little Rascals* movies), who was quite spiteful (having the distinction of biting everyone in the neighborhood). One day, when we were all out visiting, Pedee mounted the living room table and urinated in the tureen. He also leaked all over the surrounding doilies. The little bastard then hopped off the table and went about his merry way.

We discovered all of this on return, and Mom lost it. Our father told her to bleach the tureen, but Mom was hysterical and told us (of course) to bundle the tureen up and dump it on the garbage cans at street side. We did so and awaited developments. Of course, someone took the tureen home from the garbage pail line. They knew not the history.

We just knew what would happen next. One of our mother's most cherished neighbors, a middle-aged woman, stopped by our stoop and bragged about how she found the treasured soup tureen that was the talk of the neighborhood just lying on the garbage pails and took it home.

We came close to fatally gagging at this point, expecting the worst, and we got it. She went on to add that she rinsed the tureen and made a great pasta lenticchia soup.

"Jesus Christ of Nazareth," was all we could say. Jesus, of course, would not drink soup from a makeshift bedpan, and neither would we. She looked at us quizzically and asked us what was the matter?

"Nothing."

To this day, and this book, no one knows just how close-mouthed we were, and today someone is using the same tureen with the added natural flavoring.

DON'T TAKE SHORTCUTS AND PAY ATTENTION TO DETAILS

This Street Smart pearl is hardest to observe as a habit. Every pain must be taken to research a Street Smart option. But you must ruthlessly pare your efforts and keep on *one* track to spot, seize, and exploit a lucky break. Scattering your efforts will not work. We have an example. It comes from the previously mentioned Manhattan Project program to build the atomic bomb, a billion-dollar research weapon development that ended World War II, barely.

The Manhattan Project civilian scientists were baffled. They had three of the best mediums to spark an atomic reaction. They divided their efforts and resources accordingly. Of course, they got nowhere.

The general in charge probably said something along the lines of, "Hey, eggheads! Here's how we do it in the army. Of the three, which is your hunch (lucky break) that *one* is the best, ignoring all the others for any and all reasons?"

The scientists indicated *one* medium. The general smiled.

"Okay, guys...throw all resources to one medium and ignore all others...not a single research hour more devoted to the others."

That medium worked. It was a Street Smart moment. The scientists spotted, seized, and exploited *one* option. You must be able to do the same. Keeping the solutions and the pursuit of them simple is also Street Smart. You have only so much time in a day. And only one life. Keeping your nose to the grindstone forever is not Street Smart. Choose your battles wisely.

TRUST IS CRITICAL

Speaking about Joe DiMaggio, Rock's friendship with the Yankee Clipper underlines a Street Smart pearl reinforced by our Street Scholars. In fact, it begs the question: Why did this cynical, worldly, and famous man trust Rock?

After all, they were a few generations apart.

Further after all, Joe had already made it, and Rock was just getting started. People from the highest walks of life couldn't get within a continent of DiMaggio. The super powerful and wealthy, royalty, other sports legends were always kept at the DiMaggio arm's length. There is no doubt that Joe was comfortable after the start out in the negative column with the street boy. Rock learned not to ask anything of the Clipper. No autographs, no baseball memorabilia, no nothing. Joe was so accustomed to people asking for favors, and street etiquette prohibited such activity, unless of course it was a matter of life and death. Many people love to nurture others, and that was also a street thing. Joe nurtured Rock, which made him feel that he had some control and hand in the ascent of his career and even his mannerisms.

Furthest after all, on the surface, Joe and Rock came from different cities, professions, and eras. Harshest still, Rock received all the benefits of an Ivy League professional education and Joe was a high-school dropout. To boot, Joe was the son of working-class Italian immigrants who spoke broken English, while Rock came from American stock and a coal-mining family from Freeland and Hazleton, both small towns in Pennsylvania.

As pointed out in our book *Dinner with DiMaggio*, Joe had certain rules that Rock adhered to strictly from the beginning. Dinner was sacred to him. The dinner table was a sanctuary for him in so many ways. No questions or conversations ever about

Marilyn Monroe, the Kennedys, or Frank Sinatra unless Joe volunteered the information. This wasn't easy to do, as most people were overtly intrigued with these three topics, and they were always relationship and conversation terminators when these topics were spoken of. Dinner or conversation was over, and off to Siberia the unlucky ones would go and never be given another opportunity again.

Also, all dinner guests had to be approved first by Joe. It didn't matter if it was your mother, brother, best friend, the Pope, anybody. Rock broke that rule only once and wound up having two separate dinner conversations because Joe refused to acknowledge the presence of the non-approved guest!

But there was commonality in Rock and Joe. They shared ethnicity, poverty, religion, intellectual curiosity (DiMaggio was a voracious reader who read *The New York Times*, *Financial Times*, and *Wall Street Journal* cover to cover daily), and Street Smart wisdom. Rock was the son Joe never had; mind you, Joe had a biological son who he was estranged from. Rock and Joe used that commonality to bounce ideas and wisdom off each other. That theme will be picked up in the Street Smart Memoirs: trust and keeping confidence first, Street Smart later. No good listening to, let alone opening up to, some asshole. There are enough assholes out there.

Joe eventually warmed up to trust Rock, and this was slow and often painful. This trust itself arose in the streets, though differently located streets, for this Street Smart friendship: Joe from the Bay Area fishing community of San Francisco and Rock from the P.S. 226 schoolyard in Brooklyn, New York.

WHAT'S IN A NAME?

Well...everything. When you first meet someone, what do you do? Exchange introductions, of course. One of the most important rules of *any* human interaction: never, *ever* forget someone's name. Very few things in the world may be more offensive than the carelessness of forgetting someone you meet.

Developing and honing this skill, simple and yet so vital, can be the difference between creating lifelong friendships, or "being put in Siberia," a famous DiMaggio quote that was applied when he felt betrayed or ignored. And while we're at it, never misspell someone's name. This is the quickest way to incur someone's wrath. Take the extra two seconds to make sure you spell someone's name correctly. It goes a long way. It's a major part of their identity.

A famous practitioner of this skill, President Bill Clinton, not only uses his charm and ability to "work the room," but he never forgets a name. Whether it was an ambassador, congressman, or the man selling him his coffee, Clinton always makes a humble and proper introduction.

In forgetting someone's name, you've also noted that perhaps they aren't even that important enough to remember and have been implicitly told that their identity simply doesn't matter. Sadly, we're sure most of us have been the one who's been forgotten, and it's probably knocked us down a few pegs.

There's no exact way to practice this pearl, but learning mnemonic devices, patterns, or even making lists are valuable and easy. Like our other pearls, all it takes is practice, practice, practice. And common sense.

DON'T HOPSCOTCH

Speaking of ending relationships, this brings to mind another pearl: don't hopscotch.

Our street definition of hopscotch: going behind someone's back who gave you the gift of an important contact or introduction. Proper greetings and connections are invaluable for anyone wanting to build their way up in the professional world. Back in the old days and now, it's *all* about who you know.

If you decide to sneak behind someone's back for your own interest, not even extending an arm of communication, you're setting yourself up for your own downfall. You've probably not only made one but two enemies: the person who was kind enough to introduce you, and the person you tried to hopscotch your way to.

Rock learned this lesson from the one and only Fay Vincent, former commissioner of the MLB and former chairman of Columbia Pictures. Fay was a Street Smart kid from New Haven, Connecticut. The two of them had many vivid conversations about the do's and don'ts in the business world. There was no one more adept at business politics than Fay, a master strategist who has served as a top advisor to many successful CEOs and business transactions. He told Rock how important it was that as a courtesy to the person who introduced you to another, always give them some type of an update of what has transpired with the relationship that they helped create. Rock will always keep Fay informed regarding any significant conversations he had with people who Fay was kind enough to introduce him to, even three decades later.

Being one to hopscotch is almost a surefire way to create grudges and feuds. It's the quickest way to be removed from the chess board. Don't pole vault over the hand that feeds you. Or else it could short-circuit any chance you may have had to make friends in high places.

THE LAST FIVE PERCENT

What separates the achievers from the ordinary? We call it the Last Five Percent rule. Your brain is hurting, body aching, and burnout is wreaking absolute havoc. We've all experienced this feeling, but it's this critical and crucial last-five-percent effort that can mean the difference between greatness or mediocrity. It's also the most difficult part of the journey to success but equally the most important.

Mr. DiMaggio himself knew all about the Last Five Percent Rule, telling Rock during one of their dinner conversations about the importance of never giving up.

"I remember back in the season of 1940 having a terrible cold. I could barely breathe. The team doc checked me out and told Joe McCarthy, our manager at the time, who decided that I could play. I had a 101 degree temperature. To make things worse, we were going through a heat wave. It was over a hundred for a week. We were playing in uniforms made of heavy wool.

"Just talking made me lose my breath. I was sweating and that wool uniform soaked up all that sweat. It weighed twenty pounds when it was wringing wet.

"It was late in the game, and I got a hold of an outside pitch and drove it to right center over the outfielder's head. But I wasn't happy about it, because I had to run it out. I could barely breathe. I felt like I was running underwater. Somehow, I made it to third base on a hook slide. I'll never forget how I was gasping for air. It turns out I was playing with walking pneumonia."

Joe then goes on to tell Rock of the game's third base umpire calling a timeout, just to make sure Joe had a few moments to catch his breath. DiMaggio told Rock that he lost almost twenty pounds in that game alone, but the last five percent proved that the Yankee Clipper played better than most, even if he nearly passed out at third base. No matter what, Joe always wanted to give it his all. Even if that meant a trip to the emergency room after. He would have had more than his nine World Series rings, but the beginning of World War II cost Joe more than just a couple of seasons.

Another excellent example of the Last Five Percent rule in action is a story that is now revered as a baseball classic and has its own seminal place in the history of the game.

1941: The last great year in baseball. The year that two unbreakable records were achieved: DiMaggio's fifty-six-game hitting streak and Ted Williams accomplishing his famous .406 batting average. Both men recounted this phenomenal year one night at dinner with Rock and Ted's son, John Henry. Ted spoke at length about how difficult it had been to sustain his league-leading batting average for the entire season.

It was this night where Rock learned that Ted's streak was all about the Last Five Percent rule.

On September 28, 1941, when the Red Sox were playing their last two games of the season in Philadelphia, Ted was told by Joe Cronin, the team's player-manager, to sit out the double-header as the Boston Red Sox slugger's average was already .400. Why risk dropping below .400?

But no way in hell would the Splendid Splinter and the greatest natural baseball hitter ever would rest on his laurels in the final two games of the season. Ted insisted that he play in both games, because taking the easy way out was simply not an option.

He said to the three men at the table, finger pointed at the ceiling in conviction, "No matter what my average is, I'm gonna make sure I go out guns blazing. I'm leaving it all on that field."

Pushing himself further than even he thought possible, Ted got six hits in his last eight at-bats and finished his season with a .406 batting average. In the eighty years since that double-header in Philly, nobody since Ted has managed such a feat.

Ted's last five percent earned him a well-deserved spot among the greatest legends that set foot on a major league baseball diamond.

The last five percent can certainly be the difference between good and great.

THE STRENGTH OF SILENCE

In Japanese culture, silence is powerful. The Japanese have mastered this technique, and this is best seen at business conferences. The person who says the least at the negotiating table is usually the powerful decision maker. He or she is able to observe the body movements of the people at the table and assess the situation. This is also the sort of person who elicits responses from the participants. The person who talks the most is usually the least significant of the decision-making team. In other words, the active people are the ones to take much less seriously. This is contrary to the American (or Western) model where the "big Kahuna" starts directly talking, spilling information, and nuancing direction.

Another great benefit of being quiet at the table is that it often makes people feel uncomfortable and forces the others to speak and divulge what they are thinking about because the silence is deafening and also physically uncomfortable. Silence invariably forces quiet people to speak. It's an extremely effective technique. The stony, unresponsive silence of Japanese conference leaders is what often makes them invincible.

Of course, such silence is valuable in the Street Smart environs of Brooklyn. There, the local mobster rarely spoke and was smart enough to observe everyone, forming lightning-fast impressions. Some underlings did the question taking. In fact, our favorite quote from the Mafia was, "We only ask once." Once was always enough for the Street Smart. There were rarely follow-up questions. The Mafia was eloquent enough. It really was. Even though we didn't always approve of their methods, no one beat them at Street Smart.

PLAY THE BALL; DON'T LET IT PLAY YOU

It's a great strategy used to help take control of a situation. In Little League baseball at St. Athanasius in Brooklyn, one of our coaches, Tony Iati, taught this important rule that was used not only in the sports world but also in business and life.

Tony was an amazing man. He was one of the first from the "Olde Neighborhood" who went onto college, later becoming the CEO of Model Rectifier Corporation (MRC), a company that made HO scale electric trains and toy models. Tony always said that when a baseball is hit, you run to the ball, not the other way around. You have the advantage of playing that ball, and that allows you to manage and bring events under control. This is what we called "making the play."

Tony also said the same about business. "Be proactive and make the move that's going to make the person across the table make a move, and then deal with the proposal put on the table." In other words, address the proposal or problem straight on so that you have control, not the other way around. This is the opposite of the Japanese model. Still, it worked for Iati and MRC, and he was revered and respected in Japanese business circles.

Rock's friendship with the often aloof and indecipherable DiMaggio actually educated Rock in business. Rock states it better:

"DiMaggio was a brilliant strategist especially in social settings. He would always watch the dining room where we were sitting and scan the room checking for friends and potential foes. He also mentioned that in situations where you spotted someone in the room who you didn't necessarily like, the smart move was to go to their table, do a preemptive strike, and say hello and exchange the usual perfunctory pleasantries.

"Therefore, most times they would not come to your table to snoop around and find out who you were with and gather information. This was the best way to keep unwanted guests away. I saw it work over and over again with the Clipper."

STREET MENTORS

Rock's friendship with other noteworthy and important men was also further educational as a pearl of Street Smart wisdom.

Success in one field often has skills that could be transferred to other areas and pave the way for a desired outcome. Prime example: Dante scholar and Yale president A. Bartlett "Bart" Giamatti. He used his Street Smarts, academic prowess, brilliant command of the English language, and love of sports to become National League president and ultimately commissioner of baseball. He wrote a great book, *Take Time for Paradise*, where he describes baseball from a literary point of view.

"What connection does an academic professor, Renaissance scholar, and president of an Ivy League university have in common? Everything. The very skills that Bart had growing up (such as superb discipline, building interpersonal relationships, a brilliant command of the English language, as well as giving lectures and engaging a group) were used to transfer and cross over to an entirely different field," Rock said.

He has a specific memory in mind where he saw all of these skills melt into play for Giamatti.

"I remember like it was yesterday, even though it was the late '80s, when Bart was giving a talk to an Italian American group in New York run by "limousine king" Bill Fugazy, at an A-list Italian restaurant. Bart gave this extemporaneous, beautiful, and elegant speech about Dante and his connections to baseball. Unfortunately, most of the attendees didn't appreciate this world master discussing Dante.

"When Bart came back to the table he said, 'What do you think, Rock?'"

Rock could only answer honestly.

"Doctor Giamatti, I would need to translate and explain everything you said during your speech. They didn't understand a word of what you said." They were too busy eating their cannoli and drinking their espressos.

Obviously, there was not much transference there.

Jerry Della Femina, one of our Street Scholars, shared a similar transformation. Considered one of the top advertising executives in the world, he was able to cross over to a business that involved something he loved: the culinary arts. (Here, Brooklyn food was the best in the world, as you know.) Jerry built the most upscale restaurant in East Hampton where all the A-listers and those wealthy neighbors who are "Masters of the Universe" would kill to get a table on a Friday or Saturday night. During the summer months, Jerry used his talents and skills that made him legendary in the business world. All this would make him a legend in the hospitality industry in the toughest market in the country: the Hamptons. The irony of a Brooklyn boy making it even bigger in the Hamptons among the elite is not lost on you, hopefully.

BE READY FOR THE UNEXPECTED

Street Smart also involves knowing how to accomplish a goal in a more rapid way. Many times, the person who knows how to assess a situation or a project will take the mental approach that the shortest distance between two points is a straight line. You need to be decisive, but you also must learn the most important technique: knowing how and when to switch gears on the dime.

For example, whatever you are working on may take a quick turn in another direction. New variables may be rapidly introduced. You have to be able to hit the proverbial curve ball. In life, there are very few fastballs down the middle. What made baseball players great was their ability to, in a split second, alter their batting stance and swing. Most importantly, never take your eye off the ball—or in this case, a situation.

This is especially relevant in the business world. The titans who are at the top of their fields know how to make adjustments immediately and turn into bigger profits for their company. See Tony James, a Street Scholar, for example. Tony believes that our brains can be better utilized and harnessed to change circumstances themselves. His Street Smart Memoir recounts how completely different situations can be managed by proper usage of Street Smart.

In the medical world, the same rules apply. A surgeon may start out doing a procedure, and suddenly there is a rapid change in the medical condition of the patient and their circumstances.

The perfect example: an obstetrician. What starts out as a simple baby delivery can turn into a nightmare where, not only is the baby at risk, but also the mother. This sort of switch in gears is common in medicine overall. Opening a patient up might reveal a terribly different situation than revealed earlier by mere CAT scans or X-rays. There is a common attitude among doctors that you are never certain what you will find, but you always come prepared for the unexpected. There is no such thing as a simple surgical procedure. Great doctors are not measured by when they get things right, but by how they act when things go wrong.

In general, always prepare for the worst scenario. We don't care how great you think you are. Everyone is vulnerable. Being cocksure of yourself also includes room for the unexpected. A Street Smart person is always amenable to changes and can switch lanes immediately when warranted.

CAUSE FOR ACTION, NOT CAUSE FOR PANIC

If anything sucks energy from using your Street Smart, it is panic compelled by anxiety. That's a lesson that one of our Street Scholars, Governor David Paterson (D-NY) will comment further on later.

Having a plan during times of chaos puts you at an advantage to survive and thrive. Panic is the worst enemy. The time you spend panicking is lost time. Always imagine the worst scenario and have things in place and ready to go. Respond to the crisis at hand, and you will have plenty of time to panic later. Now that's easier said than done and has been written about as advice since the dawn of man's putting anything down in writing. But it's compelling Street Smart as well; that hunch you get when you feel like running down a fallout shelter in your mind will save your ass more often than not.

The military provides a clue. They provide war plans in advance for every conceivable enemy. Before World War II, they had very graphic plans, termed in colors, for potential enemies, even those countries friendly to us. This meant war against Germany, France, Italy, Japan, Mexico, even Britain. When war breaks out, they reasoned, we would have a plan in place. You can have similar plans to cover contingencies. While it is controversial for us to state it, COVID would have been better handled if we had a similar plan to handle a pandemic. There were no plans that we have read of, even after the media explored the government responses. That, sadly, is why the New World we have written this primer for was so damaging and so long lived. Where was the plan? Did you read of one either? On the street, we call it "being caught flat-footed" when you're not prepared for the unexpected.

So, when the pandemic was drifting out of the New York airports, where was the plan to state contingency options? It is ironic that COVID has swept away so many institutions that should have had commercial, governmental, and military plans. The military, again, says it right: order, counter-order, disorder!

Everyone who has a goal in mind tries to fast track and go for the proverbial home run. Many successful people have stayed away from this thinking. It's much more efficient to hit singles and move from tactical objective to objective and ultimately cross home plate. "Swinging for the fences" (meaning in baseball to strive for the longest shot, like a homerun over the fence) often puts you at a disadvantage, as it is often an expenditure of energy that can tax the process and inhibit the desired outcome. Again, easier said than done. But Street Smart assists here as well. You'll get a better hunch if you keep everything in stride and chip away in gradual deliberated steps.

BEWARE OF THE "PIPE SMOKER"

This is an interesting person. The "pipe smoker" is often the person who reads volumes on a subject and feels that they're an expert without any real experience dealing with the issue at hand. Their advice is academic but often not realistic, and it could prove fatal. We want a person on our team who is well read and schooled but, just as important, someone who has actually experienced what they are giving advice on. The term was derived from one of the authors' experiences during medical training. He brought an X-ray to show a class of medical residents and attending physicians. Once he put the X-ray up on the view box, everyone was baffled, trying to suggest what the condition could be. One of the professors approached the screen with a smoking pipe in his mouth, looking like he came right out of a Sir Walter Raleigh pipe-tobacco commercial. He was quizzical and started talking about many articles he had read, and he thought he diagnosed the condition presented on the X-ray.

After fifteen minutes of wrong guesses, they called and asked about what exactly the condition was. Nobody had a clue. It turns out that the X-ray was not that of a human foot but instead a horse's hoof that belonged to the horse of a local pizzeria owner who asked for a medical opinion!

So much for just looking intelligent! The "pipe smoker" turned out to be a horse's ass in the eyes of his peers. If you don't have the actual experience, shut up! Everyone can read about it in a book and suddenly think that they're Einstein.

COMMON SENSE

Common sense dovetails precisely with Street Smart. That should not be surprising, as any wisdom from the street will not have the dubious complexity of "wisdom" born of some idle philosopher drinking his coffee at a local Starbucks. Our Street Smart comes from people who actually work for a living. This might be critical because *you* work for a living. The life philosophy of a person remote from everyday commerce and strife will not even vaguely match yours.

The modern self-improvement guru is the equivalent of the nineteenth-century coffee-house philosopher in all ways. There is very little common sense to the present "self-improvement" genre. How could there be? Telling people to network like a lunatic avoids the inescapable observation that everyone avoided any contact in public places that could entail exposure to COVID.

Admonishing people to "think positively" is okay but has its limitations; when everything is in flux, and people you think will save you come up short, you would have to be an imbecile to think positively. Working harder is fine, but hard work, you no doubt have noticed...is *hardly* a guarantee of success. Smiling inanely is great but does not line you up on the road to success, either.

No, the self-help gurus, a multibillion-dollar market, might as well be tone deaf. Only the razor-sharp common sense of Street Smart is liberating enough in these post-COVID times. *You* decide what is success for you. Not some perpetually grinning trickster. You never figured out why they were all smiling? It had something to do with your purchase!

Only a "Rutter," a map, if you will, can assure safe and effective passage through the really uncharted reefs of this New World. The blind leading the blind is not a capable life philosophy.

Spotting a lucky break is not hard if you are actively looking for it. If you are spotting for it but not willing to seize it, you may as well not spot it. If you neither spot nor seize a lucky break, you need not exploit it. In this book, you have over three dozen successful people who are, as far as we can tell, unanimous that this raw common sense of Street Smart works where the "genre" fails miserably.

On the street, idle people spouting theories are worse than useless in the best of time. In the time of COVID, and hopefully its end or successful management, idle people and useless philosophy are literally dangerous and not merely ineffective.

None of the Street Scholars we engaged for you personally are coffee-house philosophers or ineffective counsel.

WATCH YOUR TOMATOES

A funny story from our Street Smart elementary school days: we had a summerhouse on Long Island owned by our paternal grandfather. It was our version of the Fresh Air Fund. There were nearby truck farms where we could pick our own vegetables. One blazingly hot summer day, one of our relatives took us to the truck farm and parked in the dried-out mud opposite the picking fields.

It just so happened that an overweight middle-aged man was toiling like a peasant in the fields picking tomatoes into a bushel, which would later be weighed at the farm stand. Our relative told us to stay just outside the farm picket fence and await develop-ments. The toiler in the fields later approached our relative, a denizen of the tougher streets of Brooklyn called Williamsburg.

"Hey, buddy, do me a favor. I wanna bring in another bushel from the far end of the field. Watch these tomatoes for me. I have been at this for two hours in this fuckin' sun," the hapless man asked our relative, just standing outside the picket fence.

"Sure, buddy, they'll be safe with me," our relative stated with a straight Brooklyn face. I saw a mild smile cross his face briefly. At that reassurance, the toiler returned to his fields.

With hardly a glance, our relative reached over the picket fence, picked up the tomato bushel, and deftly placed it in the back of his car. Over my father's fervent objection, we screeched off to parts unknown, leaving the peasant to ponder on the situa-tion with some vulgarity.

"If you don't watch what belongs to you, kids, it will soon belong to someone else," explained my relative with a chuckle. Oh, that's Street Smart. Watch your tomatoes and never take your eye off the ball—or the tomatoes, for that matter.

BUT...NOT EVERYONE WANTS YOU TO BE STREET SMART

It almost goes without saying that other people, some with a vested interest, would not want you Street Smart. We call them the Old World. The Old World are those intimidators who preach (sometimes literally) the rusty and obsolete rules of the Old World game.

The Old World Game, in turn, consists of the following rules: work even harder and you will succeed; give up "frivolous" pursuits like "outside the office" friendships, deep relationships, expendable people, and a home life. Go to the best B-school!

And network, network, and network further. Grin perpetually like the village idiot, maintaining a constantly faux-happy disposition of perfect optimism, and hobnob with your betters! Oh, again, nose to the grindstone until you get gristle!

Really, and what did you get for that? Not much. Instead, you got deliberately outmoded guidance from people whose main function was to keep you Street Dumb (inferior, wailing for nonexistent advice, and confused). And *they* got paid for this enforced ignorance and universal confusion.

The Street Scholars are directly giving you the rules of the New World Order. Not the widely published "New World Order" of nations or ethnicities touted about in constant periodicals and books. No, the New World Order where Street Smart is the only real key to survival and hence success in this ever-changing and hostile world.

COVID, and its many varieties, variants, and mutations, accelerated the decline of the Old World. Businesses failed, others spouted from nothing at all, individuals who were otherwise successful sickened and died, commerce stopped, businesses were closed at the whim of government and virus. So, people went to the Old World game masters: gurus, business leaders, churchmen and churchwomen, personal advisors, health advisors, and self-improvement demagogues, and they were shielded behind plastic visors, hidden in their expensive homes, clothed in MOPP outfits, triple masked, and social distanced away from the panicked masses.

But the dozens of Street Scholars in this book were self-reliant. They all agree unanimously that hard work isn't enough, that education is helpful but not decisive, that networking is insufficient, that education on the street decisively supplements book knowledge, and most importantly that the capacity for Street

Smart comes from the heart, the mind, and maybe even the soul. It is evolutionary, which is why Street Smart is itself decisive in the New World Order. It is further revolutionary in that everyone who can think can be Street Smart without much preparation or schooling.

These three dozen universally acknowledged successful people are powerful proof of the existence of this New World Order. The media provide daily accounts of the failure of the Old World Order. Which world will you reside in?

IT'S NOT EASY TO BE A MILLENNIAL

Before we bestow to you our Street Smart Memoirs, we felt it was important to further address and acknowledge the audience we want this primer to reach. We're both middle-aged guys, and we distinctly sympathize with today's millennial and the struggles that have been thrown at them through no fault of their own. COVID will define this generation much more sharply than Vietnam or the Women's Liberation Movement defined ours. And we can't say that anything good will come out of the rolling COVID pandemics. What good comes out of double masking, businesses closed by government or by infection, and how social distancing has torn the guts out of socialization?

What one can learn in the classroom versus what we've learned on the streets of New York aren't exactly the same. Though what people learn in the classroom is certainly invaluable, hopefully reading our stories and these Street Smart Memoirs can give an education classes don't teach. This primer can hopefully also serve as an opportunity to bridge the gap between our generations and relate to each other on a level that people have only dreamt of. Each person mentioned had inhabited their own definition of Street Smart. There's truly something for everyone in this treatise. We decided to write *Street Smart* not to berate or "discipline" a generation. We invited such accomplished people to take part because we saw a need to teach what we've all learned, passing it onto a younger group of people who haven't necessarily seen such a need—yet.

STREET SMART DISCOVERIES

Every memoir of the Street Scholars we interviewed agree that Street Smart not only exists, but that every living person has access to it. The concept defies logic and perhaps reason. Street Smart is a way of life and perhaps even a biological and evolutionary skill set. It takes root in any environment but is best observed in urban areas where people of many faiths, races, and ethnicities live in real harmony and interact closely. The post-COVID world might actually set back Street Smart, as some of our Street Scholars have written. But we're optimists. Here is our breakdown and takeaways from what follows ahead.

Instead, Street Smart is a mixture of intellect, hunches, feelings, and emotion. It is a composite virtue of being able to spot, seize, and exploit lucky breaks. This virtue is critical, and everyone sometimes gets a lucky break, whether realized or not, that offers success.

Accordingly, we asked the opinions of these universally acknowledged successful people about the influence of things not learned in the classroom, spanning nearly every racial, religious, and ethnic group. Spotting, seizing, exploiting, and creating Street Smart lucky breaks is both universally observed and unanimously accepted by these successful Scholars. This was a stunning, if happy, conclusion to our journey.

STREET SMART MEMOIRS

This primer follows consistently observed rules. In effect, the Street Scholars are priming the current and younger generation, and older readers as well (let's not forget that it's always better late than never), in the "New World." This New World, in turn, is totally unpredictable except for the usefulness of Street Smart. Navigating the New World without using this skill is not merely unfruitful, but dangerous. Using this "New World Primer" makes a lot of common sense, a common sense clearly absorbed by our Street Scholars.

STREET SMART MEMOIR OF DR. ANTHONY FAUCI
Brooklyn's Street Smart Used against COVID and AIDS

Dr. Anthony Fauci not only uses his Street Smart successfully, but he also says he uses his Street Smart *specifically*. Our families knew each other when his parents owned and operated a neighborhood drug store in Brooklyn around 79th Street and New Utrecht Avenues in Bensonhurst. As the delivery boy, Anthony made money from twenty-five-cent tips as he tooled around on his Schwinn bike with a delivery basket attached to his fender. He also worked at the prehistoric cash register. And he is the very first one to eloquently state that his "Old Neighborhood" Street Smart experiences helped not merely himself but the whole United States.

So, it is truthful to say that no one knew those Bensonhurst streets like Dr. Anthony Fauci. His avowed Street Smart roots go deep in the Italian/Jewish/Irish neighborhood that overlapped a working-class community. And he says so in his Street Smart journal to follow.

But you *gotta* know the neighborhood. Back then, it was just lower middle class with large streaks of working-class houses. Anthony lived in a two-family house in a neighborhood where the community was very tight-knit and people respected other people without recourse to the media, political parties, or class-action lawsuits.

Now that you have the background, Anthony's family's drug store was not a CVS, Walgreen, Kroger's, Rite Aid, or Walmart. These multibillion-dollar establishments also sell food, trinkets, sporting goods, holiday goods, and even light clothing. No, Fauci's Pharmacy basically sold both prescription and over-the-counter medications. And they had what was called a "credit account," meaning help for those families who didn't have enough money to secure vital medications. Sadly, there were a lot of these people in Anthony's neighborhood.

No such help exists today in most pharmacies. In those days, things were "on account." The Faucis were noteworthy as kind-hearted people who waited to get paid. At that time, almost all drugs were cash and carry. Very few were covered by insurance, and there was really scanty reimbursement. So, Anthony got the order (face-to-face) from his folks, grabbed a brown paper bag with meds, and set off for someone's house. He was paid for the meds and returned to the drugstore. He usually delivered via that family-owned bicycle of uncertain vintage. He then returned happier with a tip. That's if he was lucky. This was not a corporate giant. But it worked.

This system served two critically important purposes. It got Anthony to see people less fortunate than his family, always a Street Smart school setting. It also got Anthony to realize that *everyone* should be treated like family. In other words, treat others with respect and expect to be treated accordingly.

Anthony Stephen Fauci's parents, Eugenia and Stephen, were first-generation Italian Americans who earned a hard-won pharmacy license and lived near their business. Anthony was always nicknamed "Tony," and he was an outgoing, enthusiastic, and friendly young boy who did the menial jobs around the pharmacy. He attended Jesuit schools, earning their respect, which was not an easy task as they were invariably difficult men. Smart young Italian boys went to Catholic schools. Anthony went to Our Lady of Guadalupe Catholic elementary school, then Regis (Catholic Jesuit) High School (Manhattan), and then to the College of the Holy Cross (Catholic Jesuit college in Massachusetts). He later went to medical school at Cornell, finishing a residency at New York Cornell Medical Center.

According to the National Institutes of Health's website, "Dr. Fauci was appointed Director of the National Institute of Allergy and Infectious Diseases (NIAID) in 1984. And NIAID's budget is $6.1 billion—that's a lot to be in charge of. Anthony has advised seven presidents. In a 2021 analysis of Google Scholar citations, Dr. Fauci ranked as the 35th most-cited living researcher. According to the Web of Science, Dr. Fauci ranked 9th out of 2.5 million authors in the field of immunology by total citation count between 1980 and January 2021. During the same period, he ranked 20th out of 2.4 million authors in the field of research and experimental medicine, and 132nd out of 992,000 authors in the field of general and internal medicine.

"Dr. Fauci has delivered major lectures all over the world and is the recipient of numerous prestigious awards, including the Presidential Medal of Freedom (the highest honor given to a civilian by the president of the United States), the National

Medal of Science, the George M. Kober Medal of the Association of American Physicians, the Mary Woodard Lasker Public Service Award, the Albany Medical Center Prize in Medicine and Biomedical Research, the Robert Koch Gold Medal, the Prince Mahidol Award, and the Canada Gairdner Global Health Award. He also has received fifty-one honorary doctoral degrees from universities in the United States and abroad.

"Dr. Fauci is a member of the National Academy of Sciences, the National Academy of Medicine, the American Academy of Arts and Sciences, and the American Philosophical Society, as well as other professional societies including the American College of Physicians, the American Society for Clinical Investigation, the Association of American Physicians, the Infectious Diseases Society of America, the American Association of Immunologists, and the American Academy of Allergy, Asthma & Immunology. He serves on the editorial boards of many scientific journals and as an author, coauthor, or editor of more than 1,300 scientific publications, including several textbooks."

Anthony serves currently, at time of writing, as chief COVID medical advisor to President Joe Biden and formerly to President Donald Trump. He held weekly, even daily press conferences detailing the nightmare of COVID. People were visually glued to their television sets and streaming devices when a Street Smart Anthony and a medical panel held court.

"As I have recounted often, my upbringing has greatly influenced my career and the principles by which I live today. I grew up in Brooklyn, New York, in a neighborhood called Bensonhurst, storied for its toughness and resilience but strong sense of caring for each other and community spirit," starts Anthony.

There were very few principles, but they were really enforced by the streets. Really. Here are Anthony's principles in being Street Smart.

"First and foremost, it was important to know how to take care of yourself. Fortunately, I learned early on that being Street Smart meant more than being able to take care of yourself," Anthony adds.

"It meant knowing how to get along with a wide range of personalities. The Italian-American community where I was raised resembled a large family where people always looked out for one another."

The kindness of Anthony's family blessed many families struggling to pay a medication bill, as we said earlier in this Street Smart Memoir. Getting medication to a sick person even if they had little money to pay the bill is distinctly looking out for other people.

"Bonds between families and friends were built out of loyalty, honesty, and trust that led to close friendships and relationships. The experience of building these relationships would teach me an invaluable lesson that would serve me well at a critical time in my career," says Anthony.

In this light, Anthony's survival and efficiency as America's "Official First Warrior" against COVID credits his Street Smart. Anthony was earlier presented with a growing HIV epidemic, which like COVID, seemed to strike across racial, ethnic, social, and economic boundaries. In fact, as it infected primarily gay men, already stigmatized, there was much anguish in the gay community that HIV (AIDS) was spread as biological warfare.

Anthony continues: "Early during my tenure as Director of the National Institute of Allergy and Infectious Diseases in the 1980s, as the HIV epidemic became a public health crisis, I encountered a group of primarily gay men whom society had treated with stigma and prejudice, and who were at high risk of HIV. They fought for a chance to have input into how we approached this disease that was killing so many of them."

Anthony noted that the loud and rowdy gay protestors outside government buildings, including his own, were comprised of panic-driven, but also genuinely aggrieved, men. But his Street Smart kicked in. He says, "Rather than ignoring them as they led a 'Storm the NIH' (National Institute of Health) protest outside my office, I decided to invite a few of them in and listen to what they had to say."

Anthony, of course, knew nothing of AIDS, HIV, or the gay community outside of science, but he was emboldened by his Bensonhurst Street Smart. Other bookish scientists literally cowered behind their metal desks and glass beakers. Street Smart translated here for Anthony very well: he spotted the opportunity to actually speak to irate gay men suffering from HIV, seized the opportunity, and really exploited it.

"At that time, many fellow research scientists were either afraid of the disruptive activist tactics or dismissive of the idea that patients might have insights valuable to their work. However, I quickly learned quite the opposite—what they had to say made a lot of sense and would be invaluable to the public health response to HIV."

Taking a bit of Street Smart from his Bensonhurst days, Anthony placed himself in the shoes of those different than him.

"If I were a gay man and living on the streets of Brooklyn again, I would have been doing exactly what they were doing. And so, I seized this *unexpected* opportunity to forge relationships and develop allies instead of enemies, thus taking a pivotal step in the fight against HIV," explains Anthony. This is really wise, because there were not many overt gay men in Bensonhurst then.

In this way, speaking *to* a different group, and not speaking *down to them*, was a Street Smart thing to do. It is hard to be judgmental during human suffering, whether fighting COVID or HIV waves. This had roots in Old Bensonhurst. Here, it was shut up and let me know what's bothering you.

But Anthony made it a mantra. "Over decades, I developed deep, personal friendships with some of my harshest activist critics from that time," states Anthony.

Wow, imagine that.... In the present era of COVID's first, second, and third wave, making friends of vocal and vicious enemies.

"Activists became partners in research, leading to highly successful collaborations that have had a lasting impact on HIV research and have more broadly informed public health responses to this day," states Anthony, who is clearly not a fan of today's yelling, screaming, blaming, and overall baseless viciousness.

Yell as much as you want, blame the unvaccinated, the vaccinated, the breakthrough cases, the naturally immune, Blue State governors, Red State governors, the immigrant, the "Trumper," and still get COVID. No media outlet has yet posted a story about how yelling, blaming, pointing fingers or being vicious leads to avoidance of COVID. But the media plays up the differences and the hatred because that's what the panic-driven mobs want to hear.

Anthony *personally* used his Street Smart to seize an opportunity to reach out to the suffering and the isolated. That was spotting (above the noise and the chanting and the screaming and the police sirens), then seizing (actually meeting with gay men, who were widely suspected of spreading the illness through hugging, talking, yelling, and lack of social distance) this rare opportunity. He then institutionally seized his Street Smart opportunity born of that first protest and made NIH policy based on that feedback.

"Being Street Smart really helped!" says Anthony, using his Bensonhurst roots so clearly...and so effectively...to fight HIV (AIDS) many years ago.

STREET SMART MEMOIR OF BO DIETL
The City Cop Uses Street Smart Every Day

There is no one tougher or more Street Smart than NYPD Detective (Ret.) Bo Dietl. Bo has seen it all. And he prosecuted it all with Street Smart every single day of his working life.

Bo had the usual modest beginnings of our Street Scholars: emerging from the working-to-lower-middle class. In fact, he is a first-generation American. Which didn't stop him from rising to the very top of law enforcement. Bo is colorful. Bo is grand. Bo is what you see, and you only get what you see with Bo. He's outspoken. He's blunt. In fact, he reminds us of our other friend, now recently deceased, legendary NYPD Detective Emeritus Sonny Grosso. Bo's more than enough for now. And as you'll see, he not only constantly uses Street Smart, his whole life is a testament to spotting, seizing, and exploiting Street Smart.

Richard "Bo" Dietl was a New York City police officer and detective from June 1969 until he retired in 1985 and is one of the most highly decorated detectives in the history of the police department, with thousands of arrests to his credit. Bo was one of the first NYPD undercover "decoy cops" and was hospitalized thirty times for injuries sustained in the line of duty. Decoy cops are plain-clothed police deliberately enticing a mugger to attack the police officer. Yes, like on *NCIS, Kojak, Hawaii Five-O*, and the like.

Richard "Bo" Dietl is also the founder and chairman of Beau Dietl & Associates and Investigations.com. Founded in 1985, Beau Dietl & Associates has grown to become one of the premier investigative and security firms in the nation and is a full-service organization providing a wide variety of investigative and security services to corporate and individual clients worldwide. In 2010, Bo formed Beau Dietl Consulting Services (BDCS), which recruits temporary and permanent placements in the IT, finance, and business verticals for global leaders and Fortune 500 companies with clients such as JP Morgan Chase, Citibank, and Ernst & Young.

Bo credits his success as a cop...and resulting success as entertainer, news commentator, and philanthropist...to his "sixth sense." This "sixth sense" comes up in our Street Smart Memoirs frequently under other names and guises, but here's Bo's take for you. To him, it's about perceiving something not readily apparent to the usual observer.

"I believe in a sixth sense. My sixth sense has helped me many times in my career as an NYPD police officer and detective. To me, a sixth sense is something that makes you aware...something that's non-tangible...something that you can't put your finger on. It's when you have a feeling. I'd like to call it Street Smart. It's when you look around and you know exactly what is going on. This awareness can save you from being robbed or even worse," related Bo.

"I believe my Street Smart is the reason I've had such an accomplished career. As a NYPD detective, I made over 1600 felony arrests. I was mugged as a decoy over five hundred times and was the recipient of over eighty medals and citations from the NYPD," Bo wrote to us.

"Work as a decoy means a lot more than you think. A decoy is an undercover policeman pretending to be a potential crime victim, such as a man returning from shopping with packages, a worker coming from a cash-checking storefront with a wad of cash, a suburban white dweeb drug shopping in an urban minority neighborhood, or just a hapless drunk waiting to be rolled by some toughs," Bo adds.

"Getting mugged five hundred times and surviving means a very high degree of Street Smart." And Bo says so. He mentions two cases proving his embrace of Street Smart, and we warn you, they are quite graphic.

Bo, for example, used his Street Smart to capture two men wanted for what then-Mayor Edward I. Koch called "the most vicious crime in New York City history" and also "a despicable act of depravity."

"I want to see the guy, figuratively, hung," added an outraged Mayor Koch. But let's see how Bo brilliantly navigated the situation and used his Street Smart first.

Two men up in the urban Bronx neighborhood raped, sodomized, tortured, mugged, and then cut twenty-seven crosses on the body of a thirty-one-year-old nun from Our Lady of Mount Carmel convent on October 10, 1981. Bo Dietl and the Mafia both sprang into action.

According to the *Associated Press*, the Mafia put a $25,000 bounty on the two men, a Harold Wells (twenty-two years old) and a Max Lindeman (twenty-three years old). The NYPD took the case with great interest as well.

Bo was assigned to the case, along with his Street Smart toolkit. These criminals didn't have a chance. Bo remembers the case directly.

"One particular case that comes to mind is when we were investigating the rape of a Roman Catholic nun in a convent on 116th Street in Pleasant Ave. It was like one of those things people say was a light switch that went on in my head.

"Vinny Rao (co-owner of Rao's restaurant in East Harlem) was outside and overheard some people in the street passing by talking about the guys that raped the nun. They were talking about seeing a tall and short man standing outside on the corner around the same time the rape happened. They said the men lived on 125th Street (Harlem precinct) and the small one walked with a limp.

"In 1981, these clues helped me in solving the entire investigation. I attribute this to a series of lights that went off as a kind of sixth sense."

This Street Smart of Bo's became quite acute and deadly accurate.

Bo seemingly interviewed the entire world based on this threadbare lead. The number of tall and short men standing on a particular New York street corner at the approximate time of the vicious attack, one with a limp, and supposedly living on 125th Street in Harlem, only narrowed the suspects to about several thousand.

And that's if Rao's lead was accurate. But Bo pounded the dirty pavement and narrowed the suspects down to Wells and Lindeman, as did the Mafia. But Bo and the NYPD would get them first. Small Street Smart clues meant a big conviction.

"You have to use your mind and go with any hunches or feelings that you have. That's what Street Smart is. If you meet someone and you have a bad feeling about them, the majority of times you are right. One of the things that I do is, I look at someone's shoes, and if they are worn down or look disgusting, that's a signal to me that that person is a loser," Bo explained to us.

It was still up to him to nab the young creeps. Meanwhile, he was aware that the Mafia, outraged by an attack on a nun in their neighborhood, was also pounding the streets of Harlem. But Bo had his Street Smart. Bo interviewed hundreds of suspects, scrutinizing each one physically rather than mentally. The "Sixth Sense" kicked in on two suspects.

And that was not the only celebrated and baffling case Bo solved with Street Smart. Another horrendous crime awaited his use of Street Smart. The case was termed the "Palm Sunday Massacre," the murder of no fewer than ten people at 1080 Liberty Avenue in the East New York section of Brooklyn on April 15, 1984.

The ten included two three-year-olds, a four-year-old, a seven-year-old, and two ten-year-olds, all Hispanic, and all were shot by Christopher Thomas, who discharged nineteen shots from a .38 caliber revolver and a .22 caliber pistol execution style into reclining children and their mothers. Bo used his "1981 Nun" Street Smart power to assist him when assigned this terrible case.

"I use my Street Smart opportunities every day in my investigations when talking to people. My sixth sense gives me the acute ability of knowing when people are telling me the truth and when they are lying," explained Bo.

"As I explained before, my sixth sense has helped me solve probably one of the biggest cases in NY history, the rape of the nun I keep going back to...it was all the Street Smart breaks that led us to the capture of the men that committed heinous crimes," Bo further related.

Bo helped capture Thomas by shaving truth from lies using Street Smart. Now, these are the outstanding examples of street sense used by a crack NYPD detective, but Bo offers direct advice to you in your everyday life as well. You can be a Street Smart detective as well without a gold detective badge.

"When you have a feeling about something, follow it. For example, if you are married and all of a sudden, your other half loses weight and maybe starts going to the gym and starts acting a little unusual, that's an indicator that something is going on differently in their mind," says Bo to you. That's the start of Street Smart.

"And if you have that feeling, go with it.... 95 percent of the time when people come to me about a possible cheating spouse because they get 'that feeling,' they are correct." Bo gets even more descriptive for you in other life matters.

"That's Street Smart, when you know something is wrong, trust your intuition," Bo tells both of us and tells you. The difference between success and failure, Bo says, is the proper and efficient use of your innate street sense power.

Rock has his own street sense story with Bo as a main character.

During the Columbus Day Parade of 1991, Joe DiMaggio was the Grand Marshal. As you can imagine, every security group wanted to have the honor, privilege, and bragging rights to say that they guarded and kept the Yankee legend safe during his historic walk down Fifth Avenue from St. Patrick's Cathedral.

Rock remembers vividly introducing Bo to DiMaggio right after the mass at the Cathedral. Joe got a real sense of Bo just by looking him in the eye while shaking his hand. Joe said "Hey, Doc, I get a real good vibe from this Bo fellow. Do you think he would mind tagging along with us during the parade?" Joe later in his life had a fear of crowds and, based on his instinct, chose Bo to be his protector as he clearly felt something about him that made him safe. At the end of the parade, Joe gifted his Grand Marshal sash to Bo as a token of his appreciation which was no small feat and very unusual for the nostalgic DiMaggio.

Bo won't be shut up for political correctness. He always got his man, or his woman, using Street Smart. And so he told you here.

STREET SMART MEMOIR OF BOB COSTAS
The Gamblers, the Sportsmen, the Gentleman, and Street Smart

Sports can be the clearest example of using Street Smart: luck and skill do abound and mix in a way that a sharp, cognizant observer can discern. Opportunities are spotted, seized, and exploited. Conversely, even the most ignorant onlooker can peek at opportunities blindsided, fumbled, and wasted. What makes this clear and dynamic is, of course, technology: every conceivable camera angle summons up the video play-by-play, the zoom shot of a miserably passed off football, the baseball streaking between the legs of the shortstop, and the basketball recoiling off the rim during the playoffs. Even worse, not only can everything screwed up be played back, it can be played back instantaneously and even parsed into slivers of time, not only by the broadcaster but also at home by the viewer.

Street Smart actually compels you to watch, especially if you have money riding on a game like the Super Bowl, the World Series, or the Stanley Cup. There's a lot of sports out there and a lot of sports gambling money. With everyone stuck inside, and cardboard paste-ups of actual fans at stadiums not drinking beer or eating hot dogs as the "audience," COVID has bolstered at-home and internet gambling.

So, our next Street Scholar is none less than Bob Costas, the modern face of American sports.

Bob has garnered more than twenty-eight Emmy awards for his work, including covering the Olympics in China, where he earned the ire of Chinese and "friends of China" (like the *New York Times*) everywhere when he broke the story (later verified) that the Chinese teams all used performance-enhancing drugs. He covered another eleven Olympics, all to maximum ratings. His work in popularizing sports such as hockey, baseball, football, basketball, golf, or most other organized athletic activity is legendary and beyond question whatsoever. It would take a hundred pages to recount his accomplishments.

That being said, Bob explains just how being Street Smart is so vital in the world, a world ravaged by opportunities spotted, seized, and exploited…or lost. Bob is a fervent believer in Street Smart and says to you that "Street Smart capability is the razor-sharp difference between having success and survival, or having real problems, in the COVID world."

But he explains it better than we could.

"For the most part, I grew up in suburban surroundings on New York's Long Island. But my dad was a New York City guy, Brooklyn and Queens. Youngest of eight children of Greek immigrants who came to America and New York through Ellis Island. Starting with little, every one of those six boys and two girls made something of themselves. Every one of those Depression-era, first-generation Americans got an education. Some of it in classrooms. Some on New York City streets. My Dad's attitude, frame of reference, and manner of speech almost shouted Street Smart. He transmitted some of that to me. Especially through one aspect of his life and personality.

"John Costas was an inveterate gambler. He didn't frequent racetracks or Vegas. Didn't play high-stakes poker. He bet on ball games. Baseball. Football. Basketball. Big sums. Thousands of dollars on a given day. With bookies with names like Blinky and Nunzio. Nothing unusual about a boy bonding with his dad around sports. But this was more than just an interest in the home teams. In an era with no ESPN, and no internet, my Dad was as conversant with every team and its significant players as a non-media member in the '50s and '60s could possibly be. And he shared much of that knowledge with me as we followed the games (and his wagers) together.

"When the mortgage was riding on whether Whitey Ford could get Al Kaline out, or if Wilt Chamberlain could make a couple of free throws, it could be nerve-wracking. God knows my mother and sister felt that way. But most of the time, I saw my dad as a Runyonesque figure. A colorful, Street Smart character right out of one of Runyon's stories or a film noir offering on Channel 9's *Million Dollar Movie*. A side benefit was that by the time I was ten, I could accurately guess the line on any game on the board. They didn't teach that at school.

"Once, when he was on a winning streak, I accompanied him to meet his bookie at a donut shop in Brooklyn. It was 1966. I was fourteen. The guy was straight out of central casting. Wide lapel suit, snap-brim fedora, pinky ring, gravelly voice. Pretty safe bet he was acquainted with the Mob. After a few moments of small talk, he casually slid a paper bag across the counter. Moments later, we were back in the car. There, under a streetlight, John Costas counted out fourteen thousand tax-free dollars in one-hundred-dollar bills. In 1966, the house we lived in cost him nineteen grand on the GI Bill.

"Satisfied he had been paid in full, he announced we were headed to the Bronx to catch the Yankee game. Safe to say my youthful view of the world was shaped in large part by episodes like that.

"My Dad died of a heart attack in 1970. He was forty-two. I was eighteen. He didn't live to see the ultimate outcome of his influence on me. Since he bet not just on New York games, but on far-flung games as well, he was stuck sweating out the outcomes of contests he could not watch or listen to. That's where I came in. He would toss me the keys to his car and send me out to the driveway, where on the right night, amid the crackle and static, I might be able to pick up the Orioles on WBAL. The Tigers or Pistons on WJR. The Red Sox, Celtics, or Bruins on WBZ. The Pirates on KDKA. The Reds on WLW. Or, wonder of wonders, the Cardinals all the way from St. Louis on KMOX. Fifty-thousand-watt powerhouses all.

"My assignment, my first as a reporter, was to ascertain the score, the inning, the time remaining, and any other pertinent details, and then return to the house and relay the info, good or bad, to my dad. He was interested in how his 'investments' were going. He didn't realize he was also investing in his son's future.

"I was already enthralled with the broadcast styling of New York legends Mel Allen, Red Barber, and Marty Glickman. But now, here came Chuck Thompson from Baltimore, Bob Prince from Pittsburgh, and Ernie Harwell from Detroit. And the team of Harry Caray and Jack Buck from St. Louis. Each with a distinctive style. Each with a discernible presence. Their voices, like those of Allen, Barber, and Glickman, inseparable in my mind from the games themselves. Voices in the night. Part of the excitement and romance of sports, especially baseball. On those many nights when a kid, much too young to drive, sat behind the wheel of a car searching for those distant and soon enough familiar voices, an idea took hold. This is what I want to do. This is the world I want to be part of.

"Had my dad been more like the nice neighbors who worked nine to five and mowed the lawn on Saturday, I might never have been drawn to sports and broadcasting in quite the way I was. Had his 'Street Smart sensibility' not been such a big part of my childhood, my own world view and likely my career path would not have been the same."

Only a sportsman, like Bob, would fully appreciate that Street Smart is the very marrow of the backbone of every single sport.

STREET SMART MEMOIR OF GOVERNOR MIKE HUCKABEE
Salt of the Earth

Governor Mike Huckabee's take on Street Smart is fascinating: he believes that Street Smart directly proceeds from need, want, and the desire to do better with what you have. He'll explain this for you later.

First, you *gotta* know the governor. You then must know that his Street Smart wisdom descends from no less an authority than Jesus Christ, who praised the salt of the earth (the common man and common woman) in the Bible's New Testament itself, rooted in his Sermon on the Mount, about the same time as He formulated the Beatitudes and the Lord's Prayer. And you need not be a fellow Southerner, or a conservative, or a Christian to see that the governor's take on it comes with a high pedigree.

Some digression...for good reason. The governor is successful and knows Street Smart got him there. And he directly tells you why later.

> "Ye are the salt of the earth: but if the salt have lost his savour, wherewith shall it be salted? It is thenceforth good for nothing, but to be cast out, and to be trodden under foot of men. Ye are the light of the world." Matthew 5:13–14 (KJV)

Michael Dale Huckabee came from sturdy but humble stock: son of a firefighter and an employee of the Louisiana Transit Company. As such, like most of our other Street Scholars, he comes from the people, not the elite. He had a fascination for the media and public service. He has held true to the Baptist Church tenets throughout his life. These tenets include a remarkably Street Smart background of "soul competency," roughly meaning the responsibility and accountability of every person before God himself. The governor not only believes in serving his fellows but actually lives for service. And he combined all of these quite well.

He married his high school sweetheart, then attended Ouachita Baptist University, majoring in religion and minoring in speech, graduating early. Then he attended a Baptist seminary, mixing a short stint as a director of communications with a ministry. He set up a television station and thrived in a pastorship so far as to secure the presidency of the Arkansas Baptist Convention. Throughout, he was the cutting edge in religious-based broadcasting on a corporate level.

Using his Street Smart, Mike became governor of the sovereign state of Arkansas and immediately broke the mold by sponsoring a medical plan for children for Medicaid who were unable to secure private insurance. He passed tax-funding beneficent government programs for the environment and conservation, not hot Republican topics. He also taxed gasoline to rebuild Arkansas's rickety road systems and secured tobacco settlement funds for state health care. Again, outside thinking from a Republican and Conservative. Neither group was known for social activism.

Presciently, he sponsored Smart Start, a precursor in some ways of Street Smart, though for children of Arkansas. Smart Start bolstered math and reading skills for kids in kindergarten through fourth grade and was a success. Smart Step, another precursor of Street Smart, for fifth grade through high school, followed Smart Start. The governor has run for president of the United States (winning several primaries), chaired several Southern Governor conferences, and presently has his own hit television show, *Huckabee*, on TBN. He is a solid commentator on current affairs for Fox News and other outlets. But, to understand his Street Smart better, you *gotta* know the governor.

The governor came from a good but poor family. This is not a silver-spoon guy, and he'd be really at home in the "Olde Brooklyn." The governor, for all his ethnic, religious, and geographic differences, would have fit in nicely in the Brooklyn of our youth. He accepts people as Christ would, without labels and without regard to their poverty, wealth, or political bias.

However, the governor's take is literally priceless. He was poor, but it actually lit a fire under him.

"Growing up poor is not a disadvantage but a distinct *advantage*. As a kid, I had to figure out how to get things done with what I had, not what I wanted," the governor tells you. The theme of living without means, and certainly the theme of not having enough or having what some neighbors had, pops up with frequency among those driven to use their Street Smart to succeed.

We had to wait a week to get our father, a window trimmer, to buy us Good Humor ice cream from an ice cream tricycle. The governor must've waited for the same guy! He also had a rugged, almost universal recognition that the old-school tie, alumni connections, gurus, self-improvement experts, and a trust fund for him were not going to improve his lot. This is because he had no old-school tie, no alumni connections, no temporal guru (though he had Jesus), and no rich relatives. Forget the trust fund, too.

No, he says that his Street Smart propelled his lifetime. To use the flawed modern vernacular, the governor used his Street Smart to think "outside the box" of his circumstances, and he sure as hell did. From a poor boy in the Deep South to both a national leader and intellectual...must be a great trip.

"No one was there opening a wallet to provide me my desires. Not even all my needs! And *that* was a life-long blessing. One learns to determine where you want to go, and you'll figure out how to get there," the governor relates to us all. He was determined to use his Street Smart and acted accordingly, and it is a *helluva* ride.

That means no college trust fund, certificates of deposit, or the like for the Mike Huckabee you know of now.

"There is no school to teach resourcefulness. It comes from having to make do with what you have. Start by looking at the finish line and work backward to the starting point. Street Smart people don't need big budgets, because they have big imaginations."

Having a big imagination is directly correlated with Street Smart origins. And we have examples that he directly gave us of using his own Street Smart as governor.

The nemesis of the Gulf Coast, Hurricane Katrina, flooded no less than 80 percent of New Orleans, as well as overrunning most of the parishes outside the city back to the coast. It was a massive and vicious wake-up call for every branch of government. The governments were almost totally incompetent, and protests in defense of the governments were met with loud and sometimes vulgar responses.

Indeed, the Army Corps of Engineers, tasked with maintaining the levies around the city of New Orleans, had to report that fifty-three levies were crushed like cookie crust, and the waters behind flowed through. There were 1,800 dead and damage upwards of $125 *billion* in damages. But as we will see, Governor Huckabee, whose state was impacted only moderately by the hurricane, stepped up and used his Street Smart sense.

Relevant to using his own Street Smart, Governor Huckabee tells us of his use of Street Smart for the benefit of his neighbors in Louisiana. Mind you, he was governor of Arkansas at the time, but being a good Christian neighbor, he stepped up to the plate for tens of thousands of people who could not vote for him. How many politicians in this Red-State-versus-Blue-State world have opted for this use of scant state resources? Not many.

"When Hurricane Katrina resulted in the collapse of New Orleans, my state took in seventy-five thousand of the most needful evacuees. Most of those we received came from the Superdome and Convention Center and had nothing but the clothes on their back," stated Huckabee. Yes, you remember that there were suicides in the Superdome at that time and no water for days. He paints a graphic picture for us.

"No ID, none of their meds, personal documents, *nothing*. How to house, feed, clothe, protect, provide health care, education, and reassure that many people?"

Especially when they are coming from a neighboring state without much except the clothing on their backs.

But Huckabee was not daunted. Nor was he self-interested. He cast about his state of Arkansas and noticed something no one else ever did in times of emergency. He used his Street Smart to aid worthy neighboring people. And with no expectation of benefitting at the polls!

The governor took out a map and started reading. He noticed something his advisors didn't.

"I knew that all the church camps and scout camps had just closed their camping season but hadn't been winterized. They had beds, showers, dining halls, recreational facilities, security, and even a nurse's station. And they weren't all located in the same school district or in area of only one hospital. They were spread throughout our seventy-five counties."

The governor thought wisely, casting about in all this human misery, and found a solution, a "Street Smart solution" as he phrased it. The governor took to the telephone and email, and he started *doing* instead of lamenting. Lamenting is human but fills no bellies, clothes no kids, and shelters no homeless.

"I asked church and scout leaders for use of their camps and promised to cover any liabilities. Every community wanted to help, and this empowered them to do it by asking them to provide blankets, clothing, volunteers, and supplies," relates the governor. This was a "salt of the earth" response led by a "salt of the earth" leader using his Street Smart.

"We never treated people like 'boxes' or warehoused them in a large public facility without privacy or basic necessities. They were given good food, comfortable settings in a secure location, and most importantly, they were given dignity. There is no school to teach resourcefulness."

His Street Smart reaction equaled survival to tens of thousands of people who were never the governor's responsibility. Like a good neighbor, Huckabee made himself available without fanfare. Just a solid street sense grounded in his core Christian values.

The governor actually codifies his Street Smart in his books, taking much wisdom from our Street Smart Founding Fathers: Washington, Franklin, Hamilton, Jefferson, all of whom used Street Smart in colonial times to not merely win a war against a powerful enemy, but to cement a solid foundation to our country.

In his writings, Huckabee makes a case for "All-American Street Smart." Quoting no less than an authority than George Washington, the governor opines that "God himself" provided the wisdom to the Street Smart founding fathers who wrote a brilliant start for a young, fragile republic. But he updates this by citing recent business examples of Street Smart: first, the governor traced the start of the FedEx Corporation from its founder's term paper at Yale University, wherein the founder outlined the need for speed in some deliveries not capable of fulfillment by the United States Postal Service. This was back in 1972, when the founder barely had enough money to pay off his student loans. FedEx now is worth billions, the company's owner also owns a fleet of airplanes that rivals the biggest airlines, and FedEx is well entrenched as a Street Smart corporation. It is routinely praised for its management and marketing expertise.

The governor segues into the Nike corporation, another $1,200 shoestring operation grown into a giant by using and living up to its motto, "Just Do It." Nike started by building and selling a better sneaker when almost all sneakers were canvas knockoffs of the Keds line of sports footwear, and a humble enough start at that. Nike now has a net worth of billions of dollars and was started with the capital which could be traded for a bad used car.

The governor then caps it off by citing a fellow Arkansas businessman's literal five-and-dime store ascent into a $400 billion corporate empire. The father of Walmart was a working-class icon, and Walmart not only survived where other brick-and-mortar stores failed during these COVID waves but thrived, adding workers while the unemployment rate was several times what happened before the plagues. The governor credits Street Smart corporations for their wisdom in bad times.[4]

Governor Huckabee himself got his Street Smart from God, which is a great source, after all. Good enough for God.

---

[4] Mike Huckabee and Steve Feazel, *The Three Cs That Made America Great: Christianity, Capitalism and the Constitution* (California: Trilogy Christian Publishing, 2020).

STREET SMART MEMOIR OF VLADIMIR POZNER
The Russian Street Smart Street Kid with a Brooklyn Accent

You'll remember Vladimir Vladimirovich Pozner as the *unofficial* spokesman of the Soviet Union as it lurched toward normalization during the late 1980s. Pozner was the voice of calm and reconciliation. In this way, he is a remarkable international asset: his appearances on national American television soothed both Russian and American viewers when there were dangerous and sometimes violent confrontations between the Old Guard of Soviets and voices of democracy as the old system collapsed... essentially peacefully. Pozner was valuable internationally because he spoke to a world audience which needed reassurance.

No one person understands both Russia and the United States as Pozner does. That being said, Pozner's contribution to Street Smart is priceless, as he himself says in the following pages. Like us, he grew up in the Old New York of mixed religious and ethnic groups who lived together remarkably well. His Street Smart started by pounding the gritty city streets in search of *gelt*, and he found it. But some prologue first to see how this remarkable and brilliant man developed into a Street Smart protagonist.

"When asked to write a couple of paragraphs for this book, I agreed with no second thoughts. *Piece of cake*, I thought to myself, *I'll dash off a couple of brilliant sentences and be done with it*. Big mistake. The more I thought about Street Smart, the less sure I became," acknowledged Pozner.

"Anyway, after about a week of mulling the issue over, I came to the conclusion that Street Smart is something you cannot learn. It's like perfect pitch. Either you have it or you don't. If you do, you can hone it, perfect it, but if the good Lord did not endow you with it, well, that's just too bad."

That might be, but we stuck his feet to the fire and pried a little further. What made him state this fact of some people having perfect Street Smart pitch and others lacking it? Vladimir reached back to Roman times...classical Roman times of Caesar, Jesus, and the gladiators.

"The ancient Romans coined the words *carpe diem*, 'seize the day.' What they meant is that every day we are offered opportunities, and as I understand it, Street Smart is the ability to seize those opportunities, take advantage of what Street Smart-less people do not see or react to," he states. Segregating Street Smart-less people from Street Smart people is, in fact, consigning some fraction of the human race to failure.

An inherent Street Smart talent born onto you like perfect pitch might be accurate, but the premise of this book—and all the Street Smart Memoirs we include—seems to indicate that you most certainly have it.

In support of this Street Smart conclusion, Vladimir, without our prompting whatsoever, related a genuinely mirror image of our discovery of the Street Smart talent born on the same New York City streets as where we grew up.

In our introduction, we wrote how the confluence of the Jewish Sabbath laws of not doing any work whatsoever on the Jewish Sabbath, meaning not opening mail, turning on appliances, taking out trash, and so on, provided a Street Smart opportunity for we two brothers, still in grade school.

We could take out trash, open mail, turn on appliances, and the like because as *goyim*, meaning non-Jewish boys, we could provide the services (probably at the cost of damnation, but that is okay too) for a *per piece* or per apartment. That helped us out and helped out the religious Jewish families.

Well, here's Vladimir's take, and it will confirm the genesis of understanding Street Smart. It really will.

Some explanation is necessary. In the "Old Days," and in some areas of the United States now, daily newspapers were hand delivered by newsboys, meaning grade school and high school kids. These were almost always the first jobs they had, because "working papers" (issued by schools and local governments) allowed minors to work in this trade while prohibiting more strenuous work.

"When I was a kid growing up in New York's Greenwich Village, my dad paid me a weekly allowance of twenty-five cents for doing chores around the house (that would be $3.75 today— not bad pocket money for a nine-year-old). But I wanted more.

"When I asked for a raise, dad told me to go find a job." Pop Pozner was no doubt a little irritated with the demand from the proletariat. So, Vladimir cast about for a job, at first not successfully.

Vladimir remembers those "mom and pop" stores very well. "Well, right around the corner, there was a little store that sold candy and pop and such, and also papers. When I asked the owner, a man named Sam, if he had a job for me, he said yes, he needed a boy to deliver the paper Monday through Friday. Did I want the job? You bet your life I did!

"'Come around tomorrow at five in the morning and I'll show you your route,' said Sam."

Cold terror here as Vladimir realized what Street Smart entailed. It meant walking mean city streets in Greenwich Village (not then the Yuppified area it is now, with sushi bars, curb-to-curb BMWs, and wealthy residents) and depositing a newspaper at every subscriber's doorstep on the route.

"Whew, five in the morning! What's more, Sam said he would not pay me, but on holidays I was to ring his clients' doorbells and say: 'Happy holiday! I'm your paper delivery boy.'"

Wow, imagine working for nothing after delivering heavy papers in snow, rain, drizzle, and fog! As we said in Brooklyn, "What is the deal, anyway?"

"Sam said: 'They will give you a tip, how big is none of my business.' So, I began delivering papers. Now this was in September, so there were no holidays to speak of until Christmas." But not to worry...like Jewish Sabbaths, Christian holidays do arrive eventually. Like Jesus's delayed birthday party on Christmas.

"Well, on the morning of Christmas Eve, I began ringing doorbells, and by the time I had finished, I had received exactly one hundred dollars in tips—$1,500 in today's money," luxuriated Vladimir. That would be a lot of money today even with the pampered kids of wealthy people. Really. That would be a lot of comic books, chewing gum, Good Humor ice creams, and movie admissions.

"So where does Street Smart come in? I went and bought a beautiful bike with a large basket, and from that day on, instead of *shlepping* those papers, I delivered them on my bike. Man, did that make a difference!"

Oh, *shlepping* is Yiddish for hard work on the streets.

"In short, I seized the opportunity," concludes Vladimir. And a good place for us to conclude the Pozner Street Smart Memoir. Pozner was Street Smart enough to seemingly work for nothing and get paid handsomely for it.

STREET SMART MEMOIR OF KEN AULETTA
Street Smarted on the Coney Island Boardwalk

Ken is one of those authentic Street Smart entrepreneurs, a genuine article and open to all sides of any debate with reasoning born of his working-class origins. Working-class people, customarily and in our experience, have an insight that denied many readers who came from the homogenized, politically corrected, pillow-comfortable world of the upper middle class. They just do. And if that aggravates you, you will be further perturbed by his narrative on Street Smart.

Ken Auletta has written Annals of Communications columns and profiles for *The New Yorker* magazine since 1992. He is the author of twelve books, including five national bestsellers: *Three Blind Mice: How the TV Networks Lost Their Way*; *Greed and Glory on Wall Street: The Fall of the House of Lehman*; *The Highwaymen: Warriors of the Information Superhighway*; *World War 3.0: Microsoft and Its Enemies*; and *Googled: The End of the World as We Know It*.

Auletta has profiled the leading figures and companies of the "Information Age," including Google, Bill Gates, Rupert Murdoch, AOL Time Warner, John Malone, Harvey Weinstein, the *New York Times*, Sheryl Sandberg, and Facebook.

His 2001 profile of Ted Turner won a National Magazine Award as the best profile of the year. He covered the Microsoft antitrust trial for the magazine. In ranking him as America's premier media critic, the *Columbia Journalism Review* concluded, "no other reporter has covered the new communications revolution as thoroughly as has Auletta." *New York Magazine* described him as the "media Boswell."

In another life, Auletta taught and trained Peace Corps volunteers; served as special assistant to the US undersecretary of commerce; worked in Senator Robert F. Kennedy's 1968 presidential campaign; was executive editor of the weekly *Manhattan Tribune*; was state campaign manager for Howard J. Samuels, helping him through two unsuccessful races for governor of New York; and was the first executive director of the New York City Off Track Betting Corporation.

For four decades, Auletta has been a national judge of the Livingston Awards for journalists under thirty-five. He has been a trustee and member of the executive committee of the Public Theatre/New York Shakespeare Festival. He was a member of the

Columbia Journalism School Task Force assembled by incoming college president Lee Bollinger to help reshape the curriculum. He has served as a Pulitzer Prize juror and a trustee of the Nightingale-Bamford School. He was twice a trustee of PEN, the international writers' organization. He is a member of the New York Public Library's Emergency Committee for the Research Libraries, of the Author's Guild, PEN, the Council on Foreign Relations, and of the Committee to Protect Journalists.

Auletta grew up on Coney Island in Brooklyn. He graduated with a BS from the State University College at Oswego, NY and received an MA in political science from the Maxwell School of Citizenship and Public Affairs at Syracuse University. The State University of New York awarded him a Doctor of Letters in 1990, and in 1998, he gave an address at the inauguration of Deborah F. Stanley as President of Oswego State University.

***

Ken is a product of a mixed-religious background. His observations about power, dignity, and yet a keen sense of class explain also how a discerning young man turns out to be a compelling observer of modern American life, which shows up in his writing. And, like us, Street Smart began on the tough streets of Brooklyn, where Ken derived much of his success.

"What do I owe to the streets of Coney Island, where I grew up?

"On those streets I learned not to stereotype and make sweeping generalizations. Priests in the Catholic Church down the street sometimes preached, 'the Jews killed Christ.' But Jews and Italians lived side by side in harmony on West 17th Street. My mother was Jewish and two of her sisters married Italian men, and my father's brother Mike married Aunt Sally, who was Jewish," writes Ken.

We ourselves must mention that this was old melting-pot Brooklyn, of course. A Brooklyn of ethnicities, races, and religions...which happened to have worked brilliantly. Now Brooklyn and New York itself are a mixture of ethnic, racial, and immigrant lumps, which deters the melting pot theory. The country is blue and red, pro-life and pro-abortion, masked versus unmasked, unvaccinated versus vaccinated. In unity there is strength, and Ken's family is all successful and yet all strongly rooted in the no-nonsense love of education and family.

"The Street Smart thing I learned, and that stayed with me as a journalist and author, was that, as Christopher Morley once wrote, 'truth is a liquid, not a solid.' As an adult, never did I ever call a cop 'a pig,' nor someone I disagreed with 'a fascist' or 'a racist.'"

Ken's embrace of a vibrant Street Smart truth, that no one is a label, is hardly in vogue, but its truth is so evident in his writing.

Ken even ran into the Mafia, as we did. We grew up knowing—by how people just showed certain deference to some locals in Brooklyn—who was in the Mafia and who was not. They were avoided but *not* as evil people. In fact, with recent American and world history, we state that while not *admiring* Mafiosi...we knew them. They weren't any more evil than many politicians, judges, businessmen, clergy, with many of these other people being as corrupt and dangerous as the worst gangster. You just didn't deal with them, as they expected a *quid pro quo*—they always expected a *quid pro quo*. Ken was harsher here. We felt that these men were illegal businessmen. They handled their problems outside the courts, which anyone who has dealt with courts (and who is honest or not rich) realizes that courts are for the wealthy and the well-connected.

But Ken speaks here.

"On the streets, I learned to avoid the Mafia goons who were sometimes lionized in my Italian American community. My dad, having worked on the docks as a young man, hated mobsters and threatened to apply his shaving strap to my ass if I went near them, as some of my friends did. The Street Smart thing to do, he warned, was to stay away. Might I have had a different career had I not stayed away?"

Street Smart was to avoid them, obviously. But Ken does have a positive suggestion from hard-won personal history. The suggestion is education, which he attained, and his writing on the most complicated subject is illuminative of education and the topic he has covered. But this Street Smart lesson was at first poorly learned. His Street Smart sense, however, was redeemed by a Street Smart city school principal.

"Many of my friends on the street thought that if you read books you were a sissy. I was suspended from Abraham Lincoln High School in my junior year for swiping a book of passes in order to escape the building and hang out at the sweet shop across the street," confides Ken to us. Sweet shops were the Coney Island equivalent of the "mom and pop" stores. But trouble ahead for young Mr. Auletta. Trouble relieved by a mentor.

"The principal, Abe Lass, allowed me to return—only if I agreed to spend my free periods in his outer office reading Dickens and the books he commandeered from the library," states Ken. Lass saw in Ken a thoughtfulness and inherent scholarship, though that scholarship was slow in developing, as we will read here.

"The Street Smart thing I learned was that knowledge was priceless, and that an outside mentor—Abe Lass, my first mentor—was invaluable."

A doting mother and father raised Ken, but his rare rebellions were framed by their own Street Smart.

"While I sometimes rebelled at my parents, only after I was in college did I truly learn the importance of a loving home and parents who pushed and prodded—and hugged—their kids." (An advantage he had growing up as an Auletta.)

Ken made the connection between Street Smart and education at home, a loving education, though this connection was admittedly laggard. But he made the connections.

"Many years later, when I wrote a three-part series for the *New Yorker*, and a book, *The Underclass*, did I appreciate how disadvantaged were kids raised in poverty without a father in the home and with mothers overwhelmed by poverty."

He had no such disadvantage, though he lived on the same exact streets in Brooklyn as the black and Hispanic kids who now predominate there. But education proved the decisive influence, though he went to no elite schools or universities.

"Because I had a 64 percent (high school) average when I graduated, I learned that had I gone to an esteemed, super competitive college, I probably would have flunked."

Ken expected no Ivy League berth and got none either. Instead, he picked the low-tuition (almost no-tuition) State University of New York system perched up in the boonies!

"Because I went to the State University at Oswego (with the help of a letter of recommendation from Abe Lass, and the encouragement of the baseball coach who liked my fastball), I was allowed time to grow." Ken had to dump Coney Island, though not Coney Island Street Smart, quickly among the farmers.

"As a new reader who no longer rolled his T-shirt sleeves up to display muscles, I was burdened by a modicum of street insecurity," admits Ken. This was a different street to be smart in. Not only did Oswego not look anything like honky-tonk Coney Island, but the ethnicities were different. He had to think differently.

"I learned humility, which allows you to ask questions because you don't assume you know the answers, an essential quality for a journalist. I also became a better listener, another vital virtue for a journalist."

And perhaps the greatest skill in spotting, seizing, and exploiting Street Smart is shutting up enough to hear or see the Street Smart opportunity, which might only whisper its presence. It is our experience, from reading all the Street Smart Memoirs you have the good sense and great fortune to read here, that Street Smart talks softly. And Street Smart won't necessarily raise its voice.

"The streets of Coney Island imbued me with an attitude. I better understood the frustrations of the working class, the resentment about the signs along Brooklyn's Belt Parkway that read, 'To New York City,' as if Brooklyn was not part of the city. I learned to recoil at what we construed as elitism, the same elitism that years later saw Manhattan hotspots reject what they called 'Bridge and tunnel people.' This made me a better journalist," states Ken. Again, there are no labels. No snobbery. Street Smart coils in Brooklyn at Coney Island and tangles up in the elite canyons of Manhattan. But this working-class street sense carries over anyway in his political writing. If you're a snob, which is improbable because you are reading this book anyway, you run and hide behind the labels. Not Ken. He has strong opinions, but they are framed entirely by Street Smart.

"As a political reporter, I believed Donald Trump was a narcissist who too often lied and incited racism, but never for a minute would I join elitists who disparaged all the 75 million people who voted for him in 2020 as 'deplorables' and dumb 'racists' and 'rednecks,'" writes Ken to you. He knew, as you do, that people come to political opinion through a kind of Street Smart.

"Those who felt like outcasts on the streets of Coney Island were not so different from those on the streets of Iowa City." Maybe his Street Smart instincts are here as well?

No labels. No judgment. And maybe a little sympathy?

But Ken continues, as he must, in his exploration of Street Smart.

"Looking back on Coney Island and its streets, I became a self-confident man, (bearing) the armored vest of a writer who dares expose his words and ideas to an audience," concludes Ken of his Street Smart life. Read his many, many books and see the product of Coney Island Street Smart. He's a class act from start to finish. And if there is a better intellectual observer of today than Ken, we don't know of him.

STREET SMART MEMOIR OF RICHARD JOHNSON
Chronicler of Street Smart

The Street Smart Memoir of newsman Richard Johnson is especially newsworthy: Johnson is a happy throwback to times when New York journalists were the very best in the world: gritty, fearless, iconoclastic. Granted, his Page Six features were "gossipy," but never was Johnson a mere gossip columnist. No, he has always been a chronicler of what was happening in the elite circles of New York. And he did this for twenty-five years and set the standard to which all aspiring writers would want to be compared. In effect, he confirms our Street Smart assertions so well. What is important for our purposes, is that Richard Johnson knows the elite...make that "elite Street Smart." As they went up, as they went down, and some as they crashed and burned. Street Smart is fickle.

The *New York Times* went so far as to hail Richard Johnson, whose Page Six column was printed in the highly competitive but very conservative fellow *New York Post*, as "a journalistic descendant of Walter Winchell."

Mr. Winchell is a patron saint of lamented American print journalism. To be compared to Walter is fulsome praise for anyone.

The *Times* went so far to state that Richard "made whispers roar with a patrician manner and acerbic pen."

New York Magazine ranked Richard Johnson as the "Number One gossip columnist" in the capital of Street Smart: New York. His style is acerbic, putting that mildly, but no one has ever impugned him of inaccuracy or mere slander or pernicious libel. You'll find out why: he uses his New York-born Street Smart facility much as a bar room brawler uses a broken bottle or a knuckle buster knife. His columns could be hellish on the snobby elites! He could be the demon of the affected! He's the devil of the pompous! He's the red-hot scourge of the pompous ass! And for the affected, he's the printer's devil from Hell.

But where in hell did Richard Johnson come from? He came from Street Smart New York City streets, of course, like so many of our Street Scholars.

Richard's father was a magazine publisher. His mother was a public relations worker. So, the newsprint is in his veins as much as vibrant New York blood. He graduated from The Trinity School. He secured a communications degree, new-style wording for a degree from a "J School" (journalism school) from a stint at both the University of Colorado at Boulder and later Empire State College. Rather than a long internship at some out-of-town little town newspaper—the usual ladder back to the big-time New York media market—Richard instead came back home immediately. He then ascended to the *New York Post* as a general assignment reporter and eventually took charge as editor/reporter of the *Post's* Page Six feature.

Those in the field admired him and more likely envied his talent to find "scoops" of news culled from the fetid acres of bullshit fertilizing the city's media. Johnson never accepted the press handout, let alone believed their veracity. Today's journalists live and work on press releases and accept them without review. He was described by one fellow columnist as "fearless" and a "real reporter." Almost every other reporter in the city envied his ability to find out what the hell was really going on. He accepted no handouts and never bit the hand that fed him an inside scoop. But he did bite a lot of other hands and some well-upholstered asses.

Here's broken-bottle advice for the Street Smart set. Don't leave your brass knuckle busters at home, either. For an intellectual, Richard has a Street Smart grounded in survival among the elite, and sometimes even physical survival skills culled from his Street Smart instincts, as we were grounded as well. This is a colorful guy, like the old-time newspaper reporters depicted in *The Front Page* with press cards installed in their fedoras, their shirtsleeves rolled up to the shoulders, needing both a dry cleaning and maybe a fresh shower. And there are fistfights as well! Really.

First, unlike those stuffed shirts propped up by the national media, picked only for their star quality and teleprompter skills, Richard lived on the streets, thrived on the streets, and writes from the streets. Check that out. And here's why....

"I grew up in the city and I've never been mugged. I guess you can credit some Street Smarts—and fast feet," starts Richard. Getting mugged means the same as also getting sued for libel, pimped for slander, beaten up severely by an irate star, or over-turned on a hot tip by another media.

"When I walk down the street, I am aware of what's around me. So, when a mugger came up behind me late one night off Avenue B, I turned around just in time to keep him from putting a knife to my throat," says Richard, indicating that he used the Street Smart shuffle to survive. But this started in high school.

"Once when I was in high school at Trinity, having played in a basketball game, three toughs came at me, one with a club. I ran to a bodega, bought a soda in a glass bottle (as a weapon), and came out. After some conversation, I was allowed to go home," said Richard. The broken bottle of Street Smart guys again.

Richard waxes poetic here and further.

"Men are very quick at assessing whether or not they could beat up a rival, even if they are wrong. A look at the traffic in hospital emergency rooms will show that men get crazy on week-end nights, especially if it's hot. The fists, and even bullets, start flying. In many cases, a pretty woman was the prize."

Grabbing the most desirous woman is partly Street Smart, though dying for one, or being charged with a felony while get-ting the girl, would not be Street Smart.

But Richard is helpful here as well.

"The guys who have Street Smarts are probably unaware most of the time they are using them. They just win arguments, make deals, and seduce women as a natural right," says Richard. A natural right of Street Smart is a theme we have read before from the other Street Scholars. Natural rights are rights bestowed by God (or nature, if you are an atheist) and might well be as con-crete as the right to self-survival. So, we asked Richard directly for further wisdom.

"Richard, have you ever used Street Smart to be successful, especially at critical personal moments?" we asked. Richard said yes.

"I had the misfortune once of meeting Steven Seagal, and I think I made it clear to him that I was unimpressed with his karate moves," relates Richard. Seagal is one tough customer, and we suspect he had Street Smart. Seagal hails from Staten Island, a division of New York City separated by the Verrazano Narrows from Brooklyn. Richard hints that the encounter was less than pleasant but provided no other information. But Richard goes further. He picked on another tough guy from the movies, also from New York but upstate: Mickey Rourke.

"Another time, Mickey Rourke cursed me out after a photo ran in my column of him with a woman who was not his wife. I replied, 'Anytime. Anywhere.'" No broken beer bottle here, though. Too bad!

"And once, a *Village Voice* columnist attacked me for being 'unreliable.' When he refused to run a retraction, I went to his office and punched him in the face. My editors loved it," says Richard. Obviously, this was the last word in the conversation.

We asked him how he spotted opportunities to use Street Smart.

"Most people who are Street Smart are not starting fights and getting into fisticuffs. They use persuasion and charm to get what they want. But the undercurrent is there."

A lot of Street Smart is about undercurrent. It's also about not getting swept out to sea by the riptide. Oh, it is about surfing, after all, life's bigger waves. Both require Street Smart. If the water is too comfortable, maybe it is a Street Smart moment after all. Richard never seems to have been uncomfortable. Today, Richard works as a syndicated columnist for the *New York Daily News.*

STREET SMART MEMOIR OF CHARLIE ROSE
Street Smart in Dixie and at the Roundtable

Charlie Rose is the award-winning journalist who became Street Smart not in Brooklyn but from observing people in his parents' "cracker barrel" country store in rural Henderson, North Carolina. In a way, this frequency and volume of people passing through and around the store was a great education in Street Smart for Charlie. "Talk was the coin of the realm," Charlie says.

Charlie learned to listen first, a great Brooklyn attribute, and ask questions later. You learn more by listening than talking, a talent which is now almost extinct.

That being said, Charlie Rose has interviewed the most successful in business, politics, and the arts. To recount his biography would take five pages. So we let him talk directly to you instead. That saves time.

"In 1942, my father left Henderson, a small North Carolina town, to join the war against Germany. He landed at Normandy one week after D-Day and fought across France, Belgium, and Germany in the Battle of the Bulge. He left me, only two years old, with my mother, who moved twenty miles away to her father's home and store. My grandfather owned the country store in Warren Plains, a little village of one hundred where the family lived on the second floor. I lived in the same room with my grandmother, separated by a curtain. She was the Grand Dame of the community of one hundred, playing the piano at the church on Sunday and helping everybody with everything regardless of their problem.

"Living above the store had many advantages. One, [we] had instant access to ice cream and everything else. Second, the store was the center of the community. At some point almost everybody would stop by, to buy something and to talk about everything. Talk was the coin of the realm. A lot of it was about sports, weather, farming, and gossip—who did what to whom. In 1946, my father returned from the war, but we stayed in Warren Plains and he commuted to Henderson, eventually buying the country store from his father-in-law. When I was twelve, in 1954, we moved back to Henderson.

"The years between 1944 and 1952 had everything to do with how I spent the rest of my life. In my family, everybody worked in the store, including me. And if I had any standing, beyond taking something off the shelf and putting it in a bag, it was questions. If you asked interesting questions, people listened to you, paid attention, allowed you in the group. Since I followed sports more than most, I gained access. And because I was more curious than most about everything, my repertoire expanded.

The more I did it, the better the questions. The better the questions, the more I belonged.

"I also learned something else; people like to talk about themselves. And this too: the more you listen, not just listen but really hear what someone is saying, the more enriching the experience for everyone. I have had a lot of education in my life, from a great university to graduate school and law school. I suspect if I could weigh it all, what I learned in that country store about the art of conversation would weigh as much as any course I attended at any stage of my lifelong pursuit of learning. I have a long way to go, but I got a good start from the street. Or the store!"

Charlie's interview guests include: Zubin Mehta, Kenneth Branagh, Adam Sandler, Tom Petty, Steve Barron, Jeff Bezos, Hillary Clinton, President Bill Clinton, President Barack Obama, Jon Bon Jovi, Henry Kissinger, Ruth Bader Ginsburg, Judi Dench, Oliver Stone, Ken Burns, Sally Field, Arnold Palmer, Warren Buffett, Tiger Woods, David Bowie, Diane von Fürstenberg, Richard Gere, and unofficially at his table, Joe DiMaggio.

The store was Charlie's education! Can we liken it to the streets of Brooklyn? You bet. Whether derived from the lobby of a cracker barrel store in Dixie or a Brooklyn bodega, Street Smart is critical, and this Street Scholar says so plainly.

Charlie has started a new venture where he will bring his interviewing brilliance to the public once again via charlierose.com.

STREET SMART MEMOIR OF JUDGE JUDY SHEINDLIN
Here Comes the Judge

Street Smart means knowing when to assess possibilities, probabilities, and alternatives. Judge Judy Sheindlin, perhaps the most famous jurist in the country today, became Street Smart directly from navigating congested Brooklyn streets.

Brooklyn streets then, as now, were very hazardous, and everyone equated being Street Smart with surviving and also equated being oblivious with certain injury and maybe even death. As young boys, we played stickball and punchball alongside 65th Street in Brooklyn, and each of us saw at least three pedestrian knockdowns. When a ball was punched, or hit, it would go another twenty feet into the way of a car or tractor-trailer, neither of which was known to watch movement on the curbs. Sometimes, they did not notice what was happening in the roadway either. And there was no notion of speed limits. Really. In this way, you'd either suddenly become Street Smart, or you died.

Judge Judy took these serious lessons to heart. She was the rare woman in her classes in law school. She tried corporate law but found it unsatisfying. She was appointed by Street Smart mayor Ed Koch to a Family Court judgeship, where she earned a reputation as a sharp, no-nonsense jurist and later as a sharp, no-nonsense supervising judge of that court. She presided over a record number of cases (twenty thousand). The CBS news show *60 Minutes* spotted her as a remarkable judge who had a withering view of pompous lawyers and deceitful clients. Her television show, *Judge Judy*, based on deciding active cases, began attracting no fewer than ten million viewers, edging out Oprah Winfrey and becoming the top syndicated television program of its era. She states that a lot of this success is based on crossing streets in Brooklyn.

"I was born and grew up in Brooklyn, NY. We lived on Ocean Avenue that was two lanes of traffic in each direction and a lane for parked cars. We lived in the middle of the block. My best friend growing up was Elaine. She lived on the other side of the street. By the age of ten, I had mastered crossing in the middle of the block by timing the lights at the corners, assessing the probabilities of cars making right and left turns, checking the driveways of twenty houses for movement and the occasional bicyclist.

"Decades later, I still use those skills of assessing probabilities, possibilities, timing, and sometimes a smattering of raw guts. It's become instinctive, almost like breathing. Life is always present-ing challenges, choices, opportunities, and alternatives. Crossing in the middle of the block is my first memory of Brooklyn Street Smarts in action. It's against the law now, so of course I don't do it anymore.

"And yes, Elaine and I are still friends!"

They both survived crossing those mean streets of Brooklyn!

STREET SMART MEMOIR OF ANTHONY DECURTIS
Learning the Meaning of the Streets and Not Getting Rock 'n Rolled

Anthony DeCurtis is far away the most powerful and influential media critic of the age. But it was born of his Street Smart, which he freely admits. In fact, he had the genesis of Street Smart when a cabdriver told him that he was "prime rolling material." That confuses you only now because he will soon explain that Street Smart compels survival first and success later. In this era of COVID spikes, business failures, chronic unemployment, crime waves, and institutionalized violence, survival might just be enough.

Per his official website, Mr. DeCurtis is the author of recently published *In Other Words: Artists Talk about Life and Work*, as well as *Rocking My Life Away: Writing about Music and Other Matters*. He is also the editor of *Present Tense: Rock & Roll and Culture* and coeditor of *The Rolling Stone Illustrated History of Rock & Roll* and *The Rolling Stone Album Guide* (third edition). He is a contributing editor at *Rolling Stone*, where his work has appeared for twenty-five years, and he occasionally writes for the *New York Times* and many other publications. His essay accompanying the Eric Clapton box set *Crossroads* won a Grammy Award in the "Best Album Notes" category. Anthony is also the author of the definitive biography of Lou Reed, titled *Lou Reed: A Life*. He holds a PhD in American literature from Indiana University.

"When I think about Street Smarts, I inevitably think about class. If you grow up in a working-class environment, you have no choice but to develop Street Smarts. The alternative is taking a beating, or worse. A middle- or upper-class upbringing insulates you from the terrors of the street—or so you're taught to think. Someone is always there to pay the bill or to call the authorities, who are there to protect you in the first place, on your behalf. Such an upbringing insulates you from the streets, but it also insulates you from the 'smarts.'

"The sense of personal safety a privileged upbringing engenders is inherently false. It makes it too easy for you to make harmful, even fatal choices. You go running in the park late at night because, after all, New York is so safe, what could happen? You mistake the difficulties you handle so cleanly at work for genuine threats and take the power you can display in such situations as the ability to protect yourself in truly dangerous situations. You walk down the wrong block at the wrong time without even realizing it before it's too late.

"One of the best pieces of advice I ever got regarding Street Smarts was from a cab driver who took me home late one weekday night. I'd been to an event and was dressed up. Definitely looked like I might have a dollar or two in my pocket. I was also drunk as a lord. As we approached my apartment building, the driver said to me, 'You know, man, you are prime rolling material.' After I paid him and got out of his car, he watched to make sure I got into my building safely.

"I've been characterized many ways in my life, but that was the only time I was called 'prime rolling material,' and I've never forgotten it. First, I loved his phrasing. Tough, but with a touch of elegance, as working-class language so often is. More important, though, I feel that in some way he was trying to help me.

"What he was saying was: 'You're not taking care of yourself. You're putting yourself in danger. You're too easy a mark.' These days, we'd say he was blaming the potential victim. Why should I have to worry about what messages my clothes or my drunkenness were giving off? Why don't we concentrate on the perpetrator of the crime? But the driver didn't care about such an abstract principle. He was thinking with Street Smarts. Rather than worrying about blaming the victim, he was trying to help me not be a victim in the first place.

"A woman I know once complained to me about having to share her whereabouts with a friend every time she went on a date with a man she didn't know well. I commended her for doing that and explained that, having grown up in New York, I never walk down a street without mentally assessing it for threats. That process is pretty much unconscious at this point and may only take seconds. But I never take the safety of my environment for granted. We all have to protect ourselves, whether we're on a date or negotiating the mean streets.

"As for how Street Smarts have helped me professionally, they've made me alert and they've given me a sense of proportion. I suppose some people believe that office politics are the most dangerous situations they're ever going to face. The fact that I know that's not true, that real dangers lurk in the world, gave me a perspective on office politics I might never have had otherwise. I've been able to assess work entanglements coolly, never assuming that things are exactly as they appear. It never surprised me that others may not have my best interests at heart. It quickly became clear to me that others needed to earn my trust. My interests were mine to advance and protect.

"I realize this may sound paranoid, but that's not really how I think or how I operate. I love working collaboratively and, when I can, I try to create situations where everybody wins. I like it best that way. I'm not greedy and I like to share. If you were working with me, you would never get the sense that I was evaluating how our situation was proceeding, just as, if we were walking down the street, you wouldn't sense my checking out each block to make sure that we were safe. But in each instance, that's exactly what I would be doing."

How we derive Street Smart differs from person to person. Working cooperatively and professionally and liking a shared common benefit seems to work for Anthony. This is a constant theme for our Street Scholars and is absent from no biography in these three hundred or so pages.

STREET SMART MEMOIR OF ANTHONY SCARAMUCCI
The Memoir of a Long Island Macchiavelli

This self-acknowledged former "Long Island Guido" used his Street Smart to rise to the heights of capital management, by way of Harvard Law School and banking giant Goldman Sachs, and remained as clever an observer of Street Smart as we have met. Anthony is brilliant, but that's not enough. Anthony is clever, but that's also insufficient. Anthony is personable, and that helps, but not much. He openly and in writing credits Street Smart for the difference between his former self—clad in polyester cheap suit—and his present inarguable success.

"I grew up as the son of an hourly worker. After growing up in the Scranton/Wilkes-Barre area of Pennsylvania in a family of coal miners, my uncle and dad responded to a classified ad to take a job as a sand miner in the Long Island town of Port Washington, NY. It certainly wasn't glamorous work, but at least it was outdoors and healthier than coal mining. Today, he struggles to hear because of the damage done to his ears from operating heavy equipment. With a blue-collar upbringing, I learned the value of hard work, but also the importance of Street Smarts.

"My brother and I were the first generation of our family to go to college. We didn't grow up with any connections or understanding of what it took to get ahead. My first lucky break came thanks to my father. I was an average student in high school. All of my teachers recognized my intelligence and photographic memory, but I was more interested in driving around wearing gold chains, blasting music in the Camaro Berlinetta I bought with money saved from selling *Newsday* papers in my town. I was your typical Long Island Guido Italian!

"My dad believed in me and thought if he could help me get into a good university, then the light bulb would go on. He was right. Through his supervisor at the mine, Billy Tomasso, my dad helped me get into Tufts University outside of Boston. My mom thought it was spelled T-O-U-G-H-S, so she couldn't find it in the *US News & World Report* book. Tufts is a top-thirty national university, and my teachers and mentors there, led by the great Sol Gittleman, fostered my ambition and love of learning.

"Having performed well at Tufts, I had the opportunity to choose my next step. I still considered higher education the path to more money and a better life, so I applied and was accepted to Harvard Law School. My dear sheltered mother again thought I had been accepted to a law school in Hartford, CT. She was confused why a law school outside of Boston would be called Hartford Law School. But she was proud of me nonetheless, even if she didn't realize the prestige of Harvard. I certainly had an imposter complex at Harvard that I carried with me through the first decade of my career on Wall Street, where I felt out of place and as if I didn't belong.

"The most important thing I learned at Harvard Law School is that I didn't want to practice law. So, I set out to get what I thought was the coolest, most lucrative job in New York: investment banking at Goldman Sachs. At this stage of my life, I had gained knowledge and education, but I hadn't yet honed and applied the Street Smarts I had acquired in the neighborhood, hallways, and playgrounds of Port Washington. I got the job, despite showing up to my first interview fully flammable in a polyester suit and a pair of roach killers. The recruiter recommended I go buy myself a couple of wool suits, so I did, and off I went to Wall Street.

"Investment banking was a terrible fit for my personality. I am a people person. Sitting behind a desk cranking out financial models all day was a poor use of my skillset, and my performance reflected that. I vividly remember the day my boss, Michael Fascitelli, invited me over to his apartment to fire me. I knew it was coming. Instead of getting angry and blowing up at Mike, I thanked him for the opportunities and support he had provided me. Turns out it was a blessing in disguise. Laden with tens of thousands of dollars of student loan debt, I had no time to waste, so I grabbed a few rolls of quarters and started cold-calling potential employers from pay phones. Needless to say, there were no iPhones or LinkedIn at the time.

"Turns out, my most promising job lead came in the private client services department at...Goldman Sachs. Goldman had given me a generous severance after I was let go. When I got to an advanced stage of the interview with Goldman PCS, they said they would hire me, but I had to return my severance. Only problem was, I had already wired it all to help pay off my student loans! They reluctantly got over that fact, so I returned to Goldman in a role that better suited my personality. I flourished there, before moving on to start my first company, Oscar Capital.

"During this somewhat tumultuous early period of my professional life, my Street Smarts from Port Washington came into play on multiple occasions. When I was first fired from Goldman, I could've let my emotions get the best of me. I could've ripped into my boss for letting me go. I could've despaired about trying to repay my loans while supporting a young family. Instead, I played the long game. I gritted my teeth and maintained a good relationship with Mike, who provided me a strong recommendation and remains a close friend to this day.

"There are several other moments throughout my life and career where I have used Street Smarts, but I will zero in on two more examples in particular. As the global financial crisis was unfolding in 2008, everyone on Wall Street got scared. Investors were liquidating portfolios, banks were divesting assets, and financial institutions were canceling conferences. As a Street Smart contrarian thinker, I decided I wanted to be a buyer of risk, I wanted to try to scoop up forgotten bank assets, and I wanted to start a conference.

"My first move was starting the SkyBridge Alternatives, or SALT, conference. I founded SkyBridge in 2005 after selling Oscar to Neuberger Berman, which was in turn sold to Lehman Brothers. I didn't fit the desired Myers-Briggs personality profile at Lehman, so we mutually parted ways. By 2009, SkyBridge was on the verge of going under, as were many financial industry start-ups at that time. But I didn't panic. Instead, I plotted a course to pivot and resuscitate the firm. SALT was the first step on that journey.

"The first SALT conference in 2009 started with a few hundred people, but the next year we brought President Bill Clinton as the keynote speaker, and the event exploded. Today it is perhaps the preeminent alternative-investments-focused event in the country. At the same time, I was working on a deal for SkyBridge to acquire Citigroup's alternative investments unit, or fund of funds. The SALT conference gave the impression that SkyBridge was a massive, thriving company. In reality, we badly needed to pivot out of our current predicament. Citi signed off on a creatively structured transaction for SkyBridge to acquire CAI, and the rest is history. Today, SkyBridge has the largest independent fund of funds business in the industry, with a rapidly growing venture capital and digital assets business.

"During the financial crisis, my Street Smarts allowed me to keep a level head and spot opportunities where others saw danger and risk. Throughout my career, I have continued to try to maintain that contrarian mindset."

By the quality and complexity of his Street Smart Memoir, Anthony Scaramucci could be a professor of Street Smart. Not only was his working-class background not an impediment, but perhaps it was the catalyst for a successful man.

STREET SMART MEMOIR OF RAYMOND MCGUIRE
From Dayton, Ohio, to One of Wall Street's Top Investment Bankers

Raymond "Ray" McGuire received his BA from Harvard College and then went to the University of Nice in France after receiving a Rotary Fellowship. Coming back to the states, he graduated from Harvard Business School with a Master's in Business Administration and a Juris Doctor from Harvard Law. He began his long financial career at First Boston Corporation, then moved on to becoming one of the first members of Wasserstein Perella & Co., Inc., worked at Merrill Lynch, and was also employed at Morgan Stanley.

After years of building his impressive resume, McGuire became the global co-head of investment banking at Citigroup. During his time at Citigroup, he managed more than two thousand employees and advised multiple business mergers and acquisitions worth over $200 billion, including the Time Warner Cable, Inc.'s split from Time Warner Cable (a deal worth $45 billion). McGuire was listed as one of *Black Enterprise's* "100 Most Powerful Executives in Corporate America."

He then became one of the highest-ranked and longest-serving African American businessmen on Wall Street. In October 2020, he left his financial career and announced his campaign to become Mayor of New York City.

In addition to his successful business endeavors, McGuire is also a top art collector, being the chairman of the Studio Museum in Harlem and a member of the board of trustees for the Whitney Museum. He's also been a member on the committee of the International Center of Photography, as well as a trustee of the Lincoln Center and the chairman of the board at De La Salle Academy. He also served as a member of the Overseers and Directors Nominating Committee for Harvard University.

Adding to his diplomas and committee appointments from Harvard, the university also gave McGuire the Alumni Professional Achievement Award, and he was named a Distinguished Patron of the Arts by the Pratt Institute.

Raymond McGuire's Street Smart, he tells you, is essential to success. He's more than just one of the top investment bankers in the country: he is the personification of hard work, dedication, and overcoming obstacles.

He is the consummate example of someone who has been able to balance his academic and business acumen with his upmost Street Smart education.

"Without question, Street Smarts are and have been essential to the success of many of the country's most admired and respected leaders, especially those who started from the most humble beginnings. Notwithstanding, being the likely sole member of the 4H Club, Hotchkiss, and triple Harvard (arguably the best academic experience that money could buy), at the core of my success were the lessons taught at home and in the neighborhoods in Dayton, Ohio: Street Smarts. This virtue has been critical to my surviving from the early days of my education to however success is defined in almost four decades of leadership in the worlds of business, arts, culture and philanthropy.

"Yes, I have used Street Smarts from the beginning of my career in the world of corporate finance. In the second round of interviews for one of two summer associate jobs at The First Boston Corporation (now Credit Suisse), I had to use Street Smarts. I was invited to what was advertised as a cocktail reception at the Ritz Carlton in downtown Boston, Mass.

"When I entered the room (first time that I had ever been in a Ritz Carlton), the entire large room of First Boston Bankers/recruiters emptied except one recruiter. He invited me to pull up a chair and sit. As I sat, he pulled up a chair, turned its back towards me, and straddled the chair. He looked me in the eye and said, 'We have five minutes. Shoot your best shot.'

"I asked, 'What would you like for me to say?'

"He responded, 'You have four minutes, forty-five seconds.'

"I'm thinking to myself this is not really going down this way and this is a job interview. I know little to nothing about this corporate finance investment banking business, but what I do know is this guy is being pretty aggressive. So, I got nothing to lose and my Street Smart instincts came out.

"I responded, 'Harvard College, Harvard Law School, and Harvard Business School pride themselves on taking the cream of the crop. I pride myself on being the film off the top of the cream.'

"His next question was, 'We have half of your business school class interviewing for two summer positions. Why you?'

"I responded, 'In the heat of battle, you would rather have me on your side rather than against you, because I'll find a way to win.' I got one of the two jobs.

"Street Smart gives you a highly sensitive antenna that allows you to identify potential opportunities and to pursue/rank which of the opportunities will be most attractive. Street Smart has played an essential role in each career opportunity. It has been critical in identifying the risk in many of the options which I did not pursue.

"For the first ten years of my professional career, I worked for two industry giants, Joe Perella and Bruce Wasserstein. In the tenth year, I had the opportunity to separate and to build my own brand independent of Joe and Bruce. I seized the opportunity to go to Merrill Lynch to help build its advisory practice. Once established, I accepted a third-time offer from Morgan Stanley, where I eventually was promoted to co-global head of mergers and acquisitions. As the leadership changes occurred at Morgan Stanley, I was recruited to Citigroup, where I seized the opportunity to transform and lead the global corporate and investment banking business."

After all is said and done, Raymond's eloquence only underscores the concept of how he spotted, seized, and exploited a lucky break. Another modest beginning here, another brilliant career which Raymond attributes to Street Smart.

STREET SMART MEMOIR OF KEN BURNS
The Gift of Seeing the Big Picture

Ken Burns keeps the distance in his eyes. That means that he sees what is coming in America's horizon before anyone else does, a skill he credits firmly to his Street Smart. His Street Smarts, as you will read, were triggered by the early and tragic death of his beloved mother from cancer. Everything changed for the eleven-year-old Burns. Included was a keen awareness that survival in the future would depend entirely on his reading situations and relationships better than anyone else. He lived this potential out and informs you that even bad luck can spur Street Smart. Being born in Brooklyn, not far from where the authors were brought up, just germinated in Burns as he lived all over the world.

His mantra in Street Smart seizes upon his role as "perpetual noticer" or "observer," a fantastic talent which made him notice the American Civil War, the world of Major League Baseball, the building of the Brooklyn Bridge, in ways no one ever had before: compelling, warm, perceptive, and amazingly personal.

Ken was born in 1953, in Brooklyn, where so much Street Smart originated. Both parents were highly educated, and the family traveled far away from Brooklyn in his early childhood. He worked his way through college as a record-store clerk. He caught the entertainment bug through television and film. It would take six pages to recount Ken's accomplishments, but we encapsulate them here. He wrote/produced/directed: *The Civil War*; *Baseball*; *Jazz*; *Statue of Liberty*; *Huey Long*; *Lewis and Clark: The Journey of the Corps of Discovery*; *Frank Lloyd Wright*; *Mark Twain*; *Unforgivable Blackness: The Rise and Fall of Jack Johnson*; *The War*; *The National Parks: America's Best Idea*; *The Roosevelts: An Intimate History*; and *Cancer: The Emperor of All Maladies*.

It is no exaggeration to say that Ken Burns, through filmmaking and television, has totally remolded history for the present and coming generations. The history of his subjects contains Street Smart episodes and observations gathered over many decades. He's eloquent enough not to need commentary, and no bigger observer of Street Smart exists today than him.

"Stewart Udall, the secretary of the interior under Presidents Kennedy and Johnson, told me in an interview that Theodore Roosevelt had what he called 'distance in his eyes;' that the celebrated conservation president was able to see how things would be and should be in the future, that he played the long game, saw and understood the big picture. Street Smart is just this kind of gift. I was born in a hospital in Brooklyn but never grew up in a big city, where we naturally assume Street Smart is incubated and cultivated. Instead, I grew up in two college towns for the most part, and despite spending a lot of time and even living for a while in New York City, I've spent more than four decades living outside a tiny village in New England. But in some ways, I think I've acquired a version of Street Smarts along the way.

"The biggest and most shaping event in my life was my mother's death after a nearly ten-year struggle with cancer when I was eleven. Her sickness and passing eliminated all the safety associated with a carefree childhood. I developed coping mechanisms, a detachment from many things, and became more an observer than a participant. I began to anticipate the behavior of other people around me. A biographer of Mark Twain, Ron Powers, said that Twain was 'an enormous noticer.' That meant he could size a person up just by watching them, how they walked and carried themselves; he seemed to know what they did for a living by looking; he even knew what was in their pockets. Street Smart.

"As I grew older, still wary and on guard, I discovered that this separation from things and people was unusually detrimental to many important aspects of human relationships and the enjoyment of the moment. And I suffered. But I also found that in two areas it served me well—filmmaking and fatherhood. Both required a ferocious attention to what is happening *now*, a vigilance that manifests in every part of life, from the smallest of seemingly inconsequential things to that big picture. Shepherding a film into existence, easily a million or more decisions, and raising four daughters has required that kind of unblinking attention, that kind of Street Smarts.

"It's paying attention to detail while still getting a kind of aerial view. It's knowing when to hold your ground creatively or when to protect—or discipline—a child, and of course when to let go, to "fight" perhaps another day. It's paying attention to the crack in the sidewalk right below your feet that threatens to trip you up, at the same time scanning the next block up ahead, knowing how to avoid a potential danger or unnecessary confrontation by crossing over to the other side of the street, way ahead of trouble.

"Street Smart is also knowing that none of us are truly alone, that we are bound to each other inextricably regardless of innate wariness or obsessive vigilance; that despite the inevitable conflicts of the streets, there's only "us," no "them." We begin to understand that we need loved ones, friends, allies, and colleagues who enrich our lives and make us better at what we do—and sometimes we're able to let down our guard as well. And the choice of those people in our lives is as central to Street Smarts as the sun in the sky."

His prose here is eloquent and yet to the point, like his movies. Street Smart is not so eloquent but really to the point, isn't it? Placing all of history in terms of Street Smart is generational wisdom not so easily reduced to platitudes. Ken actually "got it." The theme we have pushed from page one is how this communal street sense depends on that interaction. There is no "isolated" Street Smart, and no "us" versus "them."

STREET SMART MEMOIR OF BONNIE FULLER
Not Just Street Smarts, but Persistence and Brilliance Paid Off

Here's being Street Smart, modified: celebrity powerhouse Bonnie Fuller believes that persistence and making your own luck are keys to wielding Street Smart. She doesn't believe that Street Smart is a separate talent or skill to wield in a hostile world. Persistence and longevity are what matter. And she takes precious time to lay out her memoir quite eloquently.

Bonnie Fuller has been twice named *Advertising Age*'s "Editor of the Year." Most recently, she relaunched HollywoodLife.com and serves as the president and editor-in-chief. She also hosts a weekly HollywoodLife podcast. She served as EVP, chief editorial director of American Media, Inc, from 2003 to 2008, where she oversaw the production of twenty-three magazines, including *Star*, *Celebrity Living*, *Shape*, and *Men's Fitness*.

Fuller previously worked as the editor-in-chief of *Us Weekly*, where she restructured, redesigned, and repackaged was what originally the monthly *Us* magazine. Under Fuller's charge, the celebrity news weekly was born, and newsstand sales increased over 100 percent. In 1989, she was named the editor-in-chief of *YM* where she redesigned and re-launched the teen title, changing the name from *Young Miss* to *Young & Modern*. She was also editor-in-chief of *Glamour* for three years, where she strengthened the magazine's renowned coverage of beauty, health, and women's issues. She also served as editor-in-chief for *Marie Claire* and *Cosmopolitan*, with both magazines greatly excelling during her tenures.

She is also author of the forthcoming book, *The Joys of Much Too Much: The Great Career, the Perfect Guy, and Everything Else You've Ever Wanted*, in which she asserts to "go for the big life," the importance for women of living a full life of romance, career, and family, even if it means having to "cram it all in."

"I'm not sure that I believe that success can often be attributed to 'Street Smarts.' I would argue that the way to success is based on three things: 1) having an original or creative idea that you feel strongly and passionately about. So strongly and passionately about that you are willing to 2) fight to realize your idea being put into action either in your own independent company or within a workplace where you are employed and then 3) persistence.

"Persistence is the most important element besides having an original business idea. There are so many obstacles in life and an extraordinary number of obstacles in establishing yourself as top in your field or in setting up a successful independent business. If you don't inherit money or have a wealthy family that is willing to help get you into the most prestigious universities or will give you the money to invest in your new product idea or independent visit, it's extremely difficult to actually realize your dream, particularly if it involves an investment of money—and what new business doesn't?

"That's why persistence is such a critical quality as a contributor to success. You have to be prepared to persist—to try to find a way to turn your idea into a big promotion, a career, or a new business. It's likely, as a mere mortal who didn't go to Harvard or Stanford, that you will fail to get investors, you will fail to get a highly sought-after job or promotion, you will fail to become profitable. You will have to persist and persist in looking for those critical investors, persist in applying for jobs to different companies, persist in getting higher-ups at your company to implement your idea, persist in learning more about the issues standing in the way of your independent company getting profitable, so you can implement solutions.

"You will have to persist for years, persist against lots of critics and naysayers, all without losing hope or faith in yourself. To me, these are qualities that are more important than the ability to 'spot, seize, and exploit luck or lucky breaks.'

"I wouldn't attribute the success I've had to 'lucky breaks'; I feel that my success has much more been the result of being creative, feeling extremely passionate about the ideas I have had, and then persisting against long odds. For some reason, I don't know exactly why, I have had at many times in my career very clear ideas of what I wanted to do—very clear concepts of what I thought needed to be done for women's magazines and then for celebrity magazines. And then I had a concept for a women's digital site focused on entertainment, celebrity, and women's issue news—HollywoodLife.

"My feelings about these things were innate. They were certainly based on my years of reading magazines as a teen and a young woman, and having given a huge amount of thought over the years as to how to make them better. As years went on and I was able to see how readers responded to my magazines, I learned from that and learned to be more skilled at what I did.

"As the editor-in-chief of a digital site, I have been on a continual learning curve. I watch what stories and content readers like best, but I also have to study changes in Google and Facebook algorithms. So again, I don't credit lucky breaks that have contributed to my success. Instead, it has been a determined march to get things done but matched with an open mind. In order to have had any level of success, I have had to continually learn and evolve. I could never ever sit still and have never felt that I knew it all; I'm always open to change and to learning how to deal with outside factors that necessitate my having to make changes to HollywoodLife, my digital site.

"That quality has never been more important than the past few years as Google algorithm changes and social media necessitated me seeking out and learning new skills in order to keep HollywoodLife competitive. Now, did I ever take advantage during my career of connections I made? Yes, I did. I got to know designer Tommy Hilfiger well when I covered his first designs before the actual Tommy Hilfiger collection.

"Tommy once offered to introduce me to the COO of Hearst Magazines, Gil Maurer, and I took up the offer. That connection led several years later to me finally getting hired to launch the American edition of *Marie Claire* magazine—a Hearst publication. That introduction was a lucky break, and absolutely I took advantage of it. But it wouldn't have led anywhere if I hadn't worked my tail off, building my career as a reporter and then as the editor of a major fashion magazine in Canada.

"Opportunities: I was willing to always take chances and to take on big challenges when the opportunities presented themselves. I decided to apply to be the editor-in-chief of that fashion magazine in Canada when I was just twenty-six. I didn't shrink from it, no matter how nervous I was about applying and then accepting the job, even though I had no experience as an editor at all. I pushed myself to go for it.

"I made my 'lucky break.' I had happened to do some freelance writing pieces for this magazine, *Flare*, in Canada, and for the editor-in-chief, who quit her job unexpectedly. I decided to take advantage of the situation—in other words, I knew the position was open, my friend Jane was a senior reporter at the *Toronto Star* and asked the publisher of *Flare* about me—she was, surprisingly, interested in talking to me. So, I followed through and went after that job. I created my lucky break by following through on what I saw as a great opportunity; I didn't allow terror to hold me back.

"Decades later, when I was persistently and desperately looking for investors to find some way, any way, to start HollywoodLife, I met with probably thirty VCs and two dozen potential investors and nothing...I wasn't able to raise one dollar.

"Finally, a good friend, Lara Shiftman, introduced to a friend of hers, Jay Penske, who had launched a media company and wanted to grow it: Was that a lucky break or was it a willingness to go through every door and follow through on every potential opportunity? It took over a year and going down countless paths before one finally led to an opportunity to realize my vision for a new women's digital news site.

"To me, it was persistence that led to my success. Persistence led to a break but not a lucky break. I pursued every single avenue I could think of. Asked everyone I knew or had met or had heard about, and finally one road yielded fruit.

"Again—I don't know if I have seized opportunities to use Street Smarts. In the business I am in—the news media—the hardest quality to have today is longevity. I can think of only one other female editor-in-chief besides myself who is still heading up a major digital property after decades in the business. This didn't used to be the case. In fact, I took over the editorship of two major magazine brands, which were each led by the same editors-in-chief, for over thirty years. But because of the digital revolution, most female leaders of the magazine world left the business instead of adapting. My secret has been that I was eager to jump into the new digital world. I was willing to leap into the abyss—voluntarily leaving the safety of a high-paying magazine-world position in order to pursue the idea of launching my own digital business.

"It has not been easy. I am in my thirteenth year into that journey now, and I have not fully achieved the goal I had. While my business has grown enormously, is still in business, and is running in the black, I remain determined to take it to a much bigger level. I still believe—even more strongly than ever—that it can boom.

"But just to get to where we are has involved so much continual learning and being willing to change my brand's editorial, technological, and business practices in so many ways. The digital world is constantly evolving, and just to give one example, search engine optimization requirements and practices have changed dramatically over the years. Therefore, I would say that I seize on learning. I remain open to advancing new skills and practices at all times. It's my openness to change and willingness to adapt that has enabled me to seize or take advantage of opportunities, whether this means I have been using Street Smarts or not.

"I don't believe that you can count on hunches, feelings, and emotion without educating yourself enough to trust your gut. Your gut can become outdated.

"I used to have an excellent nose for news, for example. That instinctive sense is still excellent, but that is not enough today to result in a successful women's digital news site. Covering breaking news and breaking exclusive news ourselves has to be combined with up-to-date technology and an educated full understanding of how to present our stories to Google and Facebook—the major content distributors. Without all this, our great stories, exclusive interviews, and imaginative photo galleries would never make it into the view of readers. They would never be given top positions on those platforms.

"So, my gut has had to be combined with the knowledge I have gathered on how to get our stories to 'market.' Therefore, I would advise readers to continually grow and update their skills—they have to welcome change, not make fun of it nor fear it. And if they are confident that they have a great idea or ideas and can create a new business or lead a team or division, then they need to persist.

"Persist in fully fleshing out your ideas and plans. And then persist in selling them, despite obstacles and roadblocks. Go up, go over, go around—persist—and eventually you will find a way."

We see eye to eye with Bonnie. You can take the girl out of the city but can't take the city out of the girl.

STREET SMART MEMOIR OF KEN SUNSHINE
Crafting Street Smarts and the Best Spin to Better the World

"Making the crazy world a little better" is the goal compelling Ken Sunshine to live life to the fullest, and he says to you that Street Smart is indispensable to improving both Ken's life and yours. This is idealistic to a point but also very practical. Ken was a college radical who made politics his fulcrum to doing good things. Born in Brooklyn but raised on suburban Long Island, Sunshine's advice to the reader makes a lot of practical sense. He's vibrant without the usual theatrics. And, as you read in his official biography which follows, he has almost singlehandedly revolutionized the world of political public relations.

Hailing from Long Island and graduating from Cornell University, Ken Sunshine entered the '70s social and political public relations stage in New York. He served as political advisor to some notable figures. They range from presidential candidate George McGovern to New York City mayor David Dinkins, where one of his responsibilities was to manage the young Bill de Blasio. Parlaying his consulting expertise in politics into mainstream PR, Sunshine founded Ken Sunshine Consultants in 1991.

In addition to his private-sector clientele, he continued to advise political figures like Gov. Mario Cuomo and Gov. Andrew Cuomo in their respective New York State gubernatorial campaigns.

Ken Sunshine consulted for top-tier clients such as Barbara Streisand, the National Health Care Workers' Union, and the 1992 Democratic National Convention. There, he worked alongside former US secretary of commerce and then-chairman of the Democratic Party, Ron Brown.

In 2002, Sunshine partnered with Shawn Sachs and both men found the groundbreaking PR firm Sunshine Sachs. Sachs graduated from the University of Colorado Boulder in 1995 before staffing for ND senator Byron Dorgan. He then successfully held an advisory position on the Democratic Congressional Campaign Committee. Over the past decade and a half, the firm has represented a celebrity client list that includes Ben Affleck, Leonardo DiCaprio, Jason Statham, Natalie Portman, the Michael Jackson estate, and Justin Timberlake.

Here's Ken's take on Street Smart.

"I was born in Brooklyn when Brooklyn wasn't cool. It would have been much cooler to say I was a city kid, but the truth is we quickly moved to the suburbs as so many did, for a small lawn and a small house. Life was pleasant, safe, isolated. My parents were loving and completely devoted to their three sons. We were somewhat spoiled, comfortable but hardly rich.

"My father was the sweetest guy around despite having had a more-than-challenging childhood. His parents died when he was an infant, and he was brought up in an orphan asylum. He actually had fond memories of the orphan asylum—remained active in their alumni organization. Then he fought in Europe in World War II. He would always be willing to talk all about his childhood—but almost never about his army experiences. Later, he admitted that he saw terrible things in the war. But few details.

"My mother was a hoot. Gregarious, opinionated—and a lot of fun. She would drive us all crazy—and we laughed a lot. My friends loved hanging out at our house despite my mom being a terrible cook. Discipline was never a priority.

"Thankfully we had a wonderfully eccentric grandmother who lived in Manhattan. We visited her often, and that allowed us to absorb the vibrancy, the grit, the culture of the 'city.'

"I went to sleepaway camp most summers with a lot of city kids—they seemed a little tougher, a little more aware of the world beyond the more sterile suburbs. My high school—in a middle-class/working-class community only a few miles from the Queens border—was almost 100 percent white.

"Welcome to suburbia of that era. Housing policies were overtly discriminatory. Politics there was very Republican, with small pockets of Democrats like my parents and some of their friends.

"I was mostly focused on basketball, girls, and reading. I was a pretty good shooting guard until I kind of peaked at about sixteen, when I started to become more interested in the world beyond Long Island and got to love the "city" more and more. I would take the Long Island Rail Road and the subway with my friends, sometimes alone, and explore neighborhoods, crazy art, and theater.

"By the time I left to go to college, I was more than ready to break out from safe suburbia—and join the emerging student movement that was turning most campuses into centers of activism, rebellion, and cultural upheaval.

"Cornell University was a center of all that. And I got close to students of many diverse backgrounds and became consumed with anti-Vietnam-War activism and the civil rights movement. What a wonderful time to be young, idealistic, and rebellious. Music and lifestyle were a vital part of the very serious political struggle to end a hated war and create a more equitable America.

"At Cornell, I didn't spend much time worrying about classes—and many were cancelled in these years of political turmoil. What I did struggle with was where I belonged: in the more romanticized revolutionary crowd taking over buildings or with the less exciting Democrats seeking social and political change through the political process? A visionary and later a congressman named Al Lowenstein had a big influence on me and made it clear that I should stop pretending to be a revolutionary and would be much more comfortable working to elect Democrats. He was right.

"My non-traditional career (that was the title of a lecture I gave several years ago at Cornell) started in a community center in a tough neighborhood, to being recruited to run as a delegate to the Democratic convention when I was barely old enough to vote (we won), to a long behind-the-scenes role as a political insider highlighted by helping to elect the first Black mayor of New York and serving as his first chief of staff, a delegate to many national conventions, to another career in the music business, then as an entrepreneur as the founder of a successful public relations company and a longtime civil rights activist.

"When I reflect on the journey, it was not my Ivy League education and elite cultural tastes that had much to do with whatever success I've enjoyed. No, it was Street Smarts—learned more on picket lines and demonstrations, in convincing reporters to cover your story and make that story come out favorably, in learning how to work with talented people in a world that loves to caricature celebrities. I had the privilege of getting close to three titans of NY journalism: Jimmy Breslin, Jack Newfield, and Pete Hamill—all of whom wrote about the underclass and the little guy who always got screwed. They taught me to never be impressed with wealth or privilege. I used to drive them around since they were real NYC kids and never learned to drive (Pete learned to drive later in life—Jimmy and Jack never learned to drive a car).

"I started in politics knowing virtually no one of any influence. I knew only a few low-level staffers in the music business when I got a job as a junior publicist. And I had never run anything when I started my own PR business with a staff of one. Me.

"Whatever Street Smarts really are—whatever success I've enjoyed—there was a lot more than formalized training or somebody handing me opportunities that helped me on that journey. Maybe it was the influence of a dad who never knew his parents, yet became a success and showered his kids with unlimited love.

"Hopefully there a few more chapters to go to help make this crazy world a little better," Ken concluded for us.

So, here, public relations and Street Smart go hand in glove, which actually makes perfect sense. Having a hunch about global preferences rooted in everyday life is Street Smart on a tactical level. In Ken's case, his dad showered him with love, which made the difference. And Ken's dad had to get his own Street Smart from somewhere, origin unknown.

STREET SMART MEMOIR OF STEVE AIELLO
Trust and Vision is Critical to Street Smart

National educator Steve Aiello knows Street Smart...as he was educated by his parents. Son of Sicilian immigrants, Aiello's working-class parents taught him that loyalty to friends and family is reciprocated by a healthy dose of Street Smart. Like fellow Brooklynite Arthur Miller's quote, "Anyone from outside the neighborhood was a stranger," Steve learned that a wariness in even the best cultured and powerful circles was Street Smart. His philosophy is a little different: you were to use both body and mind. In his explanation, we even get a brief narrative from Steve about his father and Al Capone, perhaps the greatest Street Smart-er in history.

Steve brings more than thirty-five years of extensive national, state, and local political and government affairs work as well as corporate public relations experience to the Wagner College board. He currently serves as a senior counselor in Hill+Knowlton Strategies. His government, crisis, labor, and coalition-building expertise has helped a number of major clients build or repair relationships with key communities and constituencies. He was formerly executive vice president and director of public affairs for Burson-Marsteller Worldwide.

Steve served in the White House as special assistant to President Carter on ethnic/urban affairs. He also held the office of president of the New York City Board of Education for three years. He was the president of the New York Educational Construction Fund and has taught at the university level and in secondary schools. He is a former director of the National Italian American Foundation, Kappa Delta Pi, a former trustee of the NYS Democratic Committee, and lifetime trustee of the Community Services Society of New York. He has received numerous honors from educational, community, government, and business organizations and has been honored by the governments of Italy and Ireland for his work in promoting greater understanding and cooperation between their countries and the United States.

Steve holds a doctorate in urban studies from Union Graduate School/Columbia University, a master's degree in history from Columbia University, a bachelor's degree in history from New York University, and a Professional Certificate in educational administration from New York University.

"To this day, I still remember the life lessons learned from my parents, family members, and close friends from my Brooklyn neighborhood. But it was my mother, through many a Sicilian proverb and her emotional intelligence, who instilled in me from a very early age the importance of being Street Smart. Mom was only three years old when her father and mother left to come to America. Left behind in Sicily, she was raised by an aunt, and when she was sixteen made the trip to New York on her own.

"Upon arrival in a new country, she went right to work and created a life for herself. She taught me not to trust anyone outside of closest family and friends because they don't always have your welfare at heart, and some will be jealous of your success. That has sadly proven true over the years. From a Sicilian proverb, 'Only your mother and real friends will tell you that you have dirt on your face.'

"When I was very young, two years old, and still recovering from a serious illness that ended with my father taking me home (basically kidnapping me) from the hospital and saying, 'If he is going to die, he is going to die at home,' my mother kept an extra close watch on me. Our Brooklyn landlord had a vicious dog that roamed free and continuously tried to bite me. When my mother complained, the landlord responded with a 'sue me or move.'

"My mother took him to court without legal counsel but with a lot of nerve. Mom recognized the judge as a fellow Sicilian who came from a very similar background. She used this common ground to come up with responses that she thought this judge would react to favorably and to gain his sympathy. The landlord had a lawyer, but Mom won the judge over and he sided with her and told the owner to either keep the dog tied up and away from me or he would fine him five thousand dollars.

"Second only to my mother, my father also provided me valuable guidance on the importance of being Street Smart. As a young boy growing up in immigrant Bushwick Brooklyn, Pop had to learn how to navigate the mean streets in the early 1920s. At eleven years old, Pop worked for a *paisan* whose business was to sell ice to both stores and private homes and apartments. Pop had to make sure that the money collected wasn't stolen by street thugs. Because of this, he quickly acquired the necessary Street Smarts that helped him years later while being a musician during prohibition.

"My father was a touring musician in New York, Chicago, and Gary, Indiana. During prohibition, he had to deal with all kinds of people and situations, many illegal. In Chicago, he worked in a speakeasy. The people who ran it worked for the Capone organization and would drive him to the boarding house at night and pick him up the next day to bring him back to work. Pop usually sat in front of the car, until one time when there were three people in the car and he was told to sit in the back and 'try to go to sleep.'

"That incident ended up in the disappearance of the third person in that car that was unknown to my father. Pop decided this was not an experience he wanted to ever live through again and left Chicago immediately. He found work in New York with a major Broadway production called *George White's Scandals*.

"Pop went on to become a successful businessman, and he taught my brother and I that the lessons he learned from the time he was eleven were invaluable to his success. He stressed, 'Use your mind and body to understand and seize opportunities when they arise, but most of all, depend on your feelings and what your inner voice is telling you.' He ended this lesson with the advice to never back down from a bully, even if you have to take a 'beating' once in a while.

"I remember the first time I had a chance to demonstrate Street Smart on my own. I was in elementary school in the sixth grade. The school had a basketball court and a few of us would go play. Eventually older kids would come and take the court and throw us off. We knew we were no match for them physically, so we'd just give up. I eventually overheard their leader talking to someone about the new Charlie Parker record. Charlie Parker was and is considered the greatest jazz alto sax player of all time and someone who I was very familiar with. My thought was I could use the fact that I have been playing sax since the third grade to my advantage. The next time we played the court, I just so happened to bring an album I had of Charlie Parker with me and left it strategically in view.

"He saw it and asked, 'Whose record is that?'

"When I said it's mine, we began to talk about his music, which led to a mutual understanding and respect. He never threw us off the court again! This was an example of how you can identify common ground and use it to your benefit.

"As I have grown older and dealt with many different types of people, I've learned that sometimes the more formal education you have may inadvertently act as a barrier to getting to the real truth of the situation. Street Smart is listening to your gut primarily and keeping aware of the ability to feel and anticipate things, whether it's relationships, business, or just walking down a street.

"Over the years, I have found the above to be true, whether in my role as an assistant to President Carter, commissioner and president of the New York City Board of Education, president and CEO of major public relations organizations, chairman and trustee of not-for-profits and institutions of higher education, or as advisor to many elected officials and major corporations.

"In summary, remember when an opportunity presents itself to seize it! Don't give away all your thinking in the beginning. Instead, wait until you've formed a trusting relationship. Maintain loyalty and use your word as your bond. And finally, as best as you can, never let them see you sweat."

That's fine advice from Steve Aiello. Trust is a precursor to Street Smart itself. Here the capability that you now have in Street Smart actually becomes empowered with time in trust. This is subtle and obviously competes with the New York pace of life. But it's still powerful wisdom.

STREET SMART MEMOIR OF JERRY DELLA FEMINA
Street Smarts from the Only Man who Ever Made DiMaggio Jealous

Competing with the snobby WASP cliques of the classic advertising world, or riding along with the Mafia characters in his
neighborhood in Gravesend Brooklyn, Jerry Della Femina is an
eloquent, if sometimes shocking, advocate of Street Smart. Jerry
lives in the Hamptons a big part of the year, meaning that he lives
among people who probably can lay claim to Street Smarts as
well. But his story, which he relates to you now, is an eye opener.

Just for the record, which he will confirm shortly for you,
Jerry is the real-life foundation of the hit television series *Mad
Men*. He was never a martini-jiggling moron seeking relief in

mediocrity and an expensive Italian tailored suit. He was always vibrant and remains so today.

Advertising Age named Jerry Della Femina one of the 100 Most Influential Advertising People of the Century.

For years he was the most sought-after advertising expert in the country, and Mr. Della Femina has appeared in almost every major television network, magazine, and newspaper. He is the winner of Lions from Cannes, Good Keys for copywriting, Clios, Andys, and just about every creative award in the advertising business. He also was chosen to be head judge at the Cannes Advertising Festival. In 2008, Mr. Della Femina was inducted into The Creative Hall of Fame.

He co-founded Della Femina Travisano & Partners in 1967. The agency grew to become one of the top twenty agencies in the U.S. with billings over $800 million. DFT&P (later named Della Femina McNamee) produced some of the most successful advertising running during the "advertising creative revolution," building successful brands such as Beck's Beer, Isuzu, Blue Nun Wine, Meow Mix ("Singing Cats"), and Dow Bathroom Cleaner ("Scrubbing Bubbles").

After selling his agency in 1987, Mr. Della Femina re-entered the advertising business with Newsweek Magazine as the flagship account of his new agency, Jerry Inc. His current agency, Della Femina Advertising, handles such notable clients as Atlantic Health System, Wakefern Food Corp., Parker Jewish Institute for Health Care and Rehabilitation, Baruch College, and AgeWell New York, to name a few.

Mr. Della Femina has written one of the three best-selling books in the history of advertising, *From Those Wonderful Folks Who Gave You Pearl Harbor. From Those Wonderful Folks* is still required reading at many universities and has been credited by many as the book that inspired them to start a career in advertising.

Mr. Della Femina was born in Brooklyn and attended Brooklyn College. He received honorary doctorates from the University of Missouri in 1983 and Long Island University in 1989. He also holds the distinction of being the only person Joe DiMaggio ever held any jealousy over. After hearing all of these stories and praises about Jerry, DiMaggio knew he had to see the man for himself. So, he had Rock arrange a meeting for the men to sit and dine at Campagna in New York. The rest is history, and Jerry's story gives justifiable reason for a man like DiMaggio to harbor any such envy.

"I came into the advertising business in 1952 at the age of sixteen, as a delivery boy for a stuffy, old-line advertising agency named Ruthrauff and Ryan, which could have served as the setting for the *Mad Men* television series without moving a desk. Needless to say, it was a difficult business to break into, especially for a teenager with a limited education.

"In 1956, I took my portfolio of sample creative work to J. Walter Thompson, the world's largest advertising agency. They had a position open for a junior writer of sales promotion on the Ford Truck account. At that time, Ford was J. Walter Thompson's largest account.

"The copy chief on the account looked at my work and said, 'This is very good, but I can't suggest you for the job.'

"'Why?' I asked.

"His answer was delivered with a nervous smile. 'Because this is Ford, and they don't want your kind working on their business.'

"It took me years to figure out what 'your kind' meant.

"Advertising agencies in those days were broken down among ethnic lines. The Mad Men flourished in large Protestant ad agencies like J. Walter Thompson and N. W. Ayer, BBDO, and Ted Bates. These agencies monopolized all the large advertising accounts (cars, food, cigarettes, soft drinks, beer). The other, smaller accounts (dress manufacturers, shoes, underwear, small retail stores) were regulated to tiny, 'Jewish' ad agencies. By 1950, only one agency whose founders were Jewish had managed to win packaged goods, cigarette, liquor, and car accounts. They did so by naming their agency after the color of the walls in their office, and by not using their Jewish names on their masthead—thus Grey Advertising was born.

"Then, in the mid-1950s, a 'Jewish' advertising agency broke through the ethnic barrier. Doyle Dane Bernbach's campaigns for advertisers like Volkswagen ('Think Small,' 'Lemon') and Levy's Bread ('You don't have to be Jewish to love Levy's') changed the advertising business. Doyle Dane Bernbach made distinctive advertising that had 'attitude' and respected the consumer's intelligence. They sold products with ads that had humor, bold language, and layouts with sharp, clean, and stylish design. It opened the door for a totally new kind of Mad Man.

"By 1961, when I got my first copywriting job, 'my kind' were suddenly in demand. The creative revolution had begun. Advertising had turned into a business dominated by young, funny, Jewish copywriters and tough, sometimes violent, Greek and Italian art directors.

"The original Mad Men did not give up without a fight.

"I once attended an advertising conference held at the Greenbrier Hotel in 1968. The dean of the original Mad Men, the great David Ogilvy, was the keynote speaker. The subject of his speech was the new creative revolution in advertising. Ogilvy knew his audience was mostly made up of desperate men who were trapped in agencies that were losing accounts to young, upstart, ethnic agencies. Ogilvy lashed out and declared, 'I say the lunatics have taken over the asylum!'

"The audience rose and gave that fighting line a standing ovation. I stood up and was clapping as loudly as the next man when I suddenly thought to myself, *What are you clapping about—he's talking about you.*"

Now, here's Jerry's priceless advice directly to you.

"No one who grew up at 800 5th Avenue on 61st Street just opposite Central Park ever had Street Smarts. From their parents they got cunning, not Street Smarts. From their friends they got nothing and gave nothing. It comes down to neighborhood.

"For those of us who lived in Brooklyn in Gravesend on Avenue U, we learned Street Smarts from Joe Jelly (a.k.a. Joe Gioielli). I only saw Joe Jelly five, maybe six times in my life, but I learned a lot from him. Everything about him said danger.

"His blazing cruel eyes and that little creepy smile he had on his face that said 'watch out.' He was a few years older than me, and I remember the first time I saw him when he decided he wanted to play softball with me and a bunch of my friends in the PS 95 schoolyard.

"Now I may have been the worst ball player in all of Brooklyn. I wore these thick glasses, and when I looked up for a fly ball, my glasses jiggled and I saw not one but three balls coming at me. The middle ball usually hits me square on the head. I was so bad that I became a perpetual right fielder.

"That was the position assigned to the worst player in the neighborhood because everyone batted right-handed, and they hit the ball to left field where the best player named Joey Depraspro made circus catches. I remember the day I was playing second base because our team captain, George Malore, felt right field was better empty than having me out there.

"The thought was even after I ran after a ball I had missed, I would pick it up and threw it back like a girl, the ball would take ten bounces, and by the time it got back the opposing player had rounded the bases and had a home run.

"So there I was playing second and there was Joe Jelly who got a hit and coming toward second base, and somehow I caught the ball thrown to me and I rushed towards him and tagged him at least ten feet from the base, so I screamed, 'You're out.'

"He stood on the base and said, 'I'm fuckin' safe. You didn't fuckin' tag me.'

"Of course I had tagged him fuckin' hard, but I looked at Joe Jelly's cruel homicidal eyes and I said, 'You're fuckin' safe. I didn't fuckin' tag you.'

"None of my friends argued. The Street Smart lesson is you don't fuckin' pick a fight with a stone-cold killer, who may be insane, over a stupid schoolyard softball game.

"Joe Jelly taught all of us about street paranoia. You don't fuckin' look for trouble, and you spend your life looking over your shoulder when you're on a dark street because you never know. You never know.

"The next time I saw Joe Jelly, he got into a fistfight with our friend Cosmo Fiorce. Cosmo was a local hero because his father ran a tiny store on West 6th Street [in Bensonhurt], and Cosmo sold individual cigarettes for three cents apiece to young children, some as old as seven. The fight was a doozy, and Cosmo landed a couple of shots at Joe Gioielli's fuckin' face. And when the fight was broken up, Joe screamed: 'I'm going to get you.'

"Cosmo then took off and disappeared.

"Not just for a day or two but forever. We never saw him again, and he was wise. He became the first Italian who hadn't fuckin' committed a crime to join his own witness protection program. He gave up his fuckin' 'selling cigarettes to little children' fortune to save his skin and live another day.

"Joe Jelly went on to neighborhood fame being one of the 'Fuckin' Barbershop Quartet' that rubbed out Albert Anastasia (legendary mobster). And he was a ranking member of the Gallo Gang (another hot-blooded legendary mobster).

"And then one day, Joe Jelly accepted an offer to go fishing from his good friend Albee, a bookie, and he was never seen again.

"His clothes with a dead fish in it were delivered to his girlfriend's house.

"How kind of the Mafia to, in the name of romance, tell her that Joe Jelly isn't fuckin' trying to avoid you, unfortunately he sleeps with the fishes.

"Joe Jelly gave us all Street Smart lessons, but going fishing with a fuckin' Mafia friend shows he was too confidant and naïve to have Street Smarts for himself. It cost him his life."

Jerry waxed poetic with another Street Smart character: he titled it, "And then, of course, there was Hoppy."

"He was big, in a neighborhood where almost everyone was five-foot-five. Hoppy was a six-foot giant and a beefy two-hundred-plus (mostly stomach) pounds. Hoppy was the mayor of 'Street Smart' Avenue U.

"Work ethic? It was cloudy. Hoppy decided when he got out of the Army right after World War II that he wasn't going to work again. He wasn't alone. There were three or four guys like Hoppy. Polock, Andrew, Sally White, Nice guys. Funny, loyal. Slightly honest.

"They decided that they didn't want to work for a living.

"They would make some money here and there.

"Hoppy worked for and against the unions. One day, he was available to march and carry a sign and yell and intimidate anyone who dared cross the line to go to work. The next day, he was available to be hired as a strike breaker threatening the strikers.

"Their headquarters was Joe's Bar and Grill on Avenue U and West Street. Just across the street from PS 95 schoolyard.

"If you had fifteen cents for a beer, you could lean against the bar all day and talk and laugh.

"Joe's Bar was dark and smelled of stale beer. The only light came from the neon signs, the neon-lit jukebox, and the ten-inch Philco television set that always seemed to show Jackie Robinson sliding safely into second base. The Miss Rheingold contest ballots were mounted on a big cardboard card that showed the smiling faces of the six hopefuls. It was perched precariously on the top of the jukebox that continuously played Jo Stafford singing the classic song 'You Belong to Me' to men who hardly ever saw the outside of the bar. The lesson for me and most of our friends, who were at least ten years younger than Hoppy and his guys, was: we never wanted to be so Street Smart that the only real joy in life came at the weekly Sunday game of shooting dice in front of Joe's.

"The Street Smart wise guys of Avenue U didn't read the *New York Times*. Of the thirty or forty sixteen-year-olds in the neighborhood, I was one of the few who had seen the inside of the Kings Highway Library. My friends read the sports pages of the *Daily News* and the *Daily Mirror*. And they devoured every word of the *Morning Telegraph*—the racing newspaper. A single copy of the *Telegraph* was handed down in the neighborhood like the Book of Mormon in Salt Lake City, Utah. It was where a sixteen-year-old could learn Street Smart statistics and Street Smart history.

"'Hey, look at this horse. He only wins when the odds are nine to one or better, and then they ship him to another track and he loses until the odds are right again.'

"Then there was Street Smart genealogy.

"'Yo. Look, this horse's grandfather came in third in the Kentucky Derby and he's the class in the race, the rest are dogs.' And let me point out the lesson in analytics you learn by going to the track or the trotters just for the last race. They let you in free for the last race, and the track is filled with people who have lost all day long and are betting long shots in the last race to try to get even.

"Meanwhile, you bet the horse who was going to be the favorite (and he has a 60 percent chance of winning), on the last race, since everyone is betting on the long shots, the favorite goes off on the best odds, three to one instead of even money.

"And don't for a second underestimate the effect our Street Smart high school, Lafayette, had on our lives. Lafayette wasn't like any other high school in Brooklyn. There was a world of difference between Avenue J, which was upper middle class, and Avenue U, where parents scraped every day to make a living.

"The kids who went to Midwood and Madison were under pressure to be lawyers, successful businessmen, doctors, and dentists like their parents. The parents of the kids who went to Lafayette put no pressure on them. They just wanted them to survive. Every single person who went to Lafayette came out with Street Smarts that stayed with them and served them well every day of their life.

"Lafayette High School is part of my Street Smart DNA. It's my youth. I can hear the music, the Penguins singing 'Earth Angel,' or the incredibly untalented Johnnie Ray scratching out the words to 'Cry.'

"Walking in the halls of Lafayette in those days, it was as if you'd stepped onto the set of *Grease*. The halls were filled with black-leather-jacketed would-be tough guys singing 'Sh-Boom.'

"There was a magic at Lafayette in those days.

"It was Lafayette that graduated a kid named Fred Wilpon, who went on to become a New York leader, and he owned the New York Mets when they became world champions.

"Okay, another kid there then, named Frankie, is now part of the witness-protection program. He admits he whacked eight or nine other mobsters.

"But another Lafayette grad is Sandy Koufax—arguably the greatest pitcher in history and one of the nicest people in the world.

"Lafayette was always a tough, Street Smart school with a low graduation rate. I know. I barely made it out, with a 59 average. I cut classes; I shot craps in front of the school. And, yes, I accidentally knocked over the principal, Mr. Grady, when I was running away as he broke up one of our crap games.

"One of [the] others in that crap game became a successful doctor. Two others are successful businessmen. One is a retired policeman; another, a retired fireman. Six of the other seven turned out fine. The seventh, I've heard, served some time.

"Those of us who stayed at Lafayette, besides Wilpon and Koufax, included Larry King, John Franco, Bob Aspromonte, Vic Damone, Larry Merchant, Maurice Sendak, Peter Max, Paul Sorvino, and billionaire hedge-fund founder Michael Steinhardt."

A more vivid depiction of where Street Smart originated cannot be found outside of Jerry's prose. Those mean streets were academic halls of Ivy League wisdom. The colorful characters he also depicts are replicated on streets here in the United States, but also around the world. And here, you got your Smarts from a master.

STREET SMART MEMOIR OF JUDITH RODIN
Hustle, but Don't Enjoy It Too Much

Judith Rodin has "made it" by any measure of success. What she tells you directly is advice on how, where, and when to use your Street Smart. She considers, firstly, the most recent information. She then looks at the competing means of attaining her goal. Then she hooks into her gut feeling. It seems to do so with active, but not overwhelming, use of the mind in considering the "hard factors" involved. She also has a warning: don't enjoy the hustle of your decisions too much.

We quote liberally from her official biography, which is still worth a thorough reading to understand what she'll say.

Judith Rodin is a pioneer, innovator, change-maker, and global thought-leader. For over two decades, Rodin led and transformed two global institutions: The Rockefeller Foundation and the University of Pennsylvania. A ground-breaking executive throughout her career, Dr. Rodin was the first woman named president to lead an Ivy League institution when she was named president of the University of Pennsylvania in 1994. She was also the first woman to serve as The Rockefeller Foundation's president. A research psychologist by training, she was one of the pioneers of the behavioral medicine and health psychology movements.

Dr. Rodin's leadership ushered The Rockefeller Foundation into a new era of strategic philanthropy that emphasized partnerships with business, government, and the philanthropic community to address and solve for the complex challenges of the twenty-first century. As a result of her vision, in 2015, *Fast Company* named The Rockefeller Foundation one of the top ten innovative non-profits in the world.

Dr. Rodin has served as a member of the board for several leading corporations including Aetna, AMR, EDS, Citigroup, Laureate Education, Inc., and Comcast NBCUniversal. She has been named to *Forbes*'s 100 Most Powerful Women list and Crain's Most Powerful Women in New York list, as well as the National Association of Corporate Directors' (NACD's) 2011 Directorship 100, in recognition of her work promoting the highest standards of corporate governance. In 2009, *US News & World Report* honored her in their list of America's best leaders.

Rodin has authored of more than 250 academic articles and chapters, and has written or co-written fifteen books, including her two most recent, *The Power of Impact Investing: Putting*

Markets to Work for Profit and Global Good (Wharton Digital Press, 2014) and *The Resilience Dividend: Being Strong in a World Where Things Go Wrong* (Public Affairs 2014). Dr. Rodin has also been featured in numerous publications and books over her career, including Tom Brokaw's volume, *Boom! Voices of the Sixties: Personal Reflections on the '60s and Today* (Random House, 2007).

In 2006, she was awarded the Pennsylvania Society's Gold Medal for Distinguished Achievement, which is bestowed upon "a prominent person in recognition of leadership, citizenship, and contributions to the arts, science, education, and industry," making her the first person ever to receive all three of these major Pennsylvania honors.

"I absolutely believe in the concept of Street Smart. I have used it often, but more typically for professional life moments; less so for more intimate personal moments when emotion seems to have the upper hand.

"Seeing an opportunity, an opening, a new direction, and knowing how to use it. Street Smart is not just a personal trait or skill; it is using that skill at the right moment that makes the magic happen. In other words, identifying when the right external, contextual factors allow you to capitalize on your Street Smart skills and know-how.

"I start with always staying tuned into the external situation, being open to new information when others may not be, then quickly seeing multiple ways to achieve the goal, and then letting both my 'gut' and my mind connect before acting.

"Using my approach, as outlined in the preceding answer, let me give an example.

"I was leading a psychology department meeting while I was chair, and my colleagues were droning on and on. It was a rehash of all the old issues, and while everyone looked irritated and bored, no one wanted to give up being heard. I was desperately late picking my kid up from daycare and they had honestly threatened to leave him out on the street if I was late one more time. Aware of the boredom and impatience in the room, I used my Street Smarts to end the meeting and get out but make it great for them too.

"So I said, 'The next agenda item, added by one of us anonymously (that would be me on the spur of the moment), is why we can't allow one another to see that we have families and things that matter outside of our incredibly competitive work environment at Yale. (We were the number-one-ranked department in the country, and not everyone could get tenure.) We don't have time to discuss it today because I, for example, want to feel comfortable telling you that I have to end this meeting because I have to pick up Alex. But let's start with this next time.'

"Not only did I get to leave and reduce my own sense of panic, but the next day, one of my colleagues came into my office to tell me he was leaving at three to go to his kid's soccer match. After giving him a big 'atta boy,' I had a great private laugh. By the way, many said our follow-up discussions of this issue changed the whole culture of the department."

But Judith explains her Street Smart philosophy by sharing her own set of rules.

"Stay aware of the situation; really pay attention to what's going on because typically others are not.

"Seize the moment.

"Enjoy the art of the hustle, but not too much.

"Practice being resilient. It is the other bookend to being Street Smart."

Judith Rodin knows Street Smart when she sees it and uses it daily. Good recommendation? Loving the hustle as art, not science—not seeing hustle as a means to a better end—can be as disastrous as not having Street Smart to begin with.

STREET SMART MEMOIR OF MICHAEL IMPERIOLI
The Refined, Polished, and Wiser Edges of a Street Smart Tough Guy

Michael Imperioli believes that sensitivity to other people is the root and reward of Street Smart. In fact, much of Michael's Street Smart wisdom stems from an unlikely source: do unto others as you would have them do unto you.

That's straight from Jesus Christ and the Bible, right? And this is even more surprising when you realize that Michael plays a lot of tough guys on television and the movies. Go figure, as we say in Brooklyn.

Before making it big in the entertainment industry, Imperioli worked numerous jobs to support himself, including waiting tables in New York. He began his film career in the late '80s, but it was 1990's *Goodfellas* that put him on the map as an actor.

The next year, Imperioli worked with director Spike Lee in *Jungle Fever*. The two later worked together on several other films, including *Malcolm X* (1992), *Clockers* (1995), and *Girl 6* (1996). During the '90s, Imperioli also appeared in several other film projects, including the Hughes brothers' *Dead Presidents* (1995) and *Trees Lounge* (1996) with Steve Buscemi.

With Spike Lee and Victor Colicchio, Imperioli wrote the screenplay for *Summer of Sam* (1999), which looked at New York City during the tense summer of 1977. The film mixed fictional tales with the real-life stories unfolding in the city's streets at the time of the spree killings done by David Berkowitz. Imperioli also had a part in the film and served as an executive producer.

In January 1999, Imperioli became part of the television phenomenon known as *The Sopranos*. The series, which looks at the life and personal struggles of fictional mob boss Tony Soprano, made an impressive debut, capturing a large television audience and critical accolades.

Imperioli impressed many with his dynamic performance as Christopher Moltisanti, a mob underling who struggles to find his place in the organization and the world at large. In 2004, he won the Emmy Award for outstanding supporting actor in a drama series and has been nominated for that same award on three other occasions. Imperioli has also put his considerable writing talents to use on the show, scripting five episodes.

During the run of *The Sopranos*, he has found time to work on a variety of projects, including lending his voice to the animated feature film *Shark Tale* in 2004. That same year, Imperioli, a veteran stage performer and director, and his wife Victoria opened a small off-Broadway theater called Studio Dante. The theater offers opportunities for theatergoers to see new works, often by new or emerging writers, and furthers the Imperiolis' commitment to improving New York's cultural life.

Imperioli also found success on television with a recurring role on *Law & Order* as detective Nick Falco. Along with his work on television and in the theater and in films, he has formed a punk rock band called La Dolce Vita. Imperioli also starred in the short-lived ABC crime drama, *Detroit 1-8-7*, before its cancellation in 2011. Recently, he has starred in the psychological thriller *Mad Dogs* and was co-host alongside Steve Schirripa of *Talking Sopranos*, a highly successful podcast that highlighted both men's time on *The Sopranos*.

Enough prelude, here's Michael's Street Smart Memoir:

"Street Smart to me is, above all, a sense, or sensitivity toward other beings...it is something that one develops through interacting with others, for better or for worse, over the course of one's life. In that respect, I see it as a personal journey. A journey of being open to, present for, and aware of other beings (both human and animal) in a very conscious way. The interactions and impressions one will manifest will usually be determined by how one sees the world at that time, or how one sees one's own place in the world. Usually, one's outlook will reflect itself in what manifests in the world, so what you bring to the streets is as much a factor in what you perceive as are the other beings you encounter in 'the streets,' and by 'the streets' I really mean 'the world.'

"If one is lucky enough to move in the direction of altruism or compassion over the course of one's life, one can bring this quality to the streets as well; of course, the converse is also true. But in general, the golden rule always seems to apply: 'Do unto others as you would have them do unto you.' Street Smart thus equals wisdom, and if one can act from a place of wisdom, in friendship, love, career, and in the streets, undoubtedly one's life will be richer, and you can perhaps then start to benefit others.

"When I was twenty-three years old, I was cast in the first significant film role of my then one-year-old career in movies. I had actually done three tiny little one-line things in three films over the course of the year prior, this after five solid years of knocking on doors, submitting fraudulent resumes, lying about my union status or additional skills. (Fluent in Italian? Of course! *Not*. Able to sing Opera? Absolutely! Thank God I never actually had to prove it!)

"Basically I finagled, conned, and scammed however I could to get my foot in the door, but the one I speak of here is different; this was a whole new ballgame, and ballgame was how I have referred to it over the years: like if I was pitching for some one-horse podunk C-level college team in Nowheresville and got called up to relief pitch for the Yankees in Game 7 of the World Series. I am talking, of course about *Goodfellas*. I am talking about Martin Scorsese, Joe Pesci, Nick Pileggi, Ray Liotta, oh yeah, and Robert De Niro!

"Now, for a kid who grew up in New York in the '70s and '80s, this crew was DiMaggio, Mantle, Maris, and Lou Gehrig. It did not get any bigger. Was I thrilled? Of course. Was I nervous? Surprisingly not!

"My enthusiasm and sheer excitement drowned out the nerves...and as deluded as this may sound for a twenty-three-year-old newbie: I felt like I belonged there, like I had earned the right to be there. I guess Marty did too, because when I got to set, he welcomed me warmly and said if I had any questions, do not hesitate and come find him. 'Oh...one last thing, Michael...treat the actors like the characters both on and off screen.'

"*Bam*! Whoa! Now, that I never heard before, but that made sense. I mean this is the team that made *Taxi Driver*, *Mean Streets*, and *Raging Bull*, for Christ's sake. Yes! Commit to the character, commit to the world, go all in or go home, so I went all in. I walked on the set and told the prop guy that I want to be in charge of the card table and reset all the props, like drinks, ashtrays, cigarettes, cards...everything. (If you haven't seen the film and don't know the scene, put this down immediately, go watch it, and we can chat later.)

"In hindsight and after three more decades of film work, I still marvel at the sheer balls I had that day to ask a crew member to basically let me do his job! A job that had strict union parameters, no less, but Marty saw where I was going and encouraged me. Then I noticed that the little bar (where I made drinks for the lovable psychopaths I would be serving) was set up with the bottles behind me, which would have me with my back turned every time I poured the booze. Bad idea, so now I became the set decorator and rearranged the bar and the bottles in a way that would allow me to make drinks and keep an eye on the guys at all times.

"Because this was my job. Like Marty said, 'treat the actors like the characters.' Well, the characters were dangerous dudes who best be served promptly, so now I was ready to work. I had made the card room mine, my place of work.

"Suddenly, *he* walked in. Yes. Travis Bickle, Jake LaMotta, Johnny Boy, Don Vito Corleone! Robert De Niro walks on set and sits down and starts shuffling a deck of cards. Again, for a twenty-three-year-old Italian American New York actor, this was the Father, Son, and Holy Ghost; it did not get more big league than this. And here I was in the same room with him. But lo and behold!

"I was not scared. No, on the contrary, my balls were as big as Brooklyn that day: 'treat the actor like the character, Michael.' So, I walked up to Jimmy Burke (yes, the character he played in the film) and said, 'What are you drinking, Jimmy?'

"He paused, looked up at me, looked back at the table, looked up at me again, and finally said, 'Shot of scotch and a glass of water.' I went back to the bar, made Jimmy his drink, and delivered it to him.

"The next thing I heard was the greatest filmmaker in history saying, 'Okay, let's rehearse.'

"The rest is history."

So, for a tough-guy actor from New York, we get a brilliant rendition of Street Smart in Hollywood. It's no accident that his Street Smarts come through in his craft and in his career. Michael, you see, is the real thing. A Street Scholar who happens to also play one on television and movies. He's not a character actor. He's a Street Smart persona who happens to use it as a living in a more direct fashion.

STREET SMART MEMOIR OF TONY LO BIANCO
After COVID, "There's A Different Human Being Out There"

Tony hails from Brooklyn, so you know he has Street Smart potential. Tony's vivid warning to you should not be ignored: Street Smart, post-COVID, is shrinking because people are being taught to emotionalize every aspect of their life. But don't take our word for it...listen to Tony's advice...in your face and very personal. Tony knows his business and has the respect and credibility from people of all walks of life.

Tony Lo Bianco has appeared in over one hundred films, television programs, and stage performances, both on-screen and off as a writer, director, and producer.

Off-Broadway, Mr. Lo Bianco won an Obie Award for best actor in Jonathan Reynolds's *Yanks 3, Detroit 0, Top of the Seventh*. Following his memorable performance as Eddie Carbone in Arthur Miller's *A View from the Bridge* on Broadway, he was nominated for the Tony Award for best actor and won the Outer Critics Circle Award. He also received an Emmy Award for *Hizzoner! The Life of Fiorello La Guardia*. Tony won two Emmys for his work on the video honoring veterans, *Just a Common Soldier*.

His best known film performances are as Sal Boca in the Academy Award-winning *The French Connection*, as Ray Fernandez in cult classic *The Honeymoon Killers*; as Peter in *God Told Me To*; *Bloodbrothers* with Richard Gere; *City Heat* with Clint Eastwood and Burt Reynolds; Oliver Stone's *Nixon* with Anthony Hopkins; *The Juror* with Alec Baldwin and Demi Moore; *F.I.S.T.* with Sylvester Stallone; *Kill the Irishman* alongside Vincent D'Onofrio, Val Kilmer, and Christopher Walken; and *The Engagement Ring* with Lainie Kazan and Patricia Heaton.

On television, Mr. Lo Bianco starred as the undefeated heavyweight champ Rocky Marciano in *Marciano*, and again in the remake, *The Rocky Marciano Story* with George C. Scott and Jon Favreau. He appeared in the miniseries *Marco Polo* and Franco Zeffirelli's *Jesus of Nazareth* with Lawrence Olivier and Anthony Quinn; and he co-starred in *La Romana* with Gina Lollobrigida and in *The Last Tenant* with legendary acting teacher Lee Strasberg.

As a director, Mr. Lo Bianco directed episodes of television series *Police Story*, *Kaz*, and the feature film *Too Scared to Scream* and is now in the process of writing and will direct in his new film based on his younger years.

Mr. Lo Bianco co-founded the Triangle Theater and served as artistic director for six years, during which time lighting designer Jules Fisher, playwright Jason Miller, and actor Roy Scheider, as well as many others, performed there. Mr. Lo Bianco himself directed eight of the productions and produced twenty-five others. He is currently teaching acting and is a lifetime member of The Actors Studio.

Mr. Lo Bianco served as the national spokesperson for the order Sons of Italy. His many humanitarian efforts have earned multiple awards, including the Eleanora Duse Award for outstanding contribution to the performing arts; Man of the Year for outstanding contributions to the Italian American community from the Police Society of New Jersey; a Man of the Year award from the State of New Jersey Senate; a lifetime entertainment award from the Columbus Day Parade Committee; the 1997 Golden Lion Award; the Humanitarian Award of the Boys' Town of Italy; and the Ellis Island Medal of honor. He is a member of the Italian American National Hall of Fame and is a recipient of the Louis Prima Arts and Entertainment Award.

We let Tony take over from here.

"Having been born in Brooklyn, yeah, of course I believe in Street Smarts. I'm not talking about being born in the Brooklyn of today. I'm talking about the Brooklyn of the past (1936) when life was a lot different and there was a lot more struggle. You got the struggle from your parents because they were struggling. Remember, WWI was over in 1918. The Depression, 1929, WWII started in 1941, and I was five years old in 1941. Think of the drama.

"My mother was a housewife, and my father a cabdriver. Not many people were taking taxis in those days.

"In truth, Street Smart is a mystery because my older brother was not Street Smart. He was a very good man, a very sweet fellow. My hero. He believed in the goodness of everything and was a real fabulous person and physically very strong. But he was also gullible and naïve, which generally comes along with all those other good qualities. And fortunately or unfortunately, I was a feisty, fighting kid who constantly challenged myself and others.

"How and why does that happen? Each of us comes from the same mother and father and have the same DNA, but we are different human beings except for our strong love for each. That love was so strong that it was noticed and admired by other family members, neighbors, and friends. We had an enviable, unbreakable bond between us.

"In my case, the Street Smarts came from what I observed and experienced. How I saw and what I learned from history. History is the teacher. It came from the stories of my mother and father and the relatives and from what was happening at that time in the world and in my surroundings, in my relationships with friends in the neighborhood and from the radio, listening and using your imagination. That's what makes a person wise and ready.

"I always say that New York is different than Los Angeles because we have more crowded streets, and more climate changes. Los Angeles has one summer, people going along and singing a song and not having any confrontations, yet confrontations are what give you education and experience.

"So, the differences between New York and Los Angeles are the four seasons, the change of weather, the people in the street that you encounter as you walk by, those people that you bump into as you pass by, and all the other stuff that goes on making conflicts. Every time you bang into something, you are learning something important. That is, if you are not a victim, and to me, a victim is someone who allows themselves to get banged into or knocked around and become someone's passive pawn for others to manipulate.

"You keep learning, and if you have an aggressive constitution, one that is going to battle against getting knocked into, and you are not kept from distasteful, unkind, terrible happenings, you will be prepared for life when you encounter it later on. And, as an actor/director, it has helped me to understand so much about people and their thought processes, fears, and actions. That's what life is all about. And you don't learn just from being passive. You don't learn from the sun shining or from every day being the same.

"What happens from that, as you can see in the world today, and the same thing in America, we as a civilized country have gotten soft. We have put a clicker in our hands. We've put in a button to press to dismiss and to answer questions. We have taken the work ethic out of a society.

"Now, Street Smart uses the word "smart." It's a very short-sounding word with a tremendous meaning, but the explanation and definition would take a long time.

"Learning from the streets and being 'street wise' comes from history, conflict, self-conflict, battling with others, other nationalities, opinions, and so on and so forth, and that is all to be learned from.

"That is what is lost in our world today. We have not seemed to learn and look to the future of what is going to happen if we do this. The saying 'Just Do It' is as stupid as can be. You don't 'just do it,' you have to know the consequences of what happens when you 'do it,' or what is in front of you before you 'do it.' You don't step into a puddle, you don't step into a hole, and you don't 'just do it' if you don't look ahead.

"If you want to call that wise, that's simplicity. That's common sense, which seems to be something we no longer have. The truth and the history and the facts seem to have all gone by the boards.

"So, hearing stories from your mother and your father who struggled and were taken out of school when they were seven or eight years old to go to work to support the big families that they had back then and to understand their mentality gives you wisdom on how to handle the future so you can add it up. You see one and one, you see two and two, you see what four people in a room is, the size of the room, how big that is. Simple things.

"I don't like to ever be in debt, so I never have been. I've made some very, very wise moves and am very self-sufficient. I'm a kid from Brooklyn with very little education, but I have three homes. I've done everything by knowledge of history, of how to get here, how to get there, and what to do if this happens.

"Get ready for all the things that are going to go bad, and that way you are going to be ready for it. You are going to be prepared.

"My hands are very quick. If something is going to fall off the table, I'm confident that I am going to catch it because I anticipate that it is going to happen.

"And I have learned to know people. I watch people's behavior most of the time and how and why they say something, and how they say it, if they are telling the truth or not, or meaning something else other than the words they speak. All of that is part of the wisdom of knowledge. That way you can tell the future.

"I have a very good ability to say what is going to happen before it happens. That is from looking from the past. I like to cook because the ingredients you put into a dish to make it taste good are what is important. The same ingredients you put into life makes your opinions and makes you see.

"I'm a very good negotiator. In order to negotiate, you have to know the value of what it is you are negotiating, of course, and how much you want it and what price you are willing to go to. At that price, you can say, well, let's say it is a car that you want to buy and it's a car that you really want; however, the price is high and after negotiating, if it is still too high for what you have in the bank, or for how you can pay for it, then you don't get it. Period. That's common sense and logic.

"It isn't a question of being disappointed; at the moment it's just out of your reach, out of your league. Period. Common sense and logic. And that shouldn't make for unhappiness. These are the facts of life, and that is what you have to follow a great deal.

"I have been great at negotiating in my life and, in fact, most of the jobs I have in terms of my career I negotiated myself, even though I have an agent. I let the agent do his job. When he says, 'that's it, that's as far as they can go,' then I make the decision whether to say no to the project, or ask for this more and that less, and to get what I want.

"I would say 99 percent of the time I have not lost a job because of negotiating. I've turned down jobs that I didn't want to do because I just didn't want to do the project. Even with apartments. I've negotiated a great deal. I won't go into that, but I have gotten remarkable things about getting an apartment for a certain amount of money, then getting another apartment and having the landlord give me $25,000 to renovate the kitchen area in that apartment.

"Then land. I bought two acres of land that was offered at $20,000, and I eventually got the seller down to $12,000. And I negotiated to pay it off at $90 per month. This was in a very expensive neighborhood in South Salem, New York.

"What advice can I give readers on how to use Street Smarts? I only know how to get Street Smarts. You need to go out and learn from history. You have to learn about people and cultures, thinking and hearing stories that will make you Street Smart, because without that knowledge in your system, you are not just going to rattle it off the top of your head—you are going to have to earn it. You learn from it, from where it comes from.

"It comes from hard work, from difficulty, and from knowing about human beings. Knowing about what people want and need.

"I know that there's a different human being out there now, in 2021 or 2022. They are being educated incorrectly. They are being taught to be racist. They are being told to be guilty for being white. They are telling males to be more feminine, and females to be more masculine, all sorts of things that really screw up your mind and your whole system. That confusion is a detriment to our country and to the whole human race.

"They want to change how we refer to each other, and yes, there are politicians who want to 'fundamentally change' America."

So says Street Scholar Tony Lo Bianco. And we don't know how to differ. Maybe it's in the DNA, as he seems to allude to. Since Street Smart has an origin, and everyone has it, it might be a nurture-versus-nature situation. But the mean streets...we believe...have a lot to do with it. Is it triggered by Street Smart or vice versa? That's for another book.

STREET SMART MEMOIR OF ARIANNA HUFFINGTON
The First Trailblazing Street Smart Internet Influencer

Arianna Huffington was the first, and most influential, "internet influencer." She agrees that Street Smart makes the difference between success and simply not succeeding. Intuition plays a major part in her Street Smart system. She boldly went where no one went...and only later followed. That she learned her wisdom in cosmopolitan Greece solidifies our argument that vibrant and overcrowded venues foster the most Street Smart.

A short set of notes for your reading follows:

Arianna Huffington is an author, philanthropist, television personality, and founder of the independently liberal online news magazine, *The Huffington Post*. Originally from Greece, she moved to England when she was sixteen and graduated from Cambridge University with an MA in economics. At twenty-one, she became president of the famed debating society, The Cambridge Union, and was the first foreign-born student to do so. After graduation, she made her mark as a conservative syndicated columnist, and with the launch of *The Huffington Post* a few years later, she created an online voice portal which offered critical observations on the political scenario. Her celebrity status helped her in getting several high-profile contributors to post their views on politics, news, and culture.

In 2003, she decided to contest as an independent candidate in the California recall election to replace then-governor Gray Davis. Apart from this, she also led a Detroit project to promote fuel-efficient cars. In 2009, she was named by *Forbes* as one of the 'Most Influential Women in Media,' gaining twelfth position in the list. In the same year, the *Guardian* included her in the "Top 100 Media" list. In 2011, AOL Inc. acquired *The Huffington Post* and made her president, which included many then-existing AOL properties too such as Engadget, AOL Music, StyleList, and Patch Media.

But she takes over here:

"Yes, having grown up in Greece, I can say that the idea of Street Smart is very much appreciated there. There's not a god of Street Smart, but if there were, it would probably be some combination of Athena, goddess of wisdom, and Tyche, goddess of chance, with a bit of Dolos, god of cunning and craftiness (though without his penchant for trickery).

"To me, it's about being able to tap into your own inner wisdom and intuition and recognize when unlikely solutions present themselves. Being Street Smart means being present and in the moment, so we can see opportunities that we might otherwise miss.

"One that comes to mind happened when I had just written my second book. It was about political leadership, and I really believed in it. Unfortunately, publishers—many publishers—didn't. I had gotten twenty-five rejections when I ran out of money. And at that point, I might have said, 'You know what, twenty-five publishers think this is not worth publishing. Maybe I've picked the wrong career.' But I didn't, because a moment of Street Smart struck instead.

"I was walking down St. James's Street in London, where I was living at the time, when I saw Barclays bank. I was out of money. But right here was a place that has lots of money—and part of their business is giving it away, at least temporarily. So armed with a bit of chutzpah and Street Smart (the two are closely related), I thought, why don't I just go in there and ask them for a loan? Can't hurt—and the worst they can say is no. So, I asked to see the bank manager and asked for an overdraft—that's what they called loans in England at the time. And for some reason, even though I had no assets to offer up as collateral, he gave the loan to me. And that extra money to live on made it possible for me to continue for another thirteen rejections until I finally got a yes from a publisher on number thirty-seven. The bank manager's name is Ian Bell, and I still send him a Christmas card every year.

"Opportunities to use Street Smart aren't always obvious or apparent. You have to be open and available to them. And for that, you have to be connected with your own antennae and intuition.

"I just put two and two together—I needed money, so why not go to the place that has money? I'm sure I passed lots of banks in the weeks leading up to that time, as I fretted about running out of money. But sometimes the simplest solution is the Street Smart solution—we just have to be in a mindset that lets us see a situation with a fresh eye.

"When faced with problems or challenges that we can't find an obvious solution to, we need to unplug, recharge, and connect with ourselves. It's in the calm eye of the hurricane that we can tap into our creativity, intuition, and insight—which is to say, our Street Smart."

Again, a Street Smart-er knows, uses (spots, seizes, and exploits) a lucky break or breaks as here in Arianna's case. As she says, you have to allow yourself to see these moments of opportunity, or they very well could go to waste.

STREET SMART MEMOIR OF MARIA BARTIROMO
Own It!!

One night, Rock wanted to introduce his daughter, Riana, to a person who he had known since childhood, Maria Bartiromo. Rock knew Maria and her brother Patty from his teen years. He and Patty had a band and would practice at Patty's house in Dyker Heights in Brooklyn on Saturday afternoons. However, to use this rehearsal space, the band struck a deal with Patty and Maria's parents: the teenagers had to babysit Maria. From an early age, everyone knew the girl nicknamed "Bullet" (attributed to her amazing speed) was clearly headed for the big time.

Riana absolutely idolized Maria, and on this particular night during dinner, Maria used a term that summed up her storied career: "own it." Go for what you want, stay focused and direct, be honest with yourself about what you want, and don't let anything stand in your way. That made quite an impression on young Riana, and it was the night Rock recognized that Maria had a PhD in Street Smart education.

First, we offer a personal word on Maria. She comes from a decent, hardworking, and amazingly industrious family, and she worked part-time at their Rex Tavern and Restaurant in Brooklyn. That was on 60th Street, not far from where Anthony Fauci lived and a little farther than where we lived on 24th Avenue and 65th Street. She was a check-coat girl: remarkably streetwise and affable.

Now, she heard a lot of street language, and we believe she heard a lot of tips on what was going on in the neighborhood of Dr. Fauci and our own. There were no wallflowers at the Rex. The Rex was located in what only can be called an industrial neighborhood.

They had great Italian food, with a fantastic brick-oven pizza (our father used to bring one home some Saturday nights). He worked there in the house band as a piano player with Maria's uncle, Carmine, who played the tenor saxophone.

Maria Bartiromo joined Fox Business Network (FBN) as global markets editor in January 2014. She is the anchor of *Mornings with Maria* on FBN (6:00–9:00 AM/ET) and anchors *Sunday Morning Futures*, the most watched Sunday morning program on cable (10:00 AM/ET) on Fox News Channel (FNC). In April 2017, Bartiromo was named the new anchor for FBN's weekly primetime investing program *Wall Street Week* (Fridays at 8:00 PM/ET).

In November 2015 Bartiromo, along with FBN's Neil Cavuto, moderated the network's inaugural Republican presidential primary debate. According to Nielsen data, the debate delivered 13.5 million total viewers and 3.7 million in the key twenty-five-to-fifty-four demo, making it the highest-rated program in network history. In January 2016, both Bartiromo and Cavuto reprised their role as debate moderators, delivering 11 million total viewers with 3 million in the twenty-five-to-fifty-four demo, making it the second highest-rated program in network history according to Nielsen Media Research.

Bartiromo has covered business and the economy for more than twenty-five years and was one of the building blocks of business cable network CNBC. During her twenty-year tenure as the face of CNBC, she launched the network's morning program, *Squawk Box*; anchored *Closing Bell with Maria Bartiromo*; and was the anchor and managing editor of the nationally syndicated *On the Money with Maria Bartiromo*, formerly *The Wall Street Journal Report with Maria Bartiromo*.

Bartiromo has been a pioneer in her industry. In 1995, she became the first journalist to report live from the floor of the New York Stock Exchange on a daily basis. She joined CNBC in 1993 after five years as a producer, writer, and assignment editor with CNN Business News, where she wrote and produced some of CNN's top business programs.

She has received numerous prestigious awards, including two Emmys and a Gracie Award. Her first Emmy was for her 2008 news and documentary coverage of the 2007–2008 financial collapse and her "Bailout Talks Collapse" coverage was broadcast on NBC Nightly News. She later won a second Emmy for her

2009 documentary, *Inside the Mind of Google*, which aired globally on CNBC. Bartiromo won a Gracie Award for "Greenspan: Power, Money & the American Dream," also broadcast globally on CNBC.

In 2009, the *Financial Times* named her one of the "50 Faces That Shaped the Decade," and she was the first female journalist to be inducted into the Cable Hall of Fame Class of 2011. In 2016, she was inducted by the Library of American Broadcasting as one of its Giants of Broadcasting & Electronic Arts. Bartiromo is the author of several books, including *The Weekend That Changed Wall Street*, published by Portfolio/Penguin, and *The 10 Laws of Enduring Success*, published by Random House; both were released in 2010.

Bartiromo has written weekly columns for *Business Week* and *Milano Finanza* magazines; as well as monthly columns for *USA Today*, *Individual Investor*, *Ticker*, and *Reader's Digest* magazines. She has been published in the *Financial Times*, *Newsweek*, *Town and Country*, *Registered Rep*, and the *New York Post*.

Bartiromo is a member of the board of trustees of New York University, the Council on Foreign Relations, and the Economic Club of New York. She graduated from New York University, where she studied journalism and economics. She also served as an adjunct professor at NYU Stern School of Business for the fall semesters of 2010 through 2013.

Maria is precise and clear-cut, and we could all learn valuable lessons from her "in your face" and honest appraisal of the many obstacles that she has overcome.

"Yes, Street Smart is something I learned in Brooklyn and from my hard-working family. It's an instinct. A confidence and a savvy.

"Yes. Every day I have to interview different people from all walks of life. My Street Smart always [gives] me an edge. It's real. Not fake. It's the ability to cut through the clutter and noise and get to the important point. People usually are attracted to real honesty, and they run from fake because it's not genuine.

"I can tell when someone is not telling me the truth. I can tell when they may be hiding something. I can tell when they are genuine and when they are not so genuine. I have become a very good judge of character. It's my instinct, and it never fails me. It's because I've seen it all in Brooklyn. I've seen people who try to take shortcuts, and I have seen people who are overachievers and work incredibly hard to accomplish something. I can see a fake coming from a mile away—that person who tries to cut corners. That's Street Smart.

"I seized on Street Smart constantly while working on the floor of the New York Stock Exchange, where I traded for twenty years. I had to read people and read the room. I had to understand who was buying and who was selling and at what price. I had to read 'poker faces.' I had to assess the situation with my instincts and sharp elbows. I had to push back on a man's world of 'suits' who thought they were smarter than me. They weren't. I had Street Smart.

"I remember when I went to Alaska right before the 2008 presidential primary to interview the governor, Sarah Palin. She was not in the spotlight at all at this time. I was doing a piece about Alaska and the potential for energy production. But while I was in her office, I had a funny feeling she wasn't telling me something. It was just an instinct. So, I asked her—has Senator John McCain called you? Are you going to be John McCain's running mate in this election? She looked at her PR guy and then looked down. And I knew it was true. I had hit a nerve. I knew because she didn't look me in the eye. She was hiding the fact that McCain called and asked her the day before. They announced it a week later. It was my Street Smarts that served me well. I kept pushing and asking more questions.

"Knowledge comes from a lot of different places. And different people. One of my strengths is I have sources everywhere. I have business sources, personal sources and friends: friends from Brooklyn, contacts in Europe, in Asia, and the Middle East. I have contacts in the Italian American community. My sources trust me because I am a woman of my word. I am not fake. I am who I say I am. And I expect the people I deal with to be true to who they say they are too. If they are not true, I do not stick around. If I do not trust you, you are out. Trust is everything.

"When pursuing your dreams, don't forget all of your sources—knowledge can come from anywhere. Tap into it. Tap into your Street Smarts. Sometimes Street Smart comes from failure. If you fall down, don't stay down. Get up. Assess what happened and what lesson can you take away from that setback. Use it as a teachable moment. Glean the Street Smarts from the situation."

All that being said, Street Smart comes from modest beginnings and a honing of the skill from daily usage. Maria is cohesive and cogent proof of its existence and of its origin. Using a failure as a teaching moment in Street Smart theory and practice is a valuable tip from a Street Scholar like Maria. Taken from an accomplished woman of means, all hard-fought means, must be graphic enough for culling wisdom from her earliest days hunched in that checkroom in Brooklyn.

STREET SMART MEMOIR OF TONY JAMES
Timing Is Everything

In the market, timing is everything, and according to the *Wall St. Journal*, Tony James times it like a maestro. But the timing of a lucky break means nothing if the timing is not married to a sense of Street Smart. So says Tony James, an admitted small-town boy who went on to achieve enormous respect, success, and wealth.

And if you were expecting a monomaniac for a billionaire's assent, Tony is as modest and forgiving as he is brilliant. His take on Street Smart exactly overlaps the dozens of other Street Smart Memoirs.

Hamilton "Tony" E. James is the former president, COO, and executive vice chairman of Blackstone, and a member of Blackstone's board of directors. He is also a former member of Blackstone's management committee and sits on the firm's various investment committees.

Prior to joining Blackstone in 2002, Mr. James was chairman of global investment banking and private equity at Credit Suisse First Boston and a member of the executive board. Prior to the acquisition of Donaldson, Lufkin & Jenrette by Credit Suisse First Boston in 2000, Mr. James was the Chairman of DLJ's banking group, responsible for all the firm's investment banking and merchant banking activities. Mr. James joined DLJ in 1975, became head of DLJ's global M&A group in 1982, founded DLJ Merchant Banking, Inc. in 1985, and was named chairman of the banking group in 1995.

Mr. James is chairman of the board of directors of Costco and has served on a number of other corporate boards. He is also is co-chair of The Metropolitan Museum of Art, chairman of the finance committee of the Mount Sinai Health System, member of the Center for American Progress board of trustees, vice chairman of Trout Unlimited's Coldwater Conservation Fund, vice chairman of the board of trustees of the Wildlife Conservation Society, among many others.

In 2018, Mr. James co-authored the second edition of *Rescuing Retirement*, a book proposing a solution to America's looming retirement crisis. The first edition was published in 2016. He has also published articles in the *New York Times*, the *Wall Street Journal*, *Financial Times*, the *Harvard Business Review* and other major publications.

Mr. James graduated magna cum laude with a BA from Harvard College in 1973 and was a John Harvard Scholar. He earned an MBA with high distinction from the Harvard Business School and graduated as a Baker Scholar in 1975.

After leaving Blackstone, Mr. James began a new business endeavor called Jefferson River Capital, which makes investments in a variety of marketable areas, which include technology and real estate. Currently, alongside his wife Amabel, Tony is focused on changing the world with the James Family Charitable Foundation, a philanthropic organization centered around funding for the arts, education, environmental conservation, and many health organizations.

"What is Street Smart? Thousands of years ago it meant knowing how to navigate safely through the jungle, understanding the habits of prey, and being able to consistently bring meat home—without ending up as someone else's main course.

"These days, we mostly think of Street Smart as being able to make your way through urban ghettos without getting into trouble. But in reality, with today's genteel streets, that is not the world most of us live in. Can it be useful in extreme circumstances? Yes, but hardly a critical life skill in modern America.

"Being Street Smart in a broader context is still helpful—even critical—for success in today's world. Politics or business, large organizations or small, social, school, community, or even family gatherings all require the same basic type of Street Smarts you would need in the jungle or ghetto. Today's threats may not be physical, but power, ego, success, recognition, and financial rewards can all be on the line. Huge gains or devastating setbacks can be at stake. You need a high level of situational awareness and the ability to instinctively read subtle signs in order to anticipate what might happen. You need a knack for pattern recognition that allows you to see around corners. When a certain set of circumstances occurs, you know the odds are elevated for a certain result. And you need to develop coping mechanisms, both offensive and defensive, to take advantage of the situation and have an instinct for the results different actions will elicit.

"Experience helps with all this, but some people can translate their learnings from past experiences to the situation at hand much more effectively than others. Though corporate boardrooms are a long way from the jungles of yesterday, being Street Smart is still necessary in the modern world.

"I certainly never thought of myself as Street Smart growing up. To the contrary, really. I was a very average small-town boy. (We all were, which was a great blessing in retrospect.) Our town was the kind of place where you rode your bike to school most days, and damming up the brook behind our house was an exciting activity every spring.

"There were no wealth, class, or status distinctions perceptible amongst us kids. The ten-cent weekly allowance I got would buy one Mars bar. If I wanted more than that, I had to work. Like everyone, I had no skills, but there was no reasonable work I wouldn't do. Nothing was beneath me or too much drudgery.

"The girls were smart, the boys clueless. I still remember what a revelation it was when one of the boys said one day: 'It is more important to be smart than it is to be a good athlete.' Clearly, I belonged in the clueless group.

"But that allowed us kids to remain kids a lot longer. We could develop at our own pace without being programmed or even pushed to excel. There were, of course, a few kids who were more focused or more talented and spurted ahead. But so what? There was no finish line, and life's road loomed long and obscure. There was no real way to know who was ahead. Although it was clear that some people were falling behind, that seemed as much a matter of their personal choice as anything else.

"Slowly I gravitated to the view that I could try harder than others. I could work harder, I could puzzle out problems longer, and I was willing to put up with more pain. Though I was slow to develop physically, I hit the big guys hard in our backyard tackle football games (no helmets or pads). My whole side might be numb, but I never showed it, and they stopped wanting to run the ball as hard. Even in elementary school, I stayed up all night long if necessary to complete homework assignments. And I always wanted to do things my way, without help or handouts from anyone.

"Our little town was too small for its own high school, so I went away to boarding school after ninth grade. That was a shock! The other students were bigger, more sophisticated, and better prepared. It was a tough place, and the environment was decidedly hostile to people who were vulnerable. I struggled to find my footing. Of course, I hated it and was under the disapproving eye of the administration for consistently failing to get basic things done on time. I finally made it through the first semester with a D in English and mediocre grades in everything else but math. But over the next two and a half years, I ground it out. I adapted. I learned first to accommodate then to beat the system. And ultimately, I ended up near the top of the heap.

"In the process, I learned some valuable lessons.

"First, failures are not fatal. In fact, you learn more from your failures than from your victories. Difficulties are inevitable. Don't get overwhelmed. Tackle big challenges one little piece at a time. Do as much as you can and never give up. How you deal with adversity will determine the course of your life.

"Second, you need to find some oases—safe spaces that are restorative where you can immerse yourself and find fun or even exuberance. As life progresses, they will evolve. But find these spaces and protect them. They were critical for me.

"Third, the brain is an amazing tool, and knowledge is its fuel. Creativity, wisdom, and even genius are often just learning something in one context and applying it to a completely different situation. So many people stop learning or never fully realize the power of their own brains.

"And finally, don't be a victim. You *can* control your own destiny. Do not concede that to others, either pro or con. There are plenty of other capable people out there, some with natural talents beyond comprehension. But we can each succeed because there is no substitute for grit, determination, and hard work.

"These may not be Street Smarts in the usual sense of those words, but they are lessons I have learned on the avenues of life, and they have guided me through hard times. Throughout my career, they have helped me develop the attitudes and habits to survive difficult or professionally dangerous situations. They have kept me safe from deception and trickery. Prioritizing learning and working harder than others has facilitated seeing new situations in the context of old ones. Being alert to signals helps with reading people and circumstances and knowing how to respond. Finally, understanding how to evolve and drive an organization's environment to be a better fit with my own skills and personality has been a powerful enabler. All of these are 'street skills' being applied in the context of elite business organizations. For me, they have worked well."

Tony James is the American Dream, of course, and he says he used Street Smart to get there. They worked well for Tony, and it separated him from the rest. Tony is also a great example of not needing to be born and bred in New York to be a Street Scholar. His humble and honest telling of how he became Street Smart serves as a model blueprint for any student wanting to learn from a master.

STREET SMART MEMOIR OF REP. PETER KING
From Loading Dock to Congress Kingmaker

Peter King is a legend in American, let alone New York, politics. When he retired from politics, New York, including his native Long Island, lost a magnificent voice of Street Smart. That may not matter that much to the reader. But in an era where COVID has divided America, the common sense of working together against a common enemy (higher crime or COVID) has been replaced by a vicious and partisan playbook on all sides.

Playbooks won't conquer COVID or crime. Nothing about this is "playing," except playing for keeps. Rep. King (Republican,

Suffolk County) is a street fighter. So who better to develop Street Smart than Peter King?

He's the rare political leader in an era of mere politicians.

Rep. King was the Republican congressional representative from New York, from January 3, 1993 to January 3, 2021. He decided not to run for reelection in 2020. Rep. King graduated from St. Francis College in Brooklyn in 1965 and earned his Juris Doctor (JD) from the University of Notre Dame Law School in 1968. His father, Peter King, Sr., was a New York City police officer.

Rep. King became involved in the Northern Ireland peace process. He served as chairman for the US House of Homeland Security and was a committee member on the US House Financial Services Committee, the Permanent Selection Committee on Intelligence, and the House Counter-Terrorism Subcommittee. All cut and dried, but here's his take on Street Smart.

"I start off with the premise that any New York City kid who grew up in a blue-collar neighborhood in the 1940s, '50s, or '60s should have Street Smarts. Even if you had the most concerned parents, there wasn't the time or money for them to guide or protect from you from all of life's harsh realities. Every neighborhood had some very tough guys. (A friend of mine's brother went to the electric chair.) But for the most part, violence wasn't random, and you learned to work your way around tough situations—and not be in the wrong place at the wrong time.

"You also learned the necessity of hard work. My father was NYPD before cops made much and always had at least two part-time jobs. He never complained. That's the way it was. Life didn't owe you a living. In my own case, during my last two years going to St. Francis College in Brooklyn full time, I had a full-time job loading and unloading trucks and freight cars at the

Railway Express Terminal on the West Side of Manhattan. This wasn't easy, but it wasn't as tough as it sounds. While the job was 'full time,' I worked deals with the foremen and bosses to let me maneuver my way to adjust my schedule when needed either by switching shifts or working just enough hours to keep my full-time status. I also made sure to keep my union membership intact in case someone dropped a letter on me for 'absenteeism.' I had to do a lot of balancing and juggling, but I kept the job for those college years. I spent more time on the loading dock than in the classroom, but I was able to pay all my college tuition and personal expenses, put a good amount of money in the bank, and still get a good education.

"In many ways though, I was living in two worlds. College student by day. Freight loader by night. The Railway Express was a college experience of its own. Many really good guys but also the numbers-runners, bookies, gamblers, and the guys trying to scrape together enough cash to pay off the loan sharks. Almost everyone I worked with was fifteen, twenty years older than me, which is a lot when you're nineteen or twenty. So not only did REA give me enough money to afford Notre Dame Law School, it gave me real world experience with people beyond my years— the good, the bad and the ugly. Street Smarts!

"The experiences of these formative years were invaluable to me surviving and getting ahead in politics. The Nassau Republican Party, with more than two thousand active committeemen and women, was by far the best organized and most tightly run in the country. When I moved to Nassau County after law school in 1971, I knew no one in or out of politics. I joined the local Seaford club off the street and showed that I had at least half a brain and was willing to work. (Getting petitions signed and handing out campaign brochures is a lot easier than loading trucks in sub-freezing weather.) Then events occurred in quick succession: becoming one of the two thousand county committeemen; taking a patronage job in the county attorney's office; getting myself assigned to the newly opened Nassau Coliseum where I met with big shots in basketball, hockey, boxing, and organized labor; managing Congressman Norm Lent's re-election campaign; and then running myself to succeed the Seaford GOP leader, who was resigning to become a judge.

"To the initiated, this might not seem so important, but winning the local leadership would put me on the County Executive Committee where Chairman Joe Margiotta called the shots. In many ways, this was my toughest race ever. There were thirty-three Seaford committeemen. All were older and most more experienced than me.

"I had been living in Seaford less than four years. My opponent had lived there for decades and was the building commissioner with control over jobs and permits. I had to piece together seventeen votes one by one—from sanitation and highway department workers to corporate officials. The seventeenth vote came when I got a guy to sign a proxy when he was on a stretcher just before being put in the ambulance on his way to the emergency room.

"The next year saw a monumental power struggle between Joe Margiotta and county executive Ralph Caso. I sided with Margiotta and along with others was soon out of my county job in a move which made the front pages and was entitled the 'New Year's Massacre.' Most observers saw this as devastating. I saw it as opportunity. In political terms, I was a victim and a standup guy. They 'owed' me.

"With (US senator) Al D'Amato's strong help and Joe Margiotta's nod, I again jumped the line and got the nomination for town councilman. A few years later I was elected county comptroller and took on a number of tough fights with more powerful and better-financed opponents, almost always coming out ahead whether the adversary was the MTA, LILCO, or local school bus companies. I also had highly publicized encounters with the British embassy over the oppression of Catholics in Northern Ireland and was elected grand marshal of the NYC St. Patrick's Cathedral in an upset win over the parade committee favorite.

"In all these instances I believed strongly in what I was doing and used my Street Smarts to gather an eclectic array of supporters and outmaneuver more powerful opponents. These Street Smarts were particularly necessary when I ran for Congress in 1992 against a millionaire who outspent me more than four to one. I gambled on letting him spend his money early and saved all mine for a final two-week surge. He was so overconfident that he basically cut off his spending just before I began to hit him hard. He was caught flatfooted, and I was able to close the gap and win by three points.

"During my time in Congress, my political obituary was written many times, such as when I would take on my own party leadership, lead controversial hearings into Islamist radicalization, support the police against left-wing attack, and take on *Newsday*, the *New York Times*, and all elements of the liberal media. Almost instinctively, my streetwise experience would kick in during tense moments no matter the issue: arguing vehemently and threatening to work against my own party if aid was not forthcoming for 9/11 victims' compensation or Hurricane Sandy relief; convincing British prime minister Tony Blair that Irish America would support the Good Friday Agreement; and working with Homeland Security officials to ensure their cooperation with NYPD counterterrorism programs in the grim aftermath of 9/11.

"While I wouldn't compromise on principle, I was not above trading votes—voting for legislation that helped another state to get what I needed for New York or Long Island. Finally, loyalty was important to me when I was growing up as well as when I was in the halls of Congress. When I made a deal or gave a commitment, I stood by it no matter what. That gave me credibility in negotiations. When, however, someone reneged on their word to me, it was known I would never forgive or forget. That also gave me credibility. When I decided to retire in 2020, I had prevailed in fourteen Congressional elections and been twice elected chairman of the House Homeland Security Committee. In Nassau County politics, I was the last man of my generation still standing.

"It was a long way from where I started in Queens and Brooklyn, but I could never have made that journey without the Street Smarts I learned on those blue-collar streets and in those neighborhoods."

So, there you have it...in the province of politics, Street Smart is supreme. And no one better to hear that from than Peter King. A kingmaker in politics, yet a sage and even a genuinely benevolent guy, Rep. King has the New York Street Smart in him: tough, savvy, but also a good guy. Politics doesn't often reward such great attributes, but it plainly did so in Rep. King. Politics is also the province of luck, but using luck is a critical part...maybe even the biggest part...of Street Smart, and Rep. King says so here.

STREET SMART MEMOIR OF JOE PISCOPO
Adaption and Survival are Significant to Street Smart

Entertainment is perhaps the cleanest and clearest example of how Street Smart operates. It is not mere luck or talent that determines success. Everyone has good or bad luck. Everyone is talented (more or less). For every superstar, there are at least several examples of equally talented artists who didn't "make it."

Joe Piscopo has made it, though his career has reflected ups and downs which never limited his talent. His idol, Frank Sinatra, perfectly suited the Street Smart mindset. Like Piscopo, Sinatra was another "New York type" originally hatched from New Jersey. Sinatra, according to Joe and written in Frank's many biographies, had the hunches that Joe relies on extensively. But Joe's still around to tell you that, as he tells you directly in his Street Smart memoir. It wasn't all laughs for either Joe or his idol, Frank.

Joe Piscopo literally saved *Saturday Night Live* (*SNL*) along with his good buddy, Eddie Murphy. The ratings and talent of their time at *SNL* were floundering. Television is all about ratings, and the hip program leaned on Piscopo and Murphy. The two comedians hit it off professionally and personally, as the best talent does.

After he left *SNL*, Joe had various stints as a radio personality, movie actor, and nightclub performer. He was *always* funny. But he was always Street Smart. Presently, and in recent times, he has hosted the *Joe Piscopo Show* (AM 970 in New York and New Jersey) and *Sundays with Sinatra* (WABC and other outlets). Here's Joe's take on Street Smart.

"When you're on stage—as a performer—you are depending on Street Smart every single second, your next joke, song, bit—I am notorious for changing our 'set list' on the spot, in the second. You 'feel' the crowd, and you know where to go (and special thanks to all of the great musicians that I've had the privilege to work with who help me make it happen)!

"When I started out as a comic at The Improv comedy club all those years ago—it was pure Street Smart to get me through. Competition was fierce, and if you wanted to survive, you need those smarts.

"Especially if you're on stage at 2:00 AM to a couple of happy but very drunk customers!

"Clubs were rough back then in NYC—I got caught in the middle of some mobbed-up gangsters one night at Catch a Rising Star—and although the audience and I were having a great time, a couple of Corleone wannabes didn't like it and came at me about four thugs at a time.

"My Street Smart really came in then. I ran. As fast as I could! Just to get outta there!

"And I survived. I believe that I am still working because I am a survivor.

"Whether it was thyroid cancer back in 1981—I had thyroid cancer that was originally misdiagnosed and thanks to the co-author of this fine book, the brilliant Dr. Rock Positano, who had enough Street Smart to tell me to get a second opinion. I did, and it saved me from what could have been a deadly turn of events.

"And I have survived in my career. Street Smart will allow you to re-invent yourself. If one thing isn't working—try a new turn.

"I have been in the radio now for almost eight years. I graduated college with a degree in broadcasting.

"Never thought I'd use it, but here we are—on two major radio network stations talking politics and playing the music of one Francis Albert Sinatra. Again, Dr. Rock to the rescue—Rocky thought I'd be good on radio and took me downtown NYC to a major New York affiliate of a national media company, and I have been in the air ever since.

"That's reinvention and radio. That's Street Smart.

"It's the way one of my aforementioned heroes, Frank Sinatra, did it. From radio to 'records' to films to TV and especially working live around the world, Mr. Sinatra kept up with the times—against all odds, by the way—and persevered to be the most iconic entertainer of our time.

"As Francis Albert might have said himself, 'Street Smart? It's the only way to fly, baby!'"

So, there you have it. Joe adapted, reinvented, and used Street Smart every step of the way, every day, and can laugh about it, even through some humorless times as well. We think that's inspiration enough. If you can laugh through pain and suffering, let alone adversity, in these post-COVID days, that's Street Smart coined in a different metal.

STREET SMART MEMOIR OF JEAN-GEORGES VONGERICHTEN
Knife, Fork, Plate, and Plenty of Tire Rubber

Restaurants come and restaurants go. But Street Smart evens the odds, according to celebrity chef and major restaurateur Jean-Georges Vongerichten. Picking a partner to go into business with is never as easy as it looks. The best of friends often makes the worst of partners. Location, location, and location...that's what also matters.

While the statistics are incomplete, it appears that restaurants fail not because of merely poor attendance (most fail within a year of opening), but because partners fail to live up to mutual expectation. This entrepreneur you will read made Street Smart the absolute decider of what he does with partners or locations. He even drives around streets looking for locations. And what is more Street Smart than that?

But first more about the man, Jean-Georges Vongerichten:

Though Jean-Georges Vongerichten is one of the world's most famous chefs, his skills extend far beyond the kitchen. A savvy businessman and restaurateur, Jean-Georges is responsible for the operation and success of over forty restaurants worldwide.

Born and raised on the outskirts of Strasbourg in Alsace, France, Jean-Georges's earliest family memories are of food. He began his training in a work-study program at Auberge de l'Ill as an apprentice to Chef Paul Haeberlin, then went on to work under Paul Bocuse and Master Chef Louis Outhier at L'Oasis in southern France. With this impressive three-star Michelin background, Jean-Georges traveled to Asia and continued his training at the Oriental Hotel in Bangkok, the Méridien Hotel in Singapore, and the Mandarin Hotel in Hong Kong.

It was during this time spent working and traveling throughout Asia that Jean-Georges developed his love for the exotic and aromatic flavors from the east. His signature cuisine abandons the traditional use of meat stocks and creams and instead features the intense flavors and textures from vegetable juices, fruit essences, light broths, and herbal vinaigrettes. Jean-Georges's culinary vision has redefined industry standards and revolutionized the way we eat and dine.

Jean-Georges is involved in every aspect of his restaurants: concept, menu, architectural design, staff selection, and training.

Here's the one story he related about when he was riding his bicycle around the Upper East Side when he saw a space for lease, which turned out to be the restaurant named JoJo on East 64th Street, where it all started:

"While working at (the restaurant) Lafayette, I was looking for my first restaurant. I was riding my bicycle around the Upper East Side and happened upon the building with the lease sign. I went inside and took one look, and I knew it was the one. The building, the location—my Street Smarts told me it couldn't be more perfect. I signed the lease two weeks later.

"I believe in Street Smart 100 percent, and yes, have always relied on Street Smarts in my life."

As to application of Street Smart, Jean-Georges states: "One in particular is looking for restaurant spaces. I am always driving around the city, and every once in a while, a location will strike me. It has to be quick with Street Smarts as opportunities, and decisions need to be made quickly."

His mantra for being Street Smart is: "Trust your instincts!"

"Growing up, I was never too good in school and eventually got kicked out. Since then, I have always relied on my Street Smarts, whether looking for new restaurant spaces or making deals. You have to trust your instincts and your gut and your Street Smarts. It has always given me an ability to really get a good read on people, which has been helpful in assessing my partners in new projects."

All this means is that when you drive around a major metropolitan city, Jean-Georges might be right behind you looking personally for Street Smart locations. Those streets are paved with gold for the chef, and why shouldn't yours be paved with gold as well? After all, you earned it with Street Smart. And so did he.

Photo credit: Sophie Elgort

STREET SMART MEMOIR OF FERN MALLIS
Great Taste and Best Fashion

Fern Mallis learned Street Smart from her parents, who made sure that Mallis's family in Brownsville, Brooklyn educated her to appreciate raising good things from the bad. This Street Smart she uses extensively was the only factor which elevated her above the clinging masses of fashion design and fashion consumption. Even her intensive internship with the fabled New York garment trade was helpful but insufficient for success. This hard-bitten internship had its dividends, but nothing paid off like the Street Smart her beloved parents handed off to her.

Widely credited with transforming New York Fashion Week into one of the big four fashion events on the international circuit, native New Yorker Fern Mallis is a celebrated fashion consultant. For ten years, from 1991–2001, she was the executive director of the Council of Fashion Designers of America (CFDA), the country's governing body of fashion designers and runway shows. In 1993, she started the initiative to organize a modern and centralized platform for American fashion designers to display their clothing and called the event "Seventh on Sixth."

The event grew quickly and was acquired by global media giant IMG in 2001, after which Mallis became a senior vice president at IMG Fashion and also became its ambassador, traveling around the world to fashion shows and competitions.

A noted philanthropist, Mallis has spearheaded charity events and initiatives that have raised millions of dollars for organizations like Design Industries Foundation Fighting Aids (DIFFA) and the CFDA's Fashion Targets Breast Cancer, which has raised more than $55 million to date. The latter celebrated twenty-five years in 2019.

For her efforts in promoting fashion as an artistic and cultural endeavor around the world, Mallis has been awarded lifetime achievement awards from the Pratt Institute, presented to her by celebrated designer Calvin Klein in 2012, and the Fashion Institute of Technology, as well as numerous trade and civic organizations. She is now an independent fashion consultant at her eponymous firm, having parted ways with IMG in 2010.

However, Mallis has remained a fixture on the fashion media scene. She hosted a series of talks at New York's 92Y, dubbed

"Fashion Icons," in which she held conversations with fashion luminaries, such as journalist Suzy Menkes; designers Kenneth Cole, Tom Ford, and Diane von Fürstenberg; photographer Bruce Weber; and so on. Mallis has also made frequent appearances on other media outlets, including as a guest judge on reality series *Project Runway*.

In recent seasons, however, the original creator of New York Fashion Week has been rethinking the utility of runway shows in general, given the media frenzy and spectacle around the biannual shows, which often detracts from the original purpose of attending—so journalists and buyers can see new-season designs. "Fashion Week needs to be rethought," she told Eric Wilson of the *New York Times* in September 2013.

Fern Mallis depicts Street Smart beyond the successes, and her story, told in her own words, further solidifies her well-earned title of Street Scholar and trendsetter.

"I grew up in Brooklyn...long before it became the coolest place on the planet. Our neighborhood was a nice middle-class community with mostly Jewish and Italian neighbors. We played in the streets, never locked the doors, always came home for dinner or homework, and we didn't have cell phones....

"My parents were the definition of Street Smart. My dad was a salesman who worked in the Garment District, and I went to work with him every chance I could on vacations and days off from school—long before Gloria Steinem coined the phrase 'Take Your Daughters to Work Day.' I loved watching him work—both in the showroom and on the streets with all the other "garmentos" (and I say that very lovingly) who filled the streets, he knew everyone and made friends with them all, especially the waitresses at Mary Elizabeth, one of the area's fabulous lunch spots. They loved him and always had a table for him, as they did at

Tony's, where they made the best meatballs I've ever tasted and everything cost $2.40. We also ate at the famous Hutton where he'd take his buyers and the department store's fashion directors and me. I learned about ordering good food and Virgin Marys—but they never called it that in front of me. I learned how to converse with adults. He told the best jokes, often 'off color.' He was 'charming'—a trait we don't hear often. I became inspired years later to pursue a career in fashion as I learned all about the industry on the streets with my father.

"My mother, on the other hand, was Martha Stewart long before we ever heard that name. She had more common sense than anyone I ever met. There was nothing she couldn't handle—from power saws to power cooking and entertaining.

"She would find lots of interesting things on the street, often in a neighbor's garbage. Small crates that housed tomatoes and vegetables from the market became a doll's bed when she took it inside and covered the interior with pretty fabric and upholstered padding for a bed and decorated the handles with bows and put our dolls in there. Broken toys were wired by her and became light fixtures. She would paint and re-paint a wall in our living room every few days until she decided on the color she liked best.

"My mom loved Broadway and went to the theater every chance she could. If she liked something, she would immediately buy more tickets to take me and my sister. My first play as a child was *Gypsy* with Ethel Merman. She took all our friends to see *Bye Bye Birdie* with Dick Van Dyke, and it was the first play they ever saw. I'll never forget when our family went to an opening at Radio City Music Hall for the movie *The Ten Commandments*, and my mom always knew when intermission was coming or could anticipate the end of a play so she could get to restrooms first or out to the parking lot before the crowds. This one time as intermission was approaching and the restrooms were calling, we raced up the long aisle and got to the back of the theater, and just before the lobby, she saw a man standing near a plush red velvet curtain, and she beelined for him, telling him how much we were loving the movie, and this strange man started patting my head saying, 'I made it for her and children just like her.' It was Cecil B. DeMille, and she didn't want to wash my hair for days. She knew how to navigate these events.

"I'll never forget the evening she and my dad had many guests over for dinner and she was serving them all the same cocktail all night. The next day they all called and said they never felt better—they weren't drunk or having a hangover and wanted to know what she served, and she told them 'Geritol on the rocks.' They wanted to kill her.

"My dad taught me how to drive by driving into the city from Brooklyn...I was scared to death to go through the tollbooth and Brooklyn Battery Tunnel...afraid the car wouldn't fit. Of course, he said, look around you. On the cities' avenues he taught me to navigate the traffic by looking ahead to which streets went east and west and to sidle over to either side to avoid the cars that would be turning.

"He and my mom were great athletes when they were younger. They played a mean game of handball on the schoolyards in Brownsville. Mom was a track star. Dad was a basketball player and played for the earliest leagues in NY, before the NBA, when the manufacturers on 7th Avenue sponsored the teams. Then he coached, and I still love basketball because of him.

"My folks never pressured their daughters to be active in sports, and we weren't. He did, however, teach me how to ride a bike. In our basement we had a pool table which would often be covered by a ping pong table. He taught me how to play both and said don't lose to the boys, if you're better, be better and win!

"He was a painter and a poet, and a gentle soul. He could never put a nail in the trunk of our backyard weeping willow tree to make a swing or a tree house, as he said it was someone's soul.

"In looking back, I realize that their Street Smarts became mine.

"I only wish they were around longer to enjoy and see my success in the fashion industry, and to have been able to come to the fashion shows in the Bryant Park Tents which I created, and to come to the 92 Street Y to listen to my 'Fashion Icons with Fern Mallis' interview series, which is celebrating its tenth anniversary this year. But I'm sure they are watching.

"Thank you, Vera and Mac!"

So, Fern Mallis, another Brooklyn kid, believes in Street Smart and uses it often. Fashion is yet another prime venue of using Street Smart. Trends change weekly, tastes evolve quickly, and the fashion world knows Street Smart luck all too well. But Fern knows the industry better than most and happens to make Street Smart the keynote of her lecture here. It is not mere luck, but it's spotting, seizing, and exploiting luck which counts. Everything else is...well...window dressing. For too many years, maybe you have been enthralled with window dressing.

STREET SMART MEMOIR OF GOVERNOR DAVID PATERSON
Overcoming a Disability and Anxiety with Street Smart

Governor David Paterson (New York) knows the meaning of Street Smart; his career has been in public service, tempered by being visually handicapped. David himself makes it for you here that sometimes making the Street Smart choice when it arrives is lost because anxiety acts as a kind of block. He says that those "silent warnings" or exciting impulses of opportunity are critical, and he proves it herein. Politics is another almost exclusive province belonging to the Street Smart. Politics is entirely living by your wits. A bad election result not only dooms a particular run for a particular office, but a real defeat can hamper a person for many years.

David A. Paterson became New York's fifty-fifth governor on March 17, 2008. He immediately raised eyebrows when he warned of an impending fiscal crisis in his inaugural address. But he was ahead of the national curve in predicting and acting on the state's fiscal downturn. Despite the greatest economic crisis that New York State has ever faced, Governor Paterson enacted sweeping reforms on a wide range of issues facing New Yorkers.

During the next three years, he would reduce New York's deficit by nearly $40 billion (twice the amount of budget-cutting in any comparable period). He became the first governor to sign legislation attaching criminal penalties to predatory lending during the worst foreclosure crisis in American history. He overhauled the Rockefeller drug laws, which excessively punished low-level drug offenders while depriving judges of discretion in sentencing for over thirty-five years. Governor Paterson would introduce landmark civil-rights legislation that eventually ended legal discrimination against same-sex couples in New York. He would also increase the welfare allowance for the neediest New Yorkers for the first time in twenty years.

In 2009, Paterson settled two hundred years of legal debate when the NY State Court of Appeals upheld his appointment of a lieutenant governor, Richard Ravitch.

Since leaving office, David Paterson has hosted a popular drive-time talk-radio show on WOR AM in New York City. Governor Paterson served as an adjunct professor of government in 2011 and 2012 at New York University and has since moved to Touro College School of Osteopathic Medicine. Governor

Paterson is a highly sought-after speaker by diverse entities and organizations and often appears as a guest commentator on political news programs.

Here's his counsel to you:

"I was sixteen or seventeen, so this incident occurred in 1970 or '71. I was walking down my block with my friend Gary Gillis when an older woman intervened to ask if we would assist her father who was trying to change a flat tire. When we came upon the gentleman, who seemed to be well over eighty, he offered to pay us to complete the job for him. We apologized that neither had ever changed a tire before.

"The gentleman, whose teaching skills were exquisite, guided Gary through the process to a beneficial conclusion and then compensated each of us with a dollar for our time. A dollar was a big deal in those days.

"Then, the gentlemen asked me if I would like to remove the tire and then replace it so that I would learn that which my friend had learned. 'Sir, I am legally blind and I don't think I could change the tire, but thank you for the offer.' He replied that with what little vision I had, he believed with his guidance I could complete the task. My instincts told me that he was right. I think I was embarrassed that I would fail at the project and declined the offer.

"Approximately twenty-eight or twenty-nine years later, I was riding from Albany with my three assistants, Karen Towns, Gina Stahlnecker, and my chief of staff, Sheila Greene. We were returning from Governor Mario Cuomo's State of the State Address. You have probably already guessed that we sustained a flat tire at around 4:00 PM on a frigid day. The three women, all of whom were licensed drivers, began an attempt to change the tire. Their mistake was that they jacked the car up but didn't take the lug nuts off of the wheel. Every time they turned the pliers, the wheel turned. As a member of the State Senate, I was then asked to place a bear hug on the wheel to stabilize it, and Karen Towns, now sitting on the roof of the car, was kicking the pliers in a failed attempt to turn the wheel. Each attempt, by the way, felt like a left hook from Mike Tyson from my position holding the tire.

"Finally, a car comes screeching off the road with its driver screaming through an open window, 'What the hell are you all doing?!'

"Nearly concussed from the previous moments, I thought I saw the old man's face in the sky. He was informing me that wherever there is an opportunity to learn something, even if one isn't sure that they will utilize the information, it is good to have that awareness should it be needed.

"At age thirty-five, I was still learning the process of honing one's instincts, being those thoughts that come into our minds in complicated situations. Many call it Street Smarts. Hypnotists believe that we actually sense what another person is going to say to us before they say it. Psychics have proven that there are people that can sense situations long before they happen. Law enforcement many times can assess criminality from responses to questions.

"And yet too often we trivialize or discount intangible messages that we all receive. The imagined intervention by the old man on that freezing thruway disabused me of my previous doubts.

"Now it is late October 2002, and I have been asked to run for the minority leadership of the State Senate by colleagues who have become disenchanted with the current leader. Initially, I was certain that I had the votes to win, but as I had observed in previous failures to overthrow leaders, the incumbents were circulating rumors that some who voiced support for my candidacy were actually spies reporting back to the leader. It is a huge price to pay if you don't kill the king. Now, days before the vote, I maintained twelve of the thirteen needed votes to win. A new state senator named Martin Dilan stated his preference for me to be the leader but asked for time to be sure. Rumors were rampant that even one of my best friends was a possible deserter. The advice that my former chief of staff Joseph Haslip gave me was, 'To win, you have to do something that no one has done before.' I did not find this pronouncement to be helpful. I could discover a cure for cancer, but that would not help me win the leadership.

"Sitting in my apartment near midnight and feeling more alone than ever, I considered the possibility that Joe's advice was an outline that could be a prelude to a strategy.

"Suddenly, a red light went off in my head. Risking verbal abuse, I telephoned all twelve of my supporters and asked them to meet me in my office at the State Office Building in Harlem at 1:00 PM the next day. I had to fly two of the members in, one from Albany and one from Buffalo. Then I called Dilan. I told him that I could produce twelve members including myself, and that if he attended the meeting, he might want to cast the thirteenth vote.

"All of the members except for Dilan arrived in a timely fashion. Quite surprised to see each other sitting in a room with all of them, I explained that in spite of the rumors, fake stories, and threats that each of them had chosen to come, and that if we stuck together, we would certainly win. All of them were elated over this new development and pledged their support. I was still aware that Dilan had not committed but advised the group that I needed a favor from them—with unanimous consent prior to hearing what the favor was. The same number of senators were agitated by my request.

"'I wish to hold a press conference at which we will all present signed oaths that we support this candidacy,' I said. The justifiable concern was that a public appearance would allow the leader to know who was not voting for him.

"My response was that there was so much gossip in this process that I was sure the leader knew exactly what was going on at that moment.

"Exercising the trust that I asked for, the members consented to holding the press conference. As the members left the room, I called a rogue member who was shifting back and forth between the candidates faster than a tennis ball in the US Open. I explained to him that I had the votes, I was holding a press conference, and that I would be a fair leader and not hold it against him that he didn't vote for me. Shocked at the breaking news, the member pleaded that he was always with me, and that he would join the press conference and bring another member to support me.

"When he arrived, I'm sure he counted to make sure there were thirteen senators in the room. Unknown to him, one of them was the uncommitted Dilan. However, Dilan now saw that there were fifteen senators in the room and asked for a conference, which we held in the men's room. 'If you treat me as the thirteenth vote making me part of your leadership team, I swear to you that I will not desert you when the leader tries to retrieve these votes,' he promised. He kept his promise.

"After the press conference, my two best friends in the Senate descended on my office to apprise me of their disdain for this process. 'I'm with you, chief, but I have no idea what you are doing. The leader is out trying to undo this at this very moment, and I don't trust ten of your supporters. They have taken their name back before.'

"I took a deep breath and responded, 'They can take their name back, but they can't take their picture back. I'm going to have their pictures and signed oaths on every TV news station this evening. Tomorrow morning, it will appear in every newspaper from Buffalo, to Brooklyn, to Montauk Point.' I won the leadership.

"Though I struggled with the vagueness of my friend Joe's advice, that inner voice that we all have urged me to consider it. This was the same inner voice that had been overruled by my fears and anxiety about changing the tire. Obstacles are only the barriers that stand between ourselves and our goals. A greater reliance on our Street Smarts, which are the total of our life experiences that propel themselves into decision making, is a very important boundary for us to cross.

"In 2006, I was offered to run for lieutenant governor, a meaningless position compared to majority leader for the State Senate, which I was close to winning. Once again, that voice which Deepak Chopra calls the 'silent witness' kept gnawing at my conscious. Why would taking this position ever be a good choice? But I accepted it, asking Governor Spitzer if he would appoint me to the United States Senate should Hillary Clinton become the president nearly three years later. This was the only way that derailing my career would pay off. But, in 2008 Governor Spitzer resigned, making me only the fourth African American governor in US history and only the second who is blind.

"The decibel level of day-to-day life, the confusion of the many challenges we face, and the anxiety of considering what is next in a volatile world can disconnect us from our beliefs and our decision-making capacity. Take it from me, those silent warnings of danger or those exciting impulses of opportunity need to be addressed because they rarely take one in the wrong direction.

"This commitment paid off for me on March 18, 2008. I had been sworn in as governor one day earlier. Rumors were swirling about affairs that my then-wife and I had during our marriage. The truth was that we viewed ourselves as separated but stayed at the same home so as not to cause grief among our children. That's the truth, but it wouldn't sound like the truth.

"Thus, we both stood before tens of media outlets and pleaded guilty to the offenses. In addition, I was asked if I had experimented with drugs in my life, so I pled to that as well. For some weeks, the media traveled the globe looking for names or details regarding our admissions. I never worried about their exploits, because I actually admitted to something that I hadn't even done.

"When you fall on your sword, you don't want anybody else to stab you. You can draw a circle around your conduct that is bigger than the accusations. So, when one headline-seeker cooked up a story about me, I didn't say that it was the lie that it was, I merely responded, 'I don't remember this happening. There was a lot going on at the time and I could be wrong.'

"This is a wily strategy, but it is not dishonest nor is it disingenuous. It is designed to address a situation honestly while not allowing any other accusations to gain momentum. Since that time, I have watched other high-profile figures tiptoe and dance, tearing up and explaining away while the public grows less trusting of their defenses. Many have been forced to leave their positions because in spite of their extraordinary ability and achievements, they lack Street Smarts. When faced with turmoil, listen to your heart, it's always beating."

Governor Paterson used Street Smart, his basic inarguable decency, and obvious truthfulness to be a very solid leader. But he also agrees that you need those Street Smarts for survival in a vicious world. Not a pretty picture, but hardly unrealistic. If you are unwilling to use them, it is as bad as not developing them in the first place. Governor Paterson is way too Street Smart to ever be blindsided.

STREET SMART MEMOIR OF BOB AND PAUL
COWSILL OF THE COWSILL FAMILY
Street Smarts, Done in Family Style

As we've said before, entertainment is definitely the province of Street Smart...not only the most talented, but also the most Street Smart entertainers make it. There are plenty of talented entertainers. The Cowsills were always quite talented but needed a quick read of Street Smart to survive and thrive. Founded by their father, a Navy veteran who was tough but fair, the Cowsills delivered talent as their father wanted them to. And Street Smart was a critical factor in delivery, as you will read from their advice to you.

The Cowsills are a family pop band. Back in the day before bands were hand mixed to demographics and marketed like household products, the "garage band" was king, meaning people played out of their garages. Their pop music biography starts simply enough: four brothers wanted to emulate the Beatles back in the 1960s: Bob Cowsill was a guitarist and organist. They had regular gigs in Newport, Rhode Island. Adding everyone else to the band over time, the Cowsills sold a lot of records. They also used a lot of Street Smarts, as Bob explains here.

"Growing up in my family I had to learn early on how to handle situations quickly and at a very young age. I realized I was living in fear within my own family because of my father, and that lead to what I believe was an early development of common sense and awareness of my surroundings. I developed Street Smarts, but the streets were within my very own 'hood'—my family.

"The trick to me with being Street Smart was to move forward and keep safe—and I learned. I kept safe by blending in within my own family. You had to learn how to minimize risks on the 'streets' and avoid the negative, and that was no different for me while growing up. Bad report card, get smacked around? Solution: good report card.

"Have Christmas taken away from you as a child because your father caught you smoking a cigarette and gave all your gifts to your siblings so you get nothing? Solution: don't smoke (or don't get caught—get smart).

"Accidentally pee your pants at your desk in the second grade and the teacher takes you from the classroom and returns with you wearing a dress for being a sissy? Solution: manage your bathroom breaks. Your father is your nemesis? Solution: learn how to deal with him and act around him to ensure your own success so he doesn't take you down.

"Our father had Street Smarts. Always outwardly confident even if not inwardly, his way or the highway with an ability on the way up to avoid the potholes, blinders on, keep going straight ahead, always alert, aware, and somewhat distrustful of anything that seemed to be a barrier to the goal of bringing his talented children and their mother to the public's attention by hitting the streets of New York City to find a record label who would sign them.

"Dad was twenty years in the Navy with a seventh-grade education...now that's a Street Smart candidate if there ever was one. Using those 'smarts,' he helped bring about the success of 'The Cowsills' family singing group. No doubt about it.

"The problem with being Street Smart, though, is once you have succeeded and reached the 'penthouse,' you have to change and morph into another type of 'smart.' You have to adjust, and some of the Street Smart qualities you employed to get there aren't going to work at the top. You don't blend in anymore and the blinders need to come off. You need to deal with success now, and that's paved with different types of streets.

"At the top, the most important risk is losing your common sense. Common sense is a Street Smart quality you need at the top more than any of the others, because if you lose your common sense—which governs a lot of decisions with Street Smart people—then you can jeopardize everything and lose it all."

Bob Cowsill used his Street Smart to morph into different incarnations. Not a bad suggestion and one shared by many of the Street Smart people we interviewed for the book. Reinventing oneself is one solution to present troubles, just easier said than done.

Bob's younger brother Paul weighs in accordingly.

Paul Cowsill: "No one ever spits on you, and no one ever says anything bad about your mom. That's what I learned growing up. And that's what I taught my kids. When they were going into the first grade, I told them just that. My youngest, when hearing that, asked me if someone was going to spit on him. And I said, 'no, but it will feel like someone did. And if that was to happen you will need to roll. You will need to engage.' That's Street Smarts.

"I taught them to avoid physical confrontation if possible, but always be ready to roll if necessary. Me and my brothers were in a coffee shop one morning, and the table across from us had some guys and their gals having coffee. The girls started flirting with our table and the guys were getting pissed. I could feel it, and I was ready to go. Those guys got up and started coming our way, and my big brother said, 'Hey, before you kick our asses, what's your name?'

"Well, that confused the guy and totally defused the whole situation. I learned on that day, be able to talk your way out of trouble. That's Street Smarts.

"Be ready to help those in trouble. I've been in many fights. But the only fights I was ever in were fights to protect my friends or someone getting bullied. That's Street Smarts.

"[There were times] in my life I needed a job and there were none to be given and none to be found. Being a carpenter my whole life, I would just show up on a construction site, tool bags in hand. Find the construction boss. And tell him, 'I'm willing to work all day for free. And at the end of the day either say no job or hire me.'

"It always worked. No one ever said no. That's Street Smarts.

"After just getting out of the military, I had lost my way. I had no money. With a wife, two kids, and a sister to feed, I got a job at a tennis racquet factory (where I almost lost both thumbs).

That paid for shelter. Now I needed food. So, I got a long trench coat, went to the local Ralph's grocery store, and packed that coat to the brim. I would have gladly paid if I had the money. I was just doing what had to be done to keep my family afloat.

"That's Street Smarts," says Paul Cowsill.

All told, the Cowsills navigated, successfully, the world of entertainment where luck, more than mere talent, rules above all. They were supremely talented, but also Street Smart, as they themselves have just told you.

The Cowsills recently completed their first record in twenty-five years called *Rhythm of the World*, filled with great music and powerful ballads that will bring in an era of nostalgia for their longtime listeners. With a planned release date of fall 2022, through Omnivore Records the album will surely usher in a new era of Cowsill fans, brimming with excitement over this Street Smart record.

STREET SMART MEMOIR OF GARY NAFTALIS
Use Street Smart, Not Just Book Smart, To Reach Judges and Juries

Gary Naftalis is proof that the old legal adage, "It is good to know the law but better to know the judge and the jury," has firm roots in Street Smart, and he says so, too.

Getting chased by the czar's Cossacks had something to do with it. Naftalis's grandfather's clashes with anti-Semitic Russian Cossacks drove him to becoming a junkman with a horse as a coworker in Newark. The junkman's grandson elevated himself, with Street Smarts...to becoming one of the leading lawyers in the country.

Naftalis knows both. His history proves it.

Mr. Naftalis is a Fellow of the American College of Trial Lawyers. For over forty years, he has represented individuals and corporations in all phases of complex bet-the-company civil, criminal, and regulatory matters, including those involving allegations of insider trading, market manipulation, accounting irregularities, stock options backdating, and other financial fraud. Mr. Naftalis also has served as counsel to audit and special committees of a number of major public companies.

Mr. Naftalis was recently named as one of the one hundred most influential lawyers in America by *The National Law Journal*, as one of the ten leading trial lawyers in the United States by *Legal 500*, and as one of the top ten lawyers in New York (top point getter 2008 and 2012) by *Super Lawyers*. He has been recognized by *Best Lawyers in America* since 1993 in three categories: bet-the-company litigation, white-collar criminal defense, and commercial litigation. He was also cited as one of America's leading lawyers by *Lawdragon 500*, as one of America's leading trial lawyers by *Chambers Global*, and as a leading white-collar defense and commercial litigator by *Chambers USA* and by *Benchmark/Institutional Investor*.

Mr. Naftalis's list of successes includes his defense of Michael Eisner, the CEO of The Walt Disney Company, in the shareholders derivative lawsuit relating to the hiring and termination of Michael Ovitz. After a thirty-seven-day trial in the Delaware Court of Chancery, Mr. Eisner and the other Disney directors prevailed on all counts. The Disney case was chosen as one of the top defense victories of 2005.

Here's the counselor's counsel on Street Smart:

"Many of the important life lessons I have learned over the years did not come from reading books or attending lectures or classes in college or law school. Rather they are a product of how I grew up in Newark, New Jersey, and the experiences I had and the values I learned.

"My parents were first-generation Americans, whose own parents had passed through Ellis Island around the turn of the twentieth century. My paternal grandfather, Max, according to family lore, had emigrated from Russia after having had one fight too many with anti-Semitic Cossacks while serving in the czar's army. Max worked as a junkman driving a horse and wagon along the streets of Newark picking up old newspapers, tin cans, and the like. My grandfather never complained and never explained.

"My parents were what is now euphemistically called lower middle class. My dad plodded the pavement as a debit agent for Prudential Insurance, a job that paid a steady but quite modest income. His customers were working-class people, whose premiums were often paid late and in cash since they frequently didn't have checking accounts. While not rich in worldly goods, my parents were rich in values. They always judged people by the content of their character rather than the contents of their wallets. The way my dad treated his customers and the way my mother fought for all her family members taught me the importance of loyalty as an exemplar of character. Simply put, you were supposed to be there for your friends and to have their backs, even if it was inconvenient and costly.

"To this day, I regard loyalty as amongst the most important character traits in a person. In assessing a person, I often ask myself, would I want that man or woman next to me in a foxhole and would they have my back?

"I also learned that there is a big difference between being book smart and being Street Smart. Having a degree from a prestigious educational institution may mean you were book smart, but it did not necessarily mean you were wise or had good judgment and common sense.

"Coaches are fond of saying that you can't coach speed. And that is certainly true. I believe it is equally true that you can't coach or teach judgment in school either.

"My dad used to colorfully refer to some of the pompous personalities who appeared on TV (our family's sole form of entertainment) as 'smart jerks'—an appellation that aptly described them. Some years later, a respected colleague in the US attorney's office similarly observed that those kinds of people were 'educated beyond their intelligence.' I often used my dad as kind of a one-man focus group, previewing arguments before I made them to the actual jury.

"My dad may not have had any formal education after high school, but his instincts about people were keen and mirrored those of many folks that sit as jurors who are able to assess whether a witness or lawyer is being candid or not. Or as Bob Dylan once famously put it, being able to 'know the difference between a real blonde and a fake.'

"From an early age, I understood the importance of hard work. I learned quickly that no one owed me anything; any success would have to be earned on the merits. With my parents' emotional support, I was the first person in our nuclear family to go to college, living at home and attending Rutgers in Newark. My scholarship only covered tuition, so I needed to work to pay the rest. During two summers, I worked as a busboy at hotels in the Catskills and Catskill-type resorts in New Jersey (I was never promoted to waiter, a post apparently reserved for law and medical students). I also honed my busboy skills by working on weekends during the school year, at weddings and bar mitzvahs.

"This was a tremendous learning experience, as I needed to consistently interact with all varieties of people—some very nice, who took a parental interest in a then-skinny-but-eager young man, and some not so very nice, who bombarded me with all sorts of seemingly endless demands and requests, and never appeared to be satisfied with the results.

"I had to learn about what made people tick and how to credibly answer their questions and persuasively respond to their concerns. It turned out to be great training for dealing with judges and jurors, who after all, are also people who have questions that need to be addressed and don't always necessarily sympathize with your client's position at the outset. And like so much of what is important about being a trial lawyer, being Street Smart is often more important than being book smart."

From Borscht Belt busboy to a leading attorney is quite a ride, afforded, Gary insists here, on Street Smart. And don't argue with him. He tends to win his arguments with legal brains, to be sure, but also application of Street Smart as well. Former Manhattan District Attorney Robert Morgenthau wasn't afraid to name Gary as his favorite defense lawyer. Morgenthau claimed that if he ever had a problem, Gary would be the first guy he'd call.

When we told Gary that others have noted that he is "silent but lethal," Mr. Naftalis' pearly white grin from ear to ear personifies such a distinct and well-earned moniker.

STREET SMART MEMOIR OF JEFF ZUCKER
Switching Gears from Law School to Media Mogul

For Jeff Zucker, former CEO of CNN, Street Smart started when he fell in love with the control room of television stations, turning his fascination with sports and news into a compelling urge to change the world. A Street Smart epiphany prompted Jeff to reluctantly give up his law career aspirations.

Law school simply wasn't his destiny. His true north turned out to be news, sports, and entertainment. But he explains it better:

"When I was in college, I dreamed of going to law school. It felt like the right path, something that would have just made sense at that point in my life. I went to a great Ivy League school for my undergraduate years, and, with a healthy dose of hubris, I suppose, made somewhat of an assumption that the fine folks at the law school would be as enamored with me as the ones that chose me for undergrad. They were not, and I got rejected. It was a tough blow.

"Little did I realize at the time that it was the best thing that ever happened to me.

"In lieu of that acceptance, I took a deferred acceptance to another, also great, school to study law. I had two years to go try something else, and then I would return to the classroom to pursue my degree. So I thought at the time.

"I embarked on an extraordinary adventure, circling the globe as a researcher for NBC's coverage of the 1988 Summer Olympics in Seoul, South Korea. It was everything a young twenty-something sports addict with a keen sense of curiosity and a penchant for journalism could ask for. Fascinating people, travel, long days and nights, rubbing elbows with some of the greatest athletes in the world, and meeting future up-and-comers that would be grabbing the sports headlines in the years to come. I loved it.

"When the games were over, that job led me to *The Today Show* at NBC where I first walked into a control room and fell in love with the pace, the immediacy, and the thrill of live television. Again, I found myself in some unbelievable places, eye to eye with people who were quite literally changing the world and being lucky enough to tell their stories. A long career in media followed at some of the most well-respected companies in the world.

"My love of sports and news has stayed with me throughout my life—and ultimately led me to where I am now. Along the way I have learned a lot—none of which could have been taught in a lecture with the aid of a book. Professionally, my passions have extended beyond news and sports to entertainment, tech, and even a passion for politics. Personally, I have celebrated great achievement and also faced some painful obstacles. In every single case, I have learned something.

"And about that law school deferment? I never went, and I have never once regretted it. The lessons I have learned in all the years since cannot be compared to what law school would have taught me. That is not to say that there is not great merit in pursuing a post-graduate degree.

"Plenty of people have chosen that path and it has served them incredibly well. But for me, I have no question that nearly all of the success I have had in life started with that disappointing rejection. What seemed like a door closing was actually one being thrown wide open. I was wise enough to run through it and never look back. Of course, I do sometimes wonder now whether I should re-apply to that law school and see what would happen now. Oh well. I'm so glad it all worked out."

Zucker's "glad it all worked out" has amounted to chairmanship of WarnerMedia News and Sports, president of CNN worldwide, and berths at NBC and other media giants. To be familiar with modern cable and broadcast media is to be familiar with Jeff Zucker. And to be familiar with Street Smart itself means to be familiar with how a hardworking, resourceful, and empathetic man like Zucker made it to the top.

STREET SMART MEMOIR OF AL ROKER
Being "Street Aware" Is a Game Changer

Al Roker's career all stems from being Street Smart. He credits what he calls being "Street Aware" for his success, and we can't differ. He also credits a commercial that aired in his childhood for signaling the wisdom of using this capacity for his personal survival and later professional success. Sadly, COVID shrunk this capacity, and we agree. Shrinking the world means exactly that; everyone retreating behind a mask, a social distance, a vaccination, a late booster, a video link, a hurried phone call. So, what can we do? Al Roker came from the streets, and his Street Smart is educational, if somewhat daunting. A genuinely good guy, his personality on and off the teleprompter is the same, which is a refreshing change of pace in the media.

If anyone agreed with our controversial statement that COVID, and modern life today, has seriously disrupted Street Smart, it would be Al Roker.

"I never really thought of myself as Street Smart. I like to think of myself as being "street aware." Growing up in Brooklyn and Queens, when it came to the street, you were taught to look both ways.

"There was a PSA (public service announcement) that ran on all the NYC TV stations that had a catchy little song: 'Don't cross the street in the middle, in the middle, in the middle, in the middle of the block.... Teach your eyes to look up.... Teach your ears to hear.... Walk up to the corner where the coast is clear.... And wait...and wait...until you see the light turn green.'

"Everything you need in life is in that little ditty. Watch, listen, learn.

"Taking the subway to Xavier High School each morning, you learned how to watch, listen, and pay attention. Sadly, our phones have turned a whole generation of New Yorkers into *The Walking Dead*. Zombies who pay no attention to their surroundings because they are transfixed by their phones.

"Besides being crazy unsafe, we miss the show that is NYC all around us. And that's not limited to New York. Unfortunately, all across this country, we are missing the street scenes, the country landscapes, and the parade of people that make being on the street special."

Al Roker is the weather and feature anchor for the highly successful and long-running *Today* program on NBC, rating "best weatherman on TV" by various accounts. He has appeared on hundreds of television shows and features. He has made it to the top of news broadcasting from the humblest of beginnings. His education in being street aware enabled him to effortlessly navigate the worlds of news, business, entertainment, and timely topics that have taken the world by storm.

STREET SMART MEMOIR OF MICHAEL STOLER
From Gun Bunny to Real Estate Titan

Michael Stoler's take on Street Smart also was born on the mean streets of Brooklyn, where bullshit artists have remarkably short lives and men like Stoler use their Street Smart to prosper, thrive, and become role models. His television show, *The Stoler Report*, covers the most volatile, and lucrative, real-estate markets in the country. His acronym "SALT" headlines a system of Street Smart which he codifies so well. He learned an adage from the Army: "The soldier who types will type in safety and never have to fire a rifle," which can be taken as luck but which he, and we, term a Street Smart observation. So, here's Stoler's take on Street Smart. His SALT system actually conveys our observations in a new and enlightening way. Before he bestows his wisdom to us, first a few words about achievements from his website that are attributed to Michael's hard work and his Street Smart.

"Michael Stoler is the president and CEO of New York Real Estate TV, LLC, a management consulting firm and television production firm.

"Mr. Stoler is the host and executive producer of two television shows: *The Stoler Report-New York's Business Report*, currently in its twenty-first season, and *Building New York-New York Life Stories*, in its seventeenth season. Both shows air eight times a week in New York City on CUNY TV and are available on numerous internet sites.

"Mr. Stoler served as managing director at Madison Realty Capital, a private equity firm from January 2009 to March 31, 2018. He previously served as a senior principal at Apollo Real Estate Advisors (AREA Property Partners) as well as SVP with First American Title Insurance Company. For more than twenty-five years, he served as president and CEO of Princeton Commercial Corporation and New York Real Estate TV, LLC, a consulting and financing firm whose clients have included financial institutions, public and private companies, commercial banks and finance companies, accounting and consulting firms, Taft Hartley Unions and Health Funds, health care organizations, and health care and business professionals."

Michael is a member of the Real Estate Committee of Yeshiva University and a member of the faculty of the Sy Syms College of Business of Yeshiva University, where he coordinates and teaches the "Titan of Real Estate" course.

He is active in numerous charitable endeavors and serves as the founder and CEO of the Foundation for Medical Evaluation and Early Detection, an organization which provides no-cost health screenings to the community. Mr. Stoler is a former overseer and member of the board of the NYU Langone Health and served as the chair of the Kaplan Comprehensive Cancer Center.

He holds a BS in accounting from the Brooklyn Center of Long Island University. Mr. Stoler served as an adjunct faculty member and the co-chair of the Fordham University Real Estate Industry Outreach Committee.

"Rock and John emphasize the importance of Street Smart, which requires an individual to think on their feet to grow and survive in the twenty-first century.

"While I do believe that one requires Street Smarts, I believe we have to add a necessary ingredient. I believe it is impossible to grow and gain some level of success unless one possesses an acronym which I call 'SALT.'

"I recognized 'SALT' over the past sixteen years in my role as the creator, host, and producer of one of my television shows. Since March 2006, I have interviewed more than four hundred individuals on my show *Building New York: NY Stories*, which profiles and provides insight on the life story of individual. Over the past sixteen seasons, I have seen firsthand that success for individuals from all walks of life including the clergy, arts, business, healthcare, education all require and need SALT.

"I have created this acronym based upon my personal experience as well as listened and interviewing individuals.

"One may ask me what 'SALT' is.

"These four letters each identify a characteristic of an individual.

"Let me start with 'T.' All successful people in life must have a certain level of tenacity. As defined in the dictionary, tenacity is the state of holding on to an idea or a thing very strongly. 'Tenacious' is a mostly positive term. If someone calls you 'tenacious,' you're probably the kind of person who never gives up and never stops trying—someone who does whatever is required to accomplish a goal. You may also be very stubborn.

"The next element is 'A' for adaptability. If you describe an individual as 'adaptable,' you mean that you can change their ideas or behavior to deal with new situations. Having adaptability skills means you are open and willing to learn new things, take on new challenges, and adjust to suit transitions in the workplace. Additionally, developing your adaptability can also mean developing other soft skills like communication and interpersonal skills. Adaptability means the ability to be flexible and adjust to changing factors, conditions, or environments.

"An individual has to have some level of 'L,' which I define as a certain level of luck. Everyone in their life needs a certain level of luck to achieve. Luck or good luck is success or good things that happen to you, which often do not come from your own abilities or efforts. Lucky people create, notice, and act upon the chance opportunities in their lives. Lucky people make successful decisions by using their intuition and gut feelings. Lucky people's expectations about the future help them fulfill their dreams and ambitions. Lucky people can transform their bad luck into good fortune.

"I believe that luck helps an individual gain insight and growth in the final letter of SALT. Seizing the opportunity can be defined as when to take advantage of an opportunity; being aware of an opportunity when offered to you and taking the necessary steps to seize or follow through with the opportunity.

"With every opportunity comes the chance of learning new skills, rounding out edges, and increasing your job prospects. Sometimes in life you are presented with an opportunity, and you must ask yourself, 'Should I take the opportunity, or should I not take the opportunity?'

"But sometimes you know that taking an opportunity might be a good thing. Sometimes taking opportunities presents you with new experiences and growth you wouldn't get otherwise.

"So, what do you do when opportunity knocks? Do you take the opportunity or do you not? Well, let's work through it.

"At this time, let me tell you about how SALT has had its impact on my life. As I reflect on my life, I often think of how important each of these categories has been in my life. I often mention to guests who have appeared on my television shows that I have been lucky to have SALT and learned how to combine each category to help my career and personal life grow.

"Looking back at my life, I realize that SALT arrived during periods of prosperity, opportunity, and personal and financial difficulties. Born and bred in Brooklyn, New York, my family had the opportunity to move when I was three years of age from the Brownsville section of Brooklyn, an emerging neighborhood directly adjacent to the Belt Parkway.

"This was the second major apartment complex that Fred C. Trump (Donald's father) built on the outskirts of Coney Island, within walking distance of Brighton Beach, called 'Beach Haven.' The complex consisted of 2,253 apartments housed in a six-story brick building.

"Me and my older sister moved from a five-story walk-up to a modern complex within the Gravesend/Ocean Parkway section of Brooklyn. We were provided the opportunity to meet thousands of similar individuals, many who returned from World War II, looking to progress, grow, and live comfortably.

"We were lucky to have a public school less than one mile from our apartment on West 2nd Street. The community had parks and public areas, as well as a shopping center where I secured one of my first jobs as a cashier and unpacker of boxes at the Bohack Supermarket.

"The community offered residents the opportunity to take a bus to nearby Brighton Beach and view the Tuesday evening fireworks of Coney Island as they arrived in the skies adjacent to the Belt Parkway.

"I learned how to adapt to circumstances at young age, upon graduation from PS 216 on Avenue X near McDonald Avenue and taking the bus to Mark Twain Junior High School. The years at Twain were uneventful and nevertheless, I graduated and moved on to the Abraham Lincoln High School on Ocean Parkway, less than a mile from our apartment 2J, on the second floor of the building.

"I was not one of the best students in high school and was fortunate to be given the opportunity to attend the State University of New York at Buffalo. Learning to live on my own adjacent to the campus was a difficult task which lasted one year when I returned to Brooklyn, attending the Brooklyn campus of Long Island University changing from a liberal arts major to business with a major in accounting.

"The three and half years at LIU allowed me to be able to adapt from a relatively underperforming student to an ambitious person who had a series of jobs ranging from business associate for a photo processing company to junior accountant from a small firm to a moderate firm named Westheimer, Fine, Berger & Co.

"In addition to these jobs in Manhattan, a place which I had not visited during my youth, I learned to understand the subway system and take advantage of life in the city and especially in Manhattan.

"Attending college in a business setting of Downtown Brooklyn allowed me to take advantage of earning additional income from the students at college selling a variety of wares including college rings, laminations of diplomas, and men's dress shoes by mail order, as well as coordinating and booking trips in the Catskills.

"In addition to the Street Smarts I gained during college, I was lucky to utilize my work experience as well as the reference of my accounting professor, Robert Rochlin, to secure a position with the nationally recognized accounting firm of J.K. Lasser & Company, located at 666 Fifth Avenue.

"With the war in Vietnam progressing when I graduated from college in January 1969, it was important that I and a number of my Brooklyn and Queens friends (very few who resided in Manhattan) pursued gaining entrance in the Army Reserve or National Guard. Each one of them sought different military bases relatively close to New York City. Call it luck or Street Smarts since I would say at least twelve to twenty of the graduates from LIU located and were selected to become a member of the reserves. My home base of training for the next five and half years was nearby Fort Tilden, in Rockway, Breezy Park, Queens.

"Reserve duty required for me a four-month all-expense (not luxury) trip for basic training at Fort Leonard Wood, in the Missouri Ozarks near St. Louis, Missouri. After ten weeks of basic training, it was time be transferred to Fort Sill, a US Army post north of Lawton, Oklahoma, about eighty-five miles southwest of Oklahoma City.

"Perhaps the greatest luck in my twenty-two years took place at Fort Sill. It was a combination of all levels of SALT and Street Smarts. Fort Sill was the place where a new soldier would spend the next eight weeks being trained to serve as a cannoneer member for the M114 155mm howitzer.

"During the second day at the base, the sergeant posed the question if anyone was an experienced typist. While I realized it was perhaps unusual for me to volunteer, nevertheless, my hand rose and I provided to the sergeant the history of my high school and college typing courses. These non-credited classes allowed me to work as the typist and an assistant to the captain and the non-commissioned officer in the local and field offices as opposed to being qualified as a cannoneer.

"I was indeed lucky to be able to have taken typing while I was young, lucky to be offered this opportunity to stay at the base as opposed to the field and seized the opportunity offered to me."

That's a very lucid testimonial to Street Smart by Michael Stoler, who...by the way...knows his business too.

That's dry in comparison to his Street Smart Memoir, right? But he's a force to be reckoned with for New York real estate, and he insists that Street Smart got him there. His SALT system is a great idea to us. Maybe you can use both as well as he does. We have no professional envy here!

STREET SMART MEMOIR OF FIIYAH
What's Needed on America's Streets? Hyper Street Smart

If we thought that Brooklyn's mean streets were a tough school to learn Street Smart, as did most of our contemporaries, Fiiyah, educates us that the modern streets of Brooklyn and Queens are more intensive by far. Somehow, he cranks up the law of probabilities here as well. And you move with an "army;" the OGs are "older guys," the officers. And no one here was drafted. You joined, you died, or you just got by.

We are white and middle-aged, but the Street Smart of someone like Fiiyah, while more intensive, stems from the same survival instinct whether you hail from the Caribbean or from Italian-Jewish Bensonhurst. The street suffers no fools.

Fiiya, a dancehall and reggae artist, also works as a music producer and is the owner of LiQwiid Fiiyah Music, a label based in Queens, New York. He's currently in the late stages of producing his album, out later this year.

"One of the main necessary aspects of survival is Street Smarts. Hailing from a Caribbean country such as Trinidad and Tobago, you'd definitely learn to sharpen up your senses. Migrating to the Americas was a huge move, but the rules still applied, as far as what to look out for or simply who. You can tell a lot by someone's movement and overall attitude, from a simple stare to the way they may respond to a given situation. Body language is Street Smarts. While many opportunities may present themselves with a ribbon and bow, your sixth sense, which is your gut feeling, is most of the time correct. If it doesn't look or feel right, then it's not.

"Words would always be words unless there is some action behind it to convince otherwise. Growing up during different time periods of music is also something to pay attention to. Many times, music, often reggae and hip-hop, will detail some of what happens in the streets once the sun is down.

"Knowing your surroundings is one thing. Knowing how to maneuver is another.

Observation and preservation is key. One must know when to take advantage of opportunities and when to strike. Not every action deserves a reaction or response as others may use your words against you. Long story short, there's a time and place for everything, you just have to know when.

"Learning how to interact with people can become a great skill in the white-collar world. The study of interactions is called sociology; so, in hindsight, the streets can turn you into a sociologist. This is a great asset for that world, but street interactions are much different. Not every interaction is the same, as people tend to present themselves from all walks of life. It is up to us to do our own due diligence to know and understand the type of beast or personality that we are dealing with.

"Even on the streets, it's very easy to become disrespectful, especially when using slang as an everyday language. A simple word can have two meanings, being the difference between you getting shot and you walking away: 'My bad.' For those who don't speak slang, it is the rough equivalent of 'I'm sorry.' Bump into someone in a crowd? 'My bad.' Step on someone's shoes? 'My bad.' On the streets, everyone will risk it all to defend their honor, and some do not have a single fuck to give. But, with a little respect, you won't have to endure much of those situations.

"Respect goes a long way on all levels, which tends to form bonds, friendships, and mutual agreements allowing us to expand our circle and learn new things about people and their interests. Not everyone would like you and not everyone would hate you, but keep in mind with progress comes 'haters.'

"When living in areas where Street Smarts are prominent, reading and deciphering gestures can go a long way. Handshakes and certain walks are very popular on the streets, and without specific credibility, you can land in a world of trouble. Witnessing and knowing the meanings behind them can also help you stay in the clear.

"Color coding is a big part of the streets. If you choose to wear the wrong colors one day, chances are you might end up in an unfriendly altercation with people who take clothing color very seriously, especially gangs.

"I remember one time when I was building my recording studio in Queens, LiqwiidFiiyah Music, I had an artist come into the studio. He was referred by another artist, but the vibe and energy were completely off. This guy was all over the place as far as his mental and body movements. I just knew and could feel that this was not a situation I wanted to be in. Little did I know, he was wanted for a robbery and was trying to use me as his hideout. On his way out, about twenty feet from LiqwiidFiiyah's entrance, he was cornered and arrested. Innocently, I myself could have been tied into something I had nothing to do with, but with my Street Smarts, I was able to observe and respond in a way that did not escalate the situation.

"The streets have an undocumented but yet universal code. This code is more than just rules, it's really a way of life. The streets have a way of knowing, and when certain rules are broken, the streets will know. They will find you, and they will give you the penalty for breaking code. With this being said, the streets offer plenty of knowledge. Oftentimes, you can see a multitude of street gambling and side hustles happening. Money changes hands very quickly, and depending on the amount of players, some people lose hands very quickly.

"Applying this knowledge of probabilities will teach you how to take chances in life and calculate a risk-to-reward ratio. Drugs and gambling can be seen as a form of side hustle. Side hustles are activities that can bring in an extra cash flow, typically requiring less effort. The most common side hustles are the sale of marijuana and coke, better known as that 'white.' Everyone uses it and it's always in demand. Other side hustles like lemonade stands and mechanic work are also common but require lots of time and effort. Everyone wants the quickest return on their investment, and nothing sells quicker than some drugs to someone who 'needs' it.

"Sometimes being 'that guy,' or who is commonly referred to as 'the plug,' can get you robbed. Robberies are very common, and for people hustling in the streets, garnering security would be optimal, but somehow not attainable without joining a gang. Gangs are a one-way street: one way in and one way out. Jump someone to get in, jump someone to get out. The other way is to replace the previous sentence's opening word with 'kill.' In these streets, safety does not exist.

"When I was ten years old, I got robbed for a sandwich and three dollars. How does that help me now? It taught me a lesson that nothing is ever safe; value everything I have and take extra care to protect the things I love most. As you get older, safety is one of your concerns in a professional world. You want to make sure you have job security and a retirement plan in place. Street Smarts can become a valuable asset to your life.

"Perhaps the most important lesson you can learn on the streets is that you make your own luck. When you become successful and you are no longer in the streets, nobody sees the eight hundred hours you've spent in a corner with a reading lamp trying to attain a college degree. Now, let's open a business and you'll see exactly how these street lessons will make you a successful entrepreneur.

"Street Smarts is not something to be taught. If you know, you know. This goes back to observation, but experience is what opens our eyes to anything new that may present itself.

"Snitching is a complete 'no go' on the streets where I come from. It's a highlight of character and would not and will *not* be tolerated, period! Once you're labeled as a snitch, you might as well move out of the hood and change your name because the code on the streets really is 'snitches get stitches.' If something does not concern you, mind your business or keep it moving.

"While many are book smart, they lack the intuition on the streets. A combination of both, on the other hand, is the ultimate mixture for success. Personally, I think exposure to both worlds tends to make or build the strongest of us. Never underestimate the thoughts of people or their mental state. Sleep with one eye open or stand with both is what I would say, and if need be, make sure to take notes.

"The word street is derived from the Latin word, *strata*, which originates in the Greek form of *stratos*, whose literal meaning is army. In the streets, most people move with an army. Moving solo is not wise for anyone coming up in rough territory, especially territory that is already owned. If you are not from that neighborhood, respect the rules of that hood. Respect the people who run the streets, the guys on the corner, the young boys, and the older guys, called OGs. The young boys are always in control, but the OGs run the show. Disrespect in any amount will get you hurt around these people. The streets are not for everyone. Not everyone is built for it, and not everyone can hang with the big boys. If you aren't about that life, the streets will eventually test you.

"Another worthy lesson is learning to fight your battles. While some battles are won before they are even started, some battles are not worth fighting. Winning a fight is very easy if you can infiltrate your opponent's mind. The streets will teach you how to fight, and ultimately when to fight. Learning this important concept can garner wins in a professional life later on.

"Street Smarts and book smarts, two things that can take you places. One is taught and one is simply natural. Street Smarts just come naturally to some; it's not something that you can teach. A person can be college educated, with many accolades showing the world how smart they are, but can still lose it all, simply because they lack the knowledge."

So, what exactly is Street Smart and what does it really mean to be Street Smart?

"Simply put, it's a natural instinct. Being Street Smart is something you learn by going through different experiences and being put into tough situations, but all in all, you come out on top. It's an easy misconception that someone who is Street Smart is not as smart as a person who is book smart. This has been proven time and time again to be false.

"Let's dive into some examples, looking into the life of some of the most successful rappers in the hip-hop industry. Many were built on pure talent and Street Smarts. From making investments in their music, to teaching themselves to play instruments and even having a gut instinct on if a business deal feels right or wrong. These are some of the things Street Smarts play a key in.

"Reading the room, it's a combination of both verbal and nonverbal communication. Ever heard of, 'it's not what you say, but how you say it?' Your tone, the way you stand, and body language are major components to delivering your message. I can say the right things, but if my face seems upset, it creates a negative tone, then my message is being received in a manner I didn't intend. For example, when you walk into a room, you should quickly analyze your audience. It always depends on the task at hand and what is the goal that needs to be accomplished. Another thing you have to ask yourself is how are you trying to be perceived? Importantly, you never want to come off as cocky and a 'know-it-all.' Always try to soften your words; a great leader always knows when to speak and when to listen.

"It's a tough place, but learning how to function on these streets can lead to a fruitful life professionally. Learning how to read emotions, situations, and body language can help assist in conference rooms or in job interviews. As a young man growing up in the streets, to now a successful adult, I've leveraged these skills to put me in places where books alone could not."

Fiiyah's memoir is specific and educational enough to be its own textbook for the streetwise entrepreneur. From reading one's body language to learning the social dos and don'ts, his entire philosophy rests on what he learned in the streets of New York City. But any street, whether Wall Street, the Garment District, or the roughest urban neighborhood, require being Street Smart for both success and, as Fiiyah so eloquently points out, survival.

STREET SMART MEMOIR OF DANNY CLINCH
The Eye of the Beholder

Celebrity photographer and documentarian Danny Clinch hails from the "wrong side of the tracks" as he says here, but that didn't stop him from being the favorite photographer for every type of entertainer from rappers to vintage singers. He credits his success to a talent which sharpens his own sense of being Street Smart; the fleeting moment when his Street Smart lulls the celebrity to relax and become him or herself for that lucky-break moment of a great photograph.

Taking celebrity photographs is definitely a hit-or-miss thing. Mostly misses. Clinch gets "the shot" by spotting, seizing, and exploiting the exact moment when he can capture the spirit of the celebrity as they become themselves, alleviating any anxiety or trepidation.

The photographer coaches every conceivable facial and body expression of their subject while the high-tech cameras whirl, click, and shutter in an effort to capture a "one in a million" moment. Even an amateur photographer knows that luck is always heavily involved in a great photograph. Whether good times or bad, "the shot" has the power to convey iconic moments, immortal forever. Think of such photographs: the sailor kissing the girl on V-J Day in Times Square; Albert Einstein sticking out his tongue at a photographer, Marines raising the flag at Iwo Jima, The Beatles crossing Abbey Road, or the beautiful blue-eyed Afghan girl staring directly into the camera.

Yes, luck had something to do with it. Danny Clinch knows that, which is why he uses the Street Smart imparted by his father to get the shots that his clients pay premium dollars for. Danny's story is an interesting one about creativity and the use of Street Smart.

Danny's photographs have appeared in the *New Yorker* and the *New York Times*, *Spin*, *Rolling Stone*, and *Vanity Fair*. His photos also grace the covers and pages of many books. You have seen many of his photographs without knowing it. Now you know where he gets it from: Street Smart. And while clicking away with a camera might seem like no territory for Street Smart, this world-famous photographer thinks otherwise.

"When I think about Street Smarts, I think about my father, who grew up with five brothers and sisters with very little means on the other side of the tracks. His education ended in eighth grade, and although he wasn't very book smart, he was Street Smart. He started his own businesses at a very young age, otherwise he would have no spending money. He had a knack for reading people and used his natural instincts to handle many situations as a young, skinny, poor kid. My father always told me that he would be just as comfortable talking to the garbage man as he would be if he was talking to the president of the United States.

"Back then, he hitchhiked everywhere he went—even as a young teenager. He once hitchhiked from Chicago back to New Jersey where he lived. My father was great at getting along with people, and he was easy to talk to; he could often find things about people that connected him with them. I always loved hearing these stories. I've used the Street Smarts he instilled in me during my career as a photographer and filmmaker to communicate with people and get on their level regardless of their celebrity status. Using Street Smarts also helps to find common interests, which sometimes helps certain people relax in order for me to capture a great photograph or portrait of them. I learned that treating people the way you want to be treated often pays off.

"As a documentary filmmaker and photographer, having Street Smarts and good instincts always helps me navigate obstacles that come when you're in someone else's space or environment. For instance, I recall early in my career when I was shooting an album cover for Big L, a legendary rapper from Harlem. We were with Big L's crew of around ten friends in his neighborhood when my battery-powered light died with no place to charge it. We were next to a very busy neighborhood chicken-and-pizza restaurant, and I walked in to try and find a place to charge my gear. I couldn't get the owner's attention, so my instinct told me that I should plug the cord into an outlet near the door. My light started to charge, and it worked perfectly until the power abruptly went out. We looked over to see what happened, and the owner was there with the plug in his hand. Everyone in the crew stopped and stared at this guy—I think he used his own instincts and Street Smarts because he plugged the light back into the out-let right away and we finished our shoot."

So speaks Danny Clinch. Even a condensed version of his biography shows how Street Smart has worked. His famous sub-jects include Blind Melon, Bruce Springsteen, Tupac Shakur, Johnny Cash, The Smashing Pumpkins, Bob Dylan, the Cowsills, Danielle Evin (*Devon Avenue*), Nicole Atkins, Björk, and the Dave Matthews Band, among others. He himself says that his "unobtrusive style," as directed by Street Smart above, makes the difference between a good photograph and a great photograph.

STREET SMART MEMOIR OF GOVERNOR PHIL MURPHY
No Lifelong Playbook, Just Street Smart Company You Keep

New Jersey governor Phil Murphy has been leading his state through the worst of the COVID pandemic. As you'll read, his Street Smart abilities originated from his family and his very humble beginnings. Sharpening all of this is the perception that doing good for others is what keeps you Street Smart anyway.

When the COVID-19 pandemic took hold in March 2020, Governor Murphy committed to protecting lives while ensuring that New Jersey emerged stronger, fairer, and more resilient. He has guided the state from being the epicenter of the national pandemic to a model state for restart and recovery with a focus on careful statewide and regional planning to protect residents and save lives. He has built broad partnerships for aggressive COVID testing and vaccinations. And his administration has provided hundreds of millions of dollars in direct relief to small businesses, schools, tenants and landlords, and middle-class families.

Under Gov. Murphy, and before the COVID pandemic, New Jersey had reemerged as a national leader in securing the dignity of working families by moving to a fifteen-dollar-per-hour minimum wage, guaranteeing earned sick days, and expanding paid family leave. He has enacted initiatives to provide a tuition-free community college education for qualified students and in-state tuition assistance to Dreamers. He has expanded protections for the state's immigrant and LGBTQ+ communities. He has also enacted numerous laws to strengthen and update New Jersey's gun laws to combat the scourge of gun violence.

Gov. Murphy has also made New Jersey a model state for social justice, signing legislation enacting among the country's strongest automatic voter registration measures and restoring voting rights to residents on parole or probation, expunging the records of numerous nonviolent offenders, and creating the nation's strongest provisions for environmental justice, alongside other new laws.

He has put a special emphasis on making New Jersey more welcoming to both established high-tech enterprises and start-up companies in the innovation economy. In January 2021, he enacted a new set of state economic incentives, focused on promoting the growth of new small businesses and innovative start-ups, enacting the state's first tax credits for historic preservation and expanding credits for brownfields reclamation and redevelopment, among other initiatives.

Under Gov. Murphy's leadership, New Jersey has also emerged as a leader in the deployment of offshore wind-energy technologies with one of the nation's most aggressive proposals for the development of offshore wind. During his time as governor, the state has also forged partnerships that will see the first wind-energy-component manufacturing facility in the United States as well as a wind port purpose-built for moving those components to market.

The youngest of four children of the late Walter F. Murphy, Sr. and Dorothy Murphy, Governor Murphy was born in Boston, Massachusetts and was raised in both Newton and nearby Needham, Massachusetts. He is a graduate of Needham High School, Harvard University, and The Wharton School of the University of Pennsylvania. Along many of his accomplishments as governor, he has been awarded numerous honorary degrees.

His "thinking man's liberalism" has held him in good political stead as well. Before he was governor of New Jersey, Murphy graduated from the world's top universities after years of hard work and persistence. The governor himself will tell you why he's a fighter who uses Street Smart.

"I didn't grow up with the advantages that many who have entered the worlds of business and politics had.

"My family was, by all modern standards, working poor—I like to say we were 'middle class on a good day.' My mother was the only one of my parents to graduate high school, and she worked as a secretary. My father was hard-working, with jobs that ranged from managing a local liquor store to even being a paid pallbearer at funerals.

"In 1950s and 1960s Greater Boston, the Murphy household definitely qualified as one striving to climb into the middle class.

"But what we lacked in wealth, my parents made sure to make up to me and my three siblings every night around the dinner table. Education. Politics and civics. Religion. Family first. These were the regular topics of conversation, and not familial chit-chat. My parents were determined that their children would not see their humble surroundings as their fates.

"'You are known by the company you keep,' my mother would admonish us.

"This was the Murphy household equivalent to earning your Street Smarts. Even though our family [was] dyed-in-the-wool Kennedy Democrats, I realized much later in life that these lessons were akin to the words of one of my other political heroes, Theodore Roosevelt: 'Do what you can, with what you have, where you are.'

"These lessons were just as valuable as those we learned in school each day. And to be sure, we were being graded on more meaningful curves.

"My siblings and I would all go on to earn college degrees—I earned my undergraduate degree from Harvard before receiving my MBA at the Wharton School at the University of Pennsylvania. In between, and to earn the money I would need for graduate school, I worked by selling college textbooks to professors, many of whom took some strange joy in slamming their office doors in the face of a salesman barely older than the students in their own classrooms.

"No classroom education could prepare me for that feeling. I had to reach back to the lessons I learned at our kitchen table.

"I chose a career in finance, from which I retired after more than twenty years of global travel and then embarked on a new chapter in politics and civic society. I have had the honor of serving as the United States ambassador to the Federal Republic of

Germany (where I had spent several years living during my business days) and now currently as the twice-elected governor of New Jersey, where my family and I have proudly and lovingly made our home for more than two decades.

"In each position, to be sure, the lessons taught in Ivy League classrooms have been valuable. But what has proven invaluable are those kitchen-table lessons. They have given me a gut instinct to know when someone is sincere, bluffing, or simply full of it. They have given me an ability to make decisions based not only on what I am told by a spreadsheet, but what I am also told from past experiences.

"There are certainly many instances from throughout my career that I could point to as proof points of this notion. But certainly nothing has tested these lessons more than governing the nation's most densely populated state, as well as one of the most economically important, during a global pandemic.

"The COVID-19 pandemic has tested all of us on multiple levels—and as I write this, it is still ongoing, and this test is not yet over. Knowing that the lives of millions of people rest on how the administration I lead will respond remains something that instills both awe and trepidation.

"In the pandemic's earliest days, especially as the state at the epicenter of the outbreak, we were very cognizant that we had only one chance to get things right—that there would be no do-overs.

"If we clamped down too hard in our efforts to contain a virus over the short term, we could save lives but suffocate our economy with little chance of its successful resuscitation. On the other hand, we knew that if we decided to let the virus just run its course, not only would we lose many tens of thousands more people, but we would still do extreme damage to our economy and our state's emotional well-being for years to come.

"And there were people arguing for both of these courses.

"To play on Teddy Roosevelt's words, I've been doing what I can, with what I am given, at the point which I am given it. Our actions are still guided by this belief.

"Leadership and Street Smarts are not about reaching for a playbook—in many cases, there won't be one. There certainly wasn't one on a shelf in my office. They are about following your instincts based on the information you are given. They are also about recognizing that having a title doesn't automatically mean you are the smartest person in the room.

"Crises require a trusted circle around you to keep you grounded, who will let you vent to them and vice versa, and whose only focus is on the task at hand and not their own futures. You are, after all, known by the company you keep.

"In the case of the pandemic, this focus enabled us to embark on one of the nation's most aggressive testing programs to more fully track the spread of COVID across our state, in real time, so we could move resources to places where they were needed. Throughout 2020, it also meant finding common ground with a president and federal administration of the opposing party—one which, pre-pandemic, I had roundly criticized on a regular basis—to get the supplies our hospitals, first responders, faith communities, and others needed to stem the tide of new infections and save lives.

"And it meant responsibly reopening our economy as soon as it was safe to do so, allowing our state to avoid the surges that many other parts of the country saw in the summer of 2020.

"Once vaccines arrived later that year, it meant creating a model for distribution and delivery—for both the vaccines and vaccine information. The challenge was not just about getting as many shots in arms as quickly as possible, but also striving for equity in our vaccination program so underserved communities would have the same level of protection as the wealthiest. As a result, our vaccination rates are among the highest in the nation, and a leader among states with large populations.

"It means listening to small businesses who were getting crushed by the economic impact of the pandemic in the early days and working quickly to deliver hundreds of millions of dollars in aid so they could remain open and be ready to lead our recovery. We have stood up innovative programs focused on our restaurants and on pairing unemployed residents with employers looking for new workers.

"It has also meant being honest and transparent with the people of New Jersey. Throughout the pandemic, we have provided New Jerseyans with regular briefings to update them on our progress as measured by the latest case numbers, figures from our hospitals, and vaccination totals, among many other data points—more than 235 briefings and counting. We haven't sugarcoated the numbers or dismissed them. When a positive trend emerges, we try to rally a weary state to keep going. When numbers begin to backslide, we try to refocus everyone to the task still at hand.

"And it also means remembering that I don't have all the answers, and in all likelihood, those around me don't, either. But working together, as a team, we can arrive at the best answers for a specific moment in time. Thankfully, I believe we have arrived at many of those answers.

"All of this is about the collective 'we'—our nine million-plus-member New Jersey family—making it through together. It is not, and can never be, about one person's political fortunes.

"And that brings it all back to those lessons taught around the kitchen table in Greater Boston all those years ago. I realize now that while my mom and dad wanted my siblings and me to be successful in our own rights, they also never wanted us to forget where we came from.

"They didn't want us to forget that no matter how successful we were, there were still going to be families just like ours, working hard every day just to make ends meet—families full of love and hopes and dreams, but without much else. Families that need someone to have their back.

"Doing what you can with what you have wherever you are, Teddy Roosevelt said. 'Keep good company,' Mom would remind us.

"Street Smarts isn't about individual survival. It's about moving everyone on that street forward."

In summary, Murphy's survival depended on a heightened form of Street Smart. Politics, and now government with COVID, both need to be infused with Street Smart abilities and characteristics. Governor Murphy says so, and who are we to disagree? He possesses the rare combination of business, street, family, and social acumen. Who knows, maybe he'll go from Gov. Murphy to President Murphy one day.

STREET SMART MEMOIR OF JACK DOUGLAS
Jumping The Boat and Using Street Smart

This Bronx-born legendary music producer for the most iconic talents started his Street Smart studies from recording everything he heard of interest as a kid, then graduating to a Greenwich Village street artist and an underaged coffee-house musician, and finally hopping on a tramp steamer to England to hear The Beatles.

Nobody can explain it better than Jack.

"So, I spent my pre-teens studying chord structure in my Mel Bay book, eventually learning to play guitar well enough to entertain family and friends. I also was obsessed with recording everything and anything. I frequently hung the microphone out of my bedroom window recording the sound of the busy street and the elevated Number Six subway that rattled by. I recorded music themes from the TV and liked to hide the microphone and record people's conversations hoping to overhear some secret or something that would embarrass a cousin or friend.

"I experimented with feedback looping and recording and playing back at different speeds. I also, over time, recorded, with increasing confidence, my own songs.

By the time the '60s rolled around, I was comfortable enough with my playing, singing, and composing skills to head down to Greenwich Village and play wherever I could. Too young to play where liquor was served, I would set up on the street or ask if I could play in a coffee house. I devoted myself to learning all I could about American traditional folk music and blues so I could play it.

"Shortly before Christmas 1963 I heard The Beatles sing, 'I Want to Hold Your Hand' on the radio. It shook me. As far as I was concerned, rock music had faded away when Chuck Berry, Bo Diddley, Little Richard, and Fats Domino were replaced by Frankie Avalon and Fabian. Elvis had long ago sold out to Hollywood, and Buddy Holly was dead. But this was different. It sounded like these English 'mop heads' were echoing all of my former favorites with a little Everly Brothers thrown in like a cherry on top.

I became more than a fan. The whole Mersey sound thrilled me. I traded in my Martin acoustic for a black 1955 Les Paul Custom. I formed a rock band with some like-minded guys and we started playing gigs.

"Exactly two years later, after much playing and dreaming, the other guitar player in the band and myself boarded a tramp steamer in New York and crossed the cold and violent North Atlantic on our way to Liverpool."

Denied legal admission to Britain, Douglas was placed on shipboard arrest but hopped over the side, sneaked inland on a bus to London, and got his true "Street Smart Epiphany" when he shared chords with famous rockers in England. That's where the legend was born. Let's let Jack take it from here.

"We arrived on a wet and foggy morning in early December after nearly two weeks of seas so high they sometimes knocked us out of our bunks. The first calm waters we enjoyed were as we sailed down the Irish Sea listening on our little transistor to Radio Caroline, a pirate station broadcasting (illegally) from a boat. They played all the rock the BBC didn't, and much of it we had never heard in the US.

"A young immigrant came aboard and asked if we were landing and what we planned.

"'We've come to play,' we answered.

"'And you have work permits to play?' he asked.

"We were so naïve. 'No,' we answered.

"'Do you have a visa? Do you have a return trip ticket?'

"'No,' to both. Wrong answers!

"We were told we would not be allowed to set foot on British soil, and when the ship left, five days hence, we would be on it. That night, as my guitar-playing fellow traveler looked on in fear, I escaped from the ship.

"It was quite easy. I expected armed guards at the bottom of the gangplank; there were none. I simply followed two merchant marines, who had just walked off another ship, through a gate and onto the street. It was obvious no one was checking the papers of men who were out for a night's drinking, only to return to their ships later to sleep off a drunk.

"So, here I was, with the only real preparation for England in my hand; a few pounds Sterling.

"I jumped on a bus that read 'Central City' on its front and held out some coins when the conductor came by. He took what he needed and returned the rest to me. I asked him when I should get off and he called out to me at my supposed destination. As soon as I stepped off, I noticed a large and very busy record store. I headed straight for it. There was a line outside, and everyone was very excited. I soon found out why."

"The inside of the record store was packed, and there was a buzz of excitement. A new Beatles album had just been released, and now I couldn't wait to get my hands on it. I stood in line and made my purchase. I quickly headed to one of the listening booths followed by fans eager to hear it. We all packed into the small space as I removed the disk from the cover and placed it on the turntable. I was astounded. The first song, 'Drive My Car,' was rocking in a way the Beatles hadn't before; almost in an R&B way. As I went deeper into the album, I realized they had made a very big move away from their former sound. The album was *Rubber Soul*. Amazed and dizzy from what I had just heard and where I was hearing it, I made my way back out onto the street, album in hand. There must be some way I can stay in this magical place, I thought to myself.

"Directly across the street, I saw a sign that read *The Liverpool Echo*. It was Liverpool's major hometown paper, I soon found out. Maybe they can help. I thought, doesn't the British press like sensational stuff? How about two American musicians held on a tramp steamer in the harbor? And this is what I expressed to the receptionist who greeted me as I entered the offices, only to realize that I was standing there and not on a ship in the harbor. She gave me a funny look and said, 'the only bit of truth I detect is that, by your accent, you are an American.' I was quick to add that I had escaped from the ship. She asked me to wait and that she would call an editor who might be interested. As I waited, I considered making a run for it if she in fact had called the police instead, but a tall gentleman in a suit entered the room and said, 'Alright tell me your story then.'

"He seemed intrigued by my tale of adventure and promised to have press cover the story if he saw me walk back onto the ship. We stopped for fish and chips on the drive back to the docks, and he watched me walk back up the gang plank and on to the ship. Needless to say, my friend Eddie was quite shocked to see me back but pleased by the new Beatles album that we played over and over on a borrowed record player all night, but (he) doubted my story about the newspaper.

"The next morning, a crewmember knocked on our cabin door yelling that a bunch of newspaper people were waiting to talk to us. We made the front page of the *Liverpool Echo* and many other papers including the *London Mirror*."

However, not all of this publicity proved to be promising for Jack and his cabinmate. Jack found the home he had made in London threatened by the English law. Immigration had discovered Jack's illegal entry into the country and weren't fond of their American visitor. However, Jack realized he had allies right down the road. Or dock.

"The citizens of Liverpool came to our defense and made supportive calls to the immigration office. A few days later, a baffled immigration officer came aboard and gave us our freedom."

Once Jack was allowed to stay, he set out to begin the music career he had dreamed of back in the states. However, his British residency was short-lived.

"We, of course, managed to get into a local band, hung out at the Cavern Club, and made the most of our Liverpool adventure until we were caught working without a permit and deported. I did have the forethought to send all our press clippings back to people in the states, and we returned triumphant, local musicians who had actually been and played in Liverpool. This landed us both some very good gigs as backup players in well-known American acts and eventually record deals of our own."

Soon after, Jack realized he wanted to focus on another aspect of the industry.

"By 1969, I grew tired of the grind of roadwork. Although both Eddie and I were recently produced by the Isley Brothers, I decided to take my chances with a career in the studios. I landed a job as the janitor at The Record Plant Studios on West 44th St. It was a hub for popular recording artists, mostly rock. I worked my way up the ladder. General worker, tape librarian, copy and editing engineer, assistant engineer, and finally novice full engineer. This I did quickly with all the New York hustle I could muster. I listened and learned, absorbing everything like a sponge.

"In early May 1971, I was informed by the studio manager that I would be working on a new John Lennon album. My job was to transfer the incoming tapes and preparing them for the overdubs that would be done in studio B. I was also to do some editing on the multi-tracks and would receive some handwritten notes to follow. I couldn't believe my good fortune!"

It only took a matter of days for Jack to realize how fortunate he had become when an unexpected visitor needed to find some solace.

"A week (or) so into the process, John Lennon walked into the room where I was working. I nearly peed myself. He asked if he could just sit for a while and rest. I believe he was trying to get away from Phil Spector for a bit and clear his head. He sat on a couch on the other side of the mixing desk, so I could only see his feet up on the glass and the smoke rising from his cigarette.

"After a few long nervous moments I said, 'I've been to Liverpool.' His head popped up and he asked why did I want to go there. 'Everyone there would like to come here.' I explained to him that I was a musician, and in 1965, (Liverpool) was certainly the place to be.

"'So how did that work out for you?' he asked.

"'Well, good and bad,' I answered. 'Bad, I got deported. Good, I made a lot of news in the press before I did.'

"He looked at me in kind of a strange way and then said, 'Were you one of those crazy Yanks that was on the front page of the Liverpool papers the same week we released an album and it should have been just us?'

"'Yes, that was me.'

"He thought that was one of the coolest things ever and invited me to come work on the overdubs and be part of the album, which was *Imagine*. My picture is on the inner sleeve. We became friends. I worked with him often for the next few years and eventually became his producer.

"My father told me that in New York, anything can happen if you work hard enough to make it happen."

Jack's dad was definitely right. Not only did Jack and John become friends, but this little studio run-in turned into one of the music industry's most impactful alliances.

In 1980, Jack produced John and Yoko Ono's album, *Double Fantasy*. Producing Lennon's final album was a task very few

could accomplish. Jack knew that John had a strange premo-
nition that this album would be his last and was aware of his
paranoia when it came to sharing his music, specifically for this
album. Being Street Smart, Jack made the conscious choice not
to betray his friend's confidence. He wasn't one to kiss and tell.
Jack's Street Smart gave Lennon the comfort he needed when
he and Yoko would meet with Jack at La Fortuna on West 71st
and Columbus Avenue and play his private demo cassette tapes.
These tapes would turn into *Double Fantasy* and later go on to
win the Grammy Award for Album of the Year in 1981, a matter
of months after Lennon's murder.

Jack has deep professional ties to Miles Davis, James Gang,
Mountain, John Lennon, Danielle Evin (*Devon Avenue*),
Aerosmith, the New York Dolls, Patti Smith, Blue Öyster
Cult, Lou Reed, Alice Cooper, The Who, and many others.
The discography alone would take five pages. But suffice it to
say, Jack used his Street Smart (or was it "Harbor Smart"?) to
become a legend.

He also discovered the band Cheap Trick in 1976 at the
Sunset Bowling Alley in Waukesha, Wisconsin. Jack then went
on to produce two of the band's most successful albums.

As stated before, entertainment is the province of luck. But
for Jack, his extreme dedication, talent, and honing his Street
Smart ideology across the Atlantic gave him one of the most
enviable and prolific careers in music. As his vivid story showed,
he is responsible for producing some of the most beloved songs
and melodies that have stood the test of time and will continue to
be cherished for many generations to come.

Street Smart is a philosophy that presents itself in many
shapes and forms and certainly, like Jack's music, is immortal and
everlasting. And as John Lennon found out, Jack is the ultimate
Stand-Up Guy.

PERSTARE ET PRAESTARE

You have experienced, not merely read, Street Smart in action, as shown in over three dozen direct memoirs. There is total commonality yet diversity in point of view. They range at all ends of the political spectrum. They come from manifestly different racial, ethnic, and religious backgrounds. They almost all come from the working and middle classes. Almost all come from urban areas. They are unanimous in the proposition that Street Smart is the critical aspect of success. Not mere talent. Not mere persistence. Not mere courage. Not an academic background. Not tied with the Old-School Tie. Not networked. Not taught in school nor by gurus, personal advice professionals, nor in other books.

Your fate really is in your own hands. Now it's up to you to go out into the world and find your own Street Smart, and hopefully, you've found that you have some very successful company for the hard road ahead. Though it can be daunting and might even seem impossible, the only way one can become Street Smart is to truly go beyond your own backyard and try it out for yourself. There is no cookie-cutter recipe for success, but the only ingredient that remains constant: try, try, and try again. The only true failures are the ones who don't give themselves permission to see what the world has to offer and what they are truly capable of achieving.

To put it a bit more bluntly, as General George S. Patton said, "Lead, follow, or get out of the way."

Ut est rerum omnium magister usus
Experience is the best teacher

ACKNOWLEDGMENTS

The authors would like to acknowledge Kendall DuPre, for her invaluable assistance in the direction and preparation of this manuscript and as project manager for *Street Smart*.

They would also like to acknowledge Laura M. Positano, in providing research and editorial support in all aspects of this project.

Special thanks to Alfred González for providing the magnificent cover photograph for this book. Alfred's photograph gallery, Gallery 71, is based in New York City. More of his work can be appreciated at www.alfredgonzalezphotography.com.

Thank you to Steve Carlis, whose amazing support and guidance was absolutely indispensable.

Special thanks to Alicia Bonanno, who masterfully supervised the day-to-day operations at the Joe DiMaggio Heel Pain Center at the Hospital for Special Surgery over the course of this project. We'd also like to acknowledge Sharmilla Ahmad.

John Positano would like to especially acknowledge Rita Guarna for her advice, stewardship, and inspiration for this project.

They'd also like to thank everyone at Post Hill Press, specifically Anthony Ziccardi, Heather King, Austin Miller, Debra Englander, Clayton Ferrell, and Brandon Rospond.

RECOMMENDED BOOKS APPENDIX

What it Takes: Lessons In The Pursuit of Excellence by Stephen A. Schwarzman (Avid Reader Press/Simon & Schuster)

The Art of War by Sun Tzu

The Art of War by Niccolo Macchiavelli

Unshakeable by Tony Robbins (Simon & Schuster)

The General and the Bomb: Biography of Leslie Groves by William Lawren (Dodd Meade and Co.)

Knight's Cross: A Life of Field Marshal Rommel by David Fraser (Harper Collins)

Armageddon by Max Hastings (Alfred Knopf)

Dinner with DiMaggio by Rock and John Positano (Simon and Schuster)

Rhinoceros Success by Scott Alexander (Rhino's Press)

Make Your Bed by William H. McRaven
(Grand Central Publishing)

Emotional Intelligence by Daniel Goleman (Random House)

*You Are a Badass: How To Stop Doubting Your
Greatness and Start Living an Awesome Life*
by Jen Sincero (Running Press Adult)

Brooklyn by Thomas J. Campanella (Princeton University Press)

Harlem to Hollywood: My Real-to-Reel Life by Sonny
Grosso with Ashley Jude Collie (soon to be published)

*From Those Wonderful Folks Who Gave You Pearl
Harbor* by Jerry Della Femina (Simon and Schuster)

Carlito's Way by Edwin Torres (E. P. Dutton & Co.)

*Black, Blind, & In Charge: A Story of Visionary Leadership
and Overcoming Adversity* by David Paterson (Skyhorse)

*Thrive: The Third Metric to Redefining Success
and Creating a Life of Well-Being, Wisdom, and
Wonder* by Arianna Huffington (Harmony)

One Tough Cop: The Bo Dietl Story by Bo Dietl (Gallery Books)

*The Three Cs That Made America Great:
Christianity, Capitalism and the Constitution* by
Mike Huckabee (Trilogy Christian Publishing)

Frenemies: The Epic Disruption of the Ad Business (and Everything Else) by Ken Auletta (Penguin Press)

Trump, the Blue-Collar President by Anthony Scaramucci (Center Street)

The Joys of Much Too Much: Go for the Big Life—The Great Career, The Perfect Guy, and Everything Else You've Ever Wanted by Bonnie Fuller (Touchstone)

An Italian Grows in Brooklyn by Jerry Della Femina (Little, Brown)

Making Money Moral: How a New Wave of Visionaries Is Linking Purpose and Profit by Judith Rodin and Saadia Madsbjerg (Wharton School Press)

Woke Up This Morning: The Definitive Oral History of The Sopranos by Michael Imperioli and Steve Schirripa (William Morrow)

The 10 Laws of Enduring Success by Maria Bartiromo with Catherine Whitney (Currency)

Rescuing Retirement: A Plan to Guarantee Retirement Security for All Americans by Tony James and Teresa Ghilarducci (Disruption Books)

Fashion Lives: Fashion Icons with Fern Mallis by Fern Mallis (Rizzoli)

Danny Clinch: Still Moving by Danny Clinch (Harry N. Abrams)

John Positano, Esq., co-author of Dinner with DiMaggio, has written extensively on law, the military, and surfing for the New York Daily News, the Huffington Post, and the Long Island Pulse. His law practice centers on federal matters, specifically as a litigation attorney in the Federal Second District of New York. John has won several awards for journalism, including the George Polk

Award, the Society of Professional Journalism Deadline Club Award, and the St. Bonaventure Award for Student Journalism. In addition to his law practice, he was head of public relations for fourteen years at a prestigious college preparatory high school in Brooklyn, New York. Father of two and a grandfather, he lives near Suffolk County in Long Island, New York.

Dr. Rock G. Positano is the Co-Director of the Non-Surgical Foot and Ankle Service and the Joe DiMaggio Heel Pain Center at the Hospital for Special Surgery in New York City. Internationally renowned and lauded as a medical pioneer in the non-surgical approach for the treatment of foot and ankle disorders, Dr. Positano graduated from Yale School of Medicine, where his thesis on foot health was approved "with Honors" and "with Distinction."

Author Photo by: Brad Hess

He is also on staff at the New York-Presbyterian Hospital/ Weill Cornell Medical College, Memorial Sloan-Kettering Cancer Center in New York City, and Lenox Hill/Northwell Health.

Dr. Positano is a clinical associate professor at the Yale School of Public Health/School of Medicine and an advisory member of both the Yale School of Management Council of Global Advisors and the Yale School of Public Health Leadership Council.

Dr. Positano has also authored and edited numerous peer reviewed articles. He has served as the editor of a wide array of medical textbooks ranging from foot and ankle orthopedics to sports medicine. Frequently quoted as a trusted and leading medical authority by national and New York City media, Dr. Positano was featured on the front page of the New York Times in an article concerning the dangers of cosmetic foot surgery.